Winnie Ruth Judd: The Trunk Murders

Winnie Ruth Judd: The Trunk Murders

by J. Dwight Dobkins and
Robert J. Hendricks

GROSSET & DUNLAP
A National General Company
Publishers   New York

Acknowledgments

The authors are indebted to the *Arizona Republic* and the *Phoenix Gazette* for their cooperation, and to the individuals who provided access to court transcripts and other official documents connected with this case.

Printed in the United States of America

CONTENTS

Authors' Note

To protect the privacy of individuals still alive, some names of those not officially connected with the trial, sanity hearings and other legal proceedings have been changed.

Although Mrs. Judd's assumed name is well known, this and the location of her present home have been disguised to assure her of the normal life for which she has steadfastly fought for the past forty years.

PREFACE

IN 1931, a lovely young woman in Phoenix, Arizona, became involved in an intrigue of love, adultery and murder—an intrigue that was to capture the attention of the world. In December, 1971, she was paroled and granted her freedom.

Continuously, for over forty years, the bizarre developments in the case of Winnie Ruth Judd created an air of unreality. It became a kind of dramatic spectacular in which the audience participated.

As wire services dispatched news of the 1931 event, crowds paid ten cents a head to visit the scene of the crime. Telephone operators worked overtime informing the world press of up-to-the-minute developments in the case. Late-night radio drama provided reenactment of the trial proceedings.

Arizona seemed somehow a curiously inappropriate setting for a case which was to explore the sophisticated relationships between "endocrine glands," heredity and sanity. The all-male jury, composed largely of farmers, ranchers and laborers, judged the events and rendered a verdict. Subsequent reports of a jury "deal" muddied the issue, and Winnie was faced with a system that limited her alternatives to insanity or the gallows.

In many ways, today's society is far different from that which, in 1932, convicted Mrs. Judd of a terrifying crime. Yet in the storm of publicity, we still lose sight of the criminal as human being and come to regard him as performing villain. We lose sight of the forces that conceive the crime. And once judgment has been rendered, the performance concluded, we give little thought to rehabilitation.

Though the widespread news reports of her escapes provided dramatic episodes through the years, little was understood of Mrs. Judd's struggle for a normal existence. Many believed that Winnie's rage for life led her to play out a demented role rather than face the gallows, and others maintained that her insanity was dictated by the circumstances of her life. Whatever the truth, this is the story of a woman who contended with forces larger than herself, a human being who struggled to preserve her sanity, escape to the real world and play a decent role in society.

Winnie Ruth Judd's struggle continued for years in the shadow of the gallows and always in the shadow of herself. We have chosen to let the events speak for themselves.

J. Dwight Dobkins
Robert J. Hendricks

Phoenix, Arizona

1. MERCY ON YOUR SOUL

"So I say, gentlemen, I have viewed this question from what I consider start to finish," continued Judge Howard C. Speakman. "I realized, as I said in the beginning, that a young woman stood before the bar of justice, her life and her liberty balanced in the scales of justice. So with that realization, I have done the thing that I think was right and just."

Judge Speakman then denied the motion for a new trial and said, "Stand up, Winnie Ruth Judd."

"I have something to say," she declared. "I have this to say. Mr. Mitchell emphatically went into the jury saying things about me. He called me names, vulgar names. He went in there with a feeling of vengeance in his heart. When he was in the jury, he told other people on the jury, 'We will hang that woman or make her talk. I have a friend who is on the Pardon Board, and if we give that woman the death penalty, she will talk.'"

"Pardon me, Mrs. Judd," said the judge, "I am sorry—"

"I have—"

"—to interrupt you, but I, as a judge of this court, must be bound by the record in this case . . . and it would do you, nor me, and no one else, any good to discuss things that are not within this record. The law so provides."

Judge Speakman then asked, "Have you anything further to say?"

"I have this to say. That neither of those girls was shot in any bedroom. There was no premeditation of any kind whatsoever. Mr. Andrews did not bring in evidence what he should have. He didn't show everything that he found in the—he knows where he found things. He knows in that breakfast room that he found blood under the molding there. That he would not prove—"

"Pardon me; I have the greatest sympathy for you, Mrs. Judd—"

"But there was no blood in the bedroom."

"—but it will do no good for us to discuss matters out of this record."

"All right. There is this: I was shot first. It was—"

"That is a matter out of this record," said the judge. "I don't care to discuss those things, Mrs. Judd. I have the kindest feeling in the world for you. I have done for you the things that I thought the law provided for me to do, but it would be useless to attempt to discuss things that are not disclosed in this record. You have been in the hands of the police of the State of California—"

"I gave myself to the police."

"Wait a minute—in the State of California and the State of Arizona for months. You should have talked before this time. Is there anything else to say within this record, nothing without?"

"Neither of the girls was murdered," she declared.

"As a conclusion . . . it is the judgment of this court that you, Winnie Ruth Judd, are guilty of murder of the first degree . . . and the sentence of this court is . . . that the superintendent of the State Prison shall therein confine you within the walls of said State Prison until the 11th day of May, 1932, and between the hours of 5 A.M. and 6 P.M. of said day . . . you shall hang by the neck until you are dead. And may God have mercy on your soul!"

So Winnie Ruth Judd protested for the first time, as she had not taken the stand during her days in court. Had she shot her two friends in their beds or in another room in self-defense? Had some members of the jury made a deal as she now claimed? What deal? But the trial had ended.

Winnie Ruth Judd stood convicted of a strange crime which, according to the record, had occurred on or about October 16, 1931.

2. BEFORE THE STORM

WINNIE, AGNES ANNE LEROI and Hedvig Samuelson were the best of friends. They had much in common, including their acquaintance with wealthy Phoenix businessman Carl Harris. It was through Winnie's husband, Dr. William C. Judd, that Winnie met Harris. And through Winnie that Harris met Anne and Sammy, as Hedvig was known by her close friends. Theirs was a happy group friendship formed in the early days of the depression year 1931.

Anne, a striking brunette, and Winnie, blue-eyed and near blond, worked at the Grunow Clinic at Tenth Street and East McDowell, Anne as an X-ray technician and Winnie as secretary-assistant to Dr. William Curtis. Both had prior nurse's training.

Winnie Ruth McKinnell, daughter of a Free Methodist minister, had been a student nurse at Southern Indiana Hospital for the Insane in Evansville, Indiana, in 1923, when she met Dr. Judd. The doctor was on the staff there for a year before he left for Lafayette, Indiana, where he soon was followed by his teenage admirer. Winnie took a job as telephone operator to be near him and they were married in Lafayette in April, 1924. The marriage certificate showed Dr. Judd's birth date and place as March 31, 1883, Gibson, Nebraska, and Winnie's as January 29, 1905, Oxford, Indiana, close to Lafayette.

It wasn't the first time Dr. Judd had been drawn to a much younger woman. He had married Lillian Colwell, seventeen-year-old daughter of Mr. and Mrs. Lee Colwell of Menard, Texas, at Junction, Texas, in July, 1920. The couple moved to Phoenix, and within a month, the bride died. Dr. Judd was reported to have written Mrs. Colwell that Lillian died of acute indigestion and heart disease. Vital statistics records show that she died in St. Joseph's Hospital, August 14, from "accidental morphine poisoning."

Anne LeRoi, whose full maiden name was Agnes Alexandra Imlah, had been in nurse's training at a hospital in Portland, Oregon, in 1925 when she married Walter Monroe, a local automobile dealer.

A few years later, Monroe recalled: "We lived together about eighteen months. We did not quarrel but it was a case of incompatibility and we agreed to a settlement and divorce. At the time of our marriage she wanted it kept secret so she could complete her training. We were not successful in this and she left the hospital soon after.

"When we were divorced, I assisted her in reentering the hospital. We saw each other occasionally and were friendly. Following her marriage to LeRoi James I saw but little of her. She divorced him, I recall, and nursed in Albany for a time and then went to Alaska. She was a fine little girl, very sweet, very pretty, but romantically inclined. She was exceedingly bright and of an understanding personality."

Anne, American-born of French parentage, adopted her husband's French-sounding first name, became superintendent of the hospital at Wrangler, Alaska, in the fall of 1929. There she met and began a close relationship with Hedvig Samuelson, whose career as a schoolteacher had led her to the same frontier town.

Miss Samuelson had graduated July 24, 1925, from North Dakota State Normal School at Minot and later taught at Landa, North Dakota, and Whitehall, Montana, before going to Alaska.

"Sammy," recalled John Troy, publisher of the *Juneau Daily Empire*, "was a little beam of sunshine. She had returned from a summer's study at the University of Chicago. She was without funds. A few weeks after school opened in the fall, she became sick. Her doctor examined her, and it was immediately manifest she had a severe case of tuberculosis."

It was also believed that Anne may have had a light case of the same disease, perhaps because of her constant association with Sammy. She wanted to take Sammy to Arizona, for the dry air, and felt she could get a job and care for Sammy at the same time. Residents of Juneau raised funds to pay the expenses of both to Phoenix.

The year 1931 was one of improvements and relapses in Sammy's long fight against tuberculosis. While Anne worked as an X-ray technician, Sammy spent her hours of recovery reading, writing letters and keeping her diary. The diary revealed the girls' morbid fascination with nighttime mystery tales—notably the horrors of the weekly murder mysteries presented for Sherlock Holmes' easy solution over the radio.

In the diary, Sammy wrote, "I have just 15 minutes of leisure before Sherlock Holmes. All doors are locked and windows barred in anticipation of an exciting time. Then we douse the lights and get deliciously frightened. Isn't it silly . . . two grown women with the mentality of children. But when it's over, we are too frightened to go to bed."

Dr. and Mrs. Judd often played bridge with Anne and Sammy in the bedroom of the girls' small duplex. "Doctor," as Winnie nearly always called her husband, had treated Sammy for tuberculosis. When Dr. Judd and Winnie separated in the spring, he went to live in Los Angeles and Winnie moved in with Anne and Sammy.

Sammy could seldom be out of bed for more than a few hours without suffering for it. When Anne, her devoted companion, was not there, Winnie nursed her. Such was the case in June, when Anne was visiting her family and fiance, Olaf F. Johnson, an electric fixtures salesman, in Portland, Oregon.

In a letter dated June 17, Anne wrote to Winnie: "Ruth, darling, I'll never thank you enough for what you've done for me, but both Sammy and I will love you always for them. Write more concerning my baby because I do worry. Love to her, Judd, and your sweet self."

All seemed well between Anne, Sammy and Winnie. Then, in early October, Winnie moved out to an apartment at 1130 East Brill Street, within easy walking distance of Grunow Clinic.

Known by her new neighbors as a calm person who spent "most of her evenings writing on a typewriter," Winnie changed suddenly and was hostess to three parties within a week prior to Friday, October 16. Carl Harris and Doris Easton, a nurse at Grunow Clinic, were among party participants. Winnie had introduced Miss Easton to Harris.

The last of the parties, held on October 15, was a long one that got "a little bit loud." One participant later told the police that Mrs. Judd was "drinking and having a great time kissing one of the men at the party." A cheap pamphlet entitled "Kissing, a Dangerous Custom" was left on a table in the apartment and a passage from it was later quoted by the press: "There is a serpent coiled behind those seemingly innocent kisses. That serpent has poisonous fangs. It is seeking to ruin your soul and body. Take the advice of one who knows, and beware!"

Such was the commonplace setting for what was to become the most widely publicized and controversial murder case in Arizona history.

Winnie Ruth Judd, twenty-six, was later described as a "most respectable person and very quiet" by Mrs. M. G. Koller, wife of Mrs. Judd's landlord, and "a level-headed woman of considerable intelligence" by Dr. C. R. Perez, the Glendale, Arizona, physician who had assisted Winnie in obtaining several jobs.

Anne LeRoi, twenty-seven and twice divorced, was to be

married to Olaf Johnson at Christmastime. "Mrs. LeRoi didn't appear to be a serious type," the mailman Homer Quist later reported. "She looked as if she'd be sure of herself anywhere."

Hedvig Samuelson, twenty-five, demure and bedridden most of the time, was looking forward to returning to Alaska in the spring.

Miss Denise Reynolds, secretary to Dr. A. J. Rood at Grunow Clinic, was believed by police to be the last person save their actual slayer or slayers to see Anne and Sammy alive. Miss Reynolds was their guest at dinner and had played cards with them in the bedroom until 9:45 P.M. "And when I left," she later said, "both walked to the door with me. Mrs. LeRoi was dressed then in red silk lounging pajamas, which she had worn during the evening. Miss Samuelson wore white washable pajamas with small figures."

3. BY THE LIGHT OF MATCHES

Mrs. Beth Springer lived at 2938 North Second Street, about a hundred feet from the scene of the crime, but knew neither of the victims. She had retired to a bed on her screen porch about 9 P.M. to read the *Phoenix Gazette* and *Arizona Republic*. It was a quiet night, with no sounds except the streetcar. At about 10:30, she heard what sounded like three muffled pistol shots—first one, then two closer together. She had a full view of the house numbered 2929, but saw nothing, not even lights in the house. She did not report the shots until several days later when she learned of the events from a newspaper.

Another neighbor, Bill Samuels, supported Mrs. Springer's testimony. The shots, he said, came within the space of "less than one minute."

On the morning of the 17th, a neighbor in the vicinity was awakened by what he thought were the screams of women. Dr. Frank Atwater later testified, "I heard the screams coming from that house for a period of several minutes, possibly five or seven minutes. I don't know how long [it was before] I recognized that the screams were coming from that house, and then

I heard two shots about five seconds apart." Dr. Atwater then got up and went about his usual business. He testified that the sounds were either shots or a screen door slamming and that the screams were similar to those he had heard from that house on other occasions.

That Saturday morning, Dr. Laurence Dunn, a physician at the Grunow Clinic, noticed the absence of his X-ray technician, Agnes LeRoi. Concerned that she might be ill, Dr. Dunn sent his wife to 2929 North Second Street. When no one responded to her knocks, Mrs. Dunn looked in the bedroom window. On one of the beds were several garments that seemed to be stained with blood.

Meanwhile, Dr. Dunn's secretary, Beverly Fox, received a telephone call "at about 9 A.M." The caller said, "This is Mrs. Judd, Mrs. Fox. Will you please have Emil open my office because I am going to be a little late this morning?"

Mrs. Fox agreed to do so. At about 9:45 A.M., she received a call from a woman who identified herself as Mrs. LeRoi. The caller asked, "Is Dr. Dunn in?"

"Yes, he is," Mrs. Fox told her, "but he is busy with a patient right now. What is the idea of your not coming down here to work? We are needing you."

The caller said, "Sammy's brother arrived, and we are taking him to Tucson today. Will you give that message to Dr. Dunn?"

Mrs. Fox replied, "I will not. I will put him on the phone, and you can transmit the message to him yourself."

Dr. Dunn spoke to the caller and objected to her announced plans. The caller finally agreed to come to work, but Mrs. LeRoi never appeared. Bev Fox had listened in on this conversation, and at its conclusion she said, "That was Mrs. Judd talking; it was not Mrs. LeRoi."

Mrs. Judd reportedly arrived at the office at 10:10 A.M. Denise Reynolds later passed by Winnie's office door and noticed that Mrs. Judd was "white as a ghost and nervous."

"Nervous!" one doctor said. "She looked like hell. She couldn't remember anything and wasn't worth a darn. Then she asked to go home early, and I didn't see her again Saturday."

That night, Winnie Ruth Judd called the Lightning Delivery Company to have a trunk picked up. John W. Pritchett, driver of the transfer truck, was accompanied by a helper by the name of Palmer on his call to 2929 North Second Street. Pritchett had trouble finding the darkened house but finally stopped at the address, walked up to the front porch and said, "I guess this is the right place after all."

Winnie appeared at the door. "Yes, this is the right house. The reason that the lights are turned off—I had the power company shut them off because I am leaving. The trunk is in the front room and we will have to transact our business by the light of matches."

When Pritchett and his helper entered the dark living room, Winnie struck a match, but they could see little by the match light, except what Winnie Ruth pointed out.

She said, "I want this trunk taken to the station immediately so that I can go down and check it out on the 10:40 train."

"All right," Pritchett said. He got out the claim check and detached the stub. He handed it to her and fastened the string portion to the handle of the trunk. The trunk had a leather handle at each end, locks in the front and two hasps to hold the lid down. It was a flat-topped packer trunk, about three feet long, with depth and width of two feet.

One of the men helped Winnie strike matches to light up the center of the living room. Then, while Winnie held the light, Palmer and Pritchett attempted to lift the trunk but couldn't get it off the floor. Pritchett later judged it to weigh four hundred pounds. "What have you in this trunk to make it so heavy?" Winnie said it contained books. As the trunk seemed to stick to the floor, Pritchett asked if it had been freshly varnished.

Winnie smiled and said, "No."

After struggling to lift the trunk on end, Pritchett and his helper told Winnie it was too heavy to go as baggage and that she could not check it on a ticket. Pritchett suggested they hold the trunk overnight and ship it by express in the morning.

Winnie hesitated. "No, I believe I will have to take it to my sister's house and have her ship it out for me tomorrow."

Pritchett and Palmer then loaded the trunk with the aid of a hand truck. Mrs. Judd was ready to leave with them when she remembered having left her keys inside the house. She offered to tip Pritchett if he would climb through a bathroom window to retrieve them. While Pritchett was attempting to climb through the window, he knocked what he thought was a bottle of medicine into the bathtub. When he returned to the truck with her keys, Mrs. Judd got into the cab and rode with the transfer men to 1130 East Brill Street. She had little to say during the ride. It was cold. She huddled up in the seat and looked straight ahead.

When they reached Apartment F, Winnie held the screen door open while the trunk was unloaded. Pritchett asked her three times to move back so he wouldn't hit her with the trunk. She maintained an expressionless look and didn't move until brushed back by the transfer men. When asked where it should be placed, she replied, "Anywhere in the front room will do." This done, Pritchett and Palmer drove away. Mrs. Judd stood in the doorway until they were gone from view.

Sunday, October 18, Winnie made arrangements for her landlord, M. G. Koller, and his son to take some baggage from her apartment to Union Depot. Koller saw Winnie three times that day—once at about 9 A.M., when she came to his home to talk to Mrs. Koller and use the telephone. Winnie used the telephone again that afternoon to call friends, asking each of them for $5 to help pay for a trip to Los Angeles. As Mrs. Judd had not eaten, Mrs. Koller insisted she stay for lunch. Winnie did not eat much and evinced little interest in some apartment drawings Koller tried to show her. Her hand was bandaged; she told Mrs. Koller she had burned it on an electric iron.

In the afternoon Koller and his son took the larger packer trunk and a smaller one from Mrs. Judd's bedroom. They strapped the larger trunk to the running board of Koller's Reo Touring car and placed the smaller trunk between the front and back seats. Mrs. Judd carried out a well-worn suitcase, a large hatbox and a little leather grip. When they reached the Union Depot, young Koller and the baggage agent carried both trunks to the baggage room. The suitcase, smaller grip and hatbox were taken to the general waiting room and placed on the seat in front of the ticket counter.

Winnie had agreed to pay Koller $1.50 for his services but found that she was short of funds and asked permission to pay him when she returned from Los Angeles. Earlier she had told him that she would return with Dr. Judd on Wednesday or Thursday.

At Union Depot, the baggage agent, after helping carry the larger trunk from Koller's car, weighed the trunks; the larger one came to 235 pounds and the smaller one 90. Later he would load them onto Train 3, the Golden State Limited, which arrived in Phoenix at 7:55 P.M. The baggage messenger received the trunks on board at 8:05, noticing, he later testified, what appeared to be blood leaking from a corner of the black packer trunk.

A baggageman checked Mrs. Judd's personal baggage to Los Angeles and collected $4.48 at "about 4:30 P.M." Winnie signed her brother's name to the baggage slips. The baggageman noticed Winnie's left hand was bandaged in a "handkerchief or something."

The head porter put Winnie's bags, the suitcase and hatbox marked "A.A.M." on the chair car of the Southern Pacific train. The only other passengers were two ladies from Miami with a baby. Winnie appeared to be nervous, and used her coat to conceal her left arm. At times she held the hatbox on her lap.

The train left at 8:10 for Los Angeles. When it arrived at 7:45 A.M., Monday, October 19, the packer trunk and smaller steamer trunk were unloaded. The baggage messenger who had earlier noticed the blood leakage from the larger trunk notified the supervisor there about his suspicions. At first, they thought the trunk contained contraband meat, perhaps from a butchered cow or deer.

Winnie took her hatbox while a porter carried her suitcase

to the women's rest room at the Southern Pacific station. The porter put the suitcase behind the door and Winnie walked across the room and sat down on the settee. A solicitous attendant asked Winnie if she were taking any of several trains.

"No," Winnie said, "I am waiting."

"What is the matter with your hand?" the maid asked.

"Oh, I got it burned," said Mrs. Judd. "Will these bags be all right behind the door?"

"Can't you check them?" asked the maid.

"I haven't the money to check them," said Winnie. "I have sent my brother a message, and if he is at the university he can't come. They won't deliver the message to him."

"Well, in a case like that I will try to keep an eye on them," said the maid. "Who will your brother be looking for?"

"Mrs. Judd."

"It is J-u-d-e?"

"No, Mrs. J-u-d-d."

"If your brother comes, shall I let him have the bags?"

"No, don't let anyone have the bags until I come back."

"When you come back, will you please come to me so I will know the right person will get the bags?"

Winnie said she would and left. She did not appear unusually nervous or excited.

At 12 noon, October 19, the baggage delivery clerk was at his post waiting on passengers when Mrs. Judd arrived with her brother, Jason. The clerk later reported, "I noticed a car back in, and this lady and a man got out of the car. He was a tall, raw-boned young man with bushy red hair; and he wore white cord trousers and didn't have any coat on. I saw her hand him the checks, and he presented me with the checks. I compared the checks with the numbers that I had copied off the two checks."

The trunks were in the baggage room, side by side on a baggage truck. The clerk had noticed an offensive odor coming from them and that one of them was leaking "a kind of fluid . . . the color of thick water or something." He notified his district baggage agent, who now asked the young man with the checks whom the baggage belonged to. Mrs. Judd stepped forward and said it belonged to her. C. B. Kaiser questioned her about the contents of the larger trunk. She said it contained personal effects and clothing.

Kaiser said, "It must contain something else that seems to be in bad order." He asked her to come with him to open the trunk and examine it. On the baggage room floor, she walked to the four-wheel truck backed up against the wall. As they approached, Kaiser asked Winnie and the young man with her if they noticed the unpleasant odor. They said they did not. He motioned them closer. They walked right up to the trunks. He asked them again if they could detect the odor.

Young Jason said he could. Kaiser turned to Mrs. Judd, and she now said she could, too. Her brother asked her "what in the world can be in the trunks" that would cause such an odor. She said she had no idea.

Kaiser again asked that the larger trunk be opened to determine what was causing the leakage. Jason said it might cause some embarrassment to open it then. He suggested that the district agent come to his residence and examine the contents there. The agent refused. Mrs. Judd opened her purse, apparently looking for the key. She said she couldn't find it, that her husband had it. Winnie was allowed to use the agent's phone to call her husband and have him bring the key to the station. When Mrs. Judd returned, she said she hadn't been able to find her husband's number in the directory and that she would get him and bring him to the station. Winnie and her brother left. They never returned to claim the baggage.

Jason drove his sister to Sixth Street and Broadway. He gave her $5 and some small change, and they parted.

4. THE SHOCK WAVES SPREAD

ABOUT 4:30 P.M., the district baggage agent reported the incident to the Los Angeles Police Department. Lieutenant Frank Ryan of the Detective Bureau, Homicide Detail, arrived about five o'clock. He noticed the offensive odor coming from the larger of the two trunks and proceeded to examine it. When he opened it, the first thing he saw was what appeared to be a piece of rug.

Lieutenant Ryan later testified, "There were a number of books and papers, also some bloody clothing and a quilt. I pulled the quilt down at the corner where the blood appeared to be coming from until I uncovered a woman's head." He closed the trunk, dropping the lid on it, and went to the baggage office where he phoned his office.

"Then I returned back out to the platform and, using the same key, opened the smaller of the two trunks. There were several sheets of blank paper, some of these blood-stained, and a light—what you would call a sheet—blanket. This, when I pulled it apart, I discovered was a bundle wrapped up in a piece of woman's clothing. When I unwrapped it, it proved to be a foot and a leg, from the knee down, of a human being. I opened down a little further through the blanket and discovered a woman's head. That was as far as the examination went at that time.

"Several sheets of that paper fell out of the smaller trunk when I opened it. Those were put back by Lieutenant Hopkins, who examined them there for fingerprints and then placed them back.

"The trunks were loaded into the coroner's wagon and taken to the county morgue. I followed behind them in the police car."

When news of the crime reached Phoenix, Chief of Police George O. Brisbois assigned several detectives including Eddie Moore, McCord Harrison, Dan Lucey and David Montgomery to the case. A police teletype was issued: "Arrest the woman on suspicion of murder—Winnie Ruth Judd, American, 26, fair complexion, grey-blue eyes, light brown hair. She weighs 125 pounds, is five feet seven inches and was wearing a black and white dress and a black hat."

Mrs. Judd's apartment at 1130 East Brill Street was searched by detectives Lucey and Montgomery. They found a bag of surgical tools, a suitcase containing men's clothing, other men's wear and a man's surgical shirt; also an article of woman's lingerie. They also found a suitcase packed with blankets, a small-caliber shell which had been fired and an album with photos of Dr. and Mrs. Judd and unidentified persons. Police learned about a missing radio, known to be in the apartment several days before Mrs. Judd left.

The stucco duplex at 2929 North Second Street was searched. Two rings of blood near the door and several spots on the carpet were found. A piece had been cut out of the carpet. One of the beds did not have a mattress, while the other was covered with a folded quilt. Orville Bechtol, superintendent of the police records department, photographed the scene of the crime and took fingerprints from three ginger ale bottles, found with a half-empty bottle of whiskey in the icebox.

The growing belief in an accomplice prompted Maricopa

County Attorney Lloyd J. Andrews to file two warrants: one charging Mrs. Judd, John Doe and Richard Doe with the crime of first degree murder in the death of Hedvig Samuelson, the second charging only Mrs. Judd with the murder of Agnes LeRoi.

"It would be foolish considering all we have learned," the county attorney told reporters, "to go on the theory Mrs. Judd alone was responsible for the slaying. She is a woman of slight build, and it would have been impossible for her alone to have handled the bodies. There is little doubt a man was involved in the packing of the bodies into the trunk."

Shortly after the corpses were discovered, Jason was located at the home of a sister-in-law of Mrs. Judd. He told police his sister had confessed killing the two women and admitted she had wanted him to pick up the trunks to throw them into the ocean. "I knew what was in those trunks," he said. "She told me. The thing I hate most about this is that it will kill my mother if she finds out about it. She is an invalid as it is. As for my sister, I hope she gets away. I wish I had $500 to give her."

Jason also explained that his sister had "insane fits of anger" while she was living with her parents. He said she liked a "good time" but that she would fly into "mad rages" and beat him with her fists. He was held after questioning.

Dr. Judd was quickly found, questioned and released. He told police he had not seen his wife in several weeks, and admitted knowing the slain women. He was variously reported as saying he didn't believe Winnie could have done such a thing, that he believed she was mentally deranged and that she had killed them and was perfectly justified in doing so.

Winnie's temperament soon became the topic of the day. She was described by some as being quiet and reserved. Others called attention to her parties during the week before the killings. Deputy County Attorney G. A. Rodgers listed narcotics and jealousy as possible motives. Investigators found several bottles of a drug then commonly known as "Luminal" among Winnie's belongings. Pharmacists gave "Luminal" as the trademark name for phenylethlmalonylurea, a sedative which they regarded as habit-forming but not narcotic. A letter from Dr. Judd to his wife was found, in which Judd pleaded with his wife to stop taking too much of a certain substance. He wrote, "You want to get hold of yourself. It will knock your nervous system to a fare-thee-well if you don't cut it out." Apart from his medical knowledge, Dr. Judd had personal experiences in such matters. He had spent time in the Oregon State Hospital as an inmate, committed from Marion County as a drug addict. The commitment had followed his return from European service with the American Expeditionary Forces in 1918.

Dr. Judd also gave Winnie advice about her mental stability in a letter written in early October: "There is nothing to be proud of in saying, 'I am going crazy' and threatening to 'do anything.' People do that every day, and you have seen hundreds of them who have. You had better just take things as easy as you can, come home at 5 o'clock and rest a bit and eat and sleep in a decent manner. I warn you that you must use a little self-control."

Jealousy between Mrs. Judd and Mrs. LeRoi was revealed by Dr. Curtis at the Grunow Clinic. He said Mrs. Judd had made several unfavorable statements about Mrs. LeRoi, and that her attitude toward her former friend had changed greatly in recent weeks. According to one news report, he told Mrs. Judd, "If you keep on saying things like that, people will think you are jealous of Mrs. LeRoi."

Hedvig Samuelson's sister, Elaine Whittmoor of Chicago, gave jealousy as a possible motive. She said, "I can hardly believe that Hedvig is dead. Hedvig visited me here last July and August to attend the Chicago Normal College and told me of the great friendship she and Mrs. LeRoi had. Later, she wrote about Mrs. Judd, saying that Mrs. Judd seemed terribly jealous of Mrs. LeRoi's friendship for Hedvig. The awful jealousy of Mrs. Judd is the only reason I can advance for the tragedy."

Olaf Johnson, Mrs. LeRoi's fiance, read of her death in a Twin Falls, Idaho, newspaper. Upon arriving in Boise, Idaho, during a sales trip, he showed inquirers some of Anne's letters.

On September 28, she had written: "Ruth is leaving us in a few days. Dr. Judd is coming home so she will take an apartment. It really hasn't worked out as well having three of us. We are very fond of her, and she is a sweet girl. But three just seems to be a wrong number when one is used to living by oneself and just one other very congenial one." On October 12, she wrote: "Went to Ruth's for luncheon today. She spent seven years in Mexico, and prides herself on Spanish dishes. I don't know what I ate. It didn't taste too bad, but I think it ruined me." Nothing in the other letters indicated any hostility between the women.

The news even touched Wrangler, Alaska. Miss Dorothy Wynn, a nurse whose picture was found in one of the trunks, was identified as a good friend of Mrs. LeRoi. Miss Wynn had served as a nurse when Mrs. LeRoi was superintendent at the Wrangler hospital, from October, 1929, to February, 1930. Six months later, Mrs. LeRoi and Miss Samuelson left for Phoenix. After hearing the news, Miss Wynn left Wrangler. It was assumed she had gone to her home in Leslie, Saskatchewan, but she was later found working in a hospital on the Olympic peninsula in Washington. She refused to discuss the case.

At his home in Darlington, Indiana, the Rev. H. J. McKinnell, Winnie's father, told reporters that his daughter had just written to him that she was happy and everything was going well. "Ruth used to teach in the Sunday School of my church here," he told them. "She always was a good girl. I am confident that my daughter had nothing to do with these murders. It must be mistaken identity. Her early training and the church would prevent such a thing. My only fear is that the suspicion thrown on Ruth will have a serious effect on Mother." Mrs. McKinnell was already in a state of "nervous collapse."

He said later, "Our first word about Ruth came from the newspapers. It struck us like a thunderbolt. As we know Ruth, there was never a discord in her life. While we have no way of knowing what later developments in her life have been, circumstantial evidence seems strongly against her. It is hard to believe she can be guilty."

News reports describing the impact of the crime on relatives ranged from the dramatic to the sentimental. In Portland, Oregon, the family of Anne LeRoi was interviewed.

"Here is her picture," said Mrs. Imlah, rousing from before the stove where solicitous friends had been attempting to quiet her.

She held forth a tear-stained portrait of her daughter in nursing uniform.

There was a family album on the table. Snapshots showed laughing children and their parents.

One of the pictures was of a baby girl, whose broken body was lifted from a blood-stained trunk in the Los Angeles railroad station.

Reporters of the Phoenix newspapers set a stark mood, the *Arizona Republic* depicting:

Silence . . . spooky silence . . . eerie silence. Not even the purr of a kitten, nor the bark of a dog. . . .

Such a condition prevailed in two Phoenix homes last night—two homes that have figured in the double trunk murder case.

The reporter was referring to 2929 North Second Street and 1130 East Brill Street, contrasting the "silence of death" found at these addresses with the "joyful" apartment courts of other Phoenix residents taking in every detail of the crime "during the last few days."

The article continued:

Aside from the two homes, the center of interest in the case was the *Gazette-Republic* newsroom. Reporters from Los Angeles joined with Phoenix newspapermen in the quest for bits of information leading to the motive of the crime or the whereabouts of Mrs. Judd.

Telephone operators worked overtime informing Phoenicians of developments in the case. Reporters, tired for want of sleep, worked fast in gathering information on the case.

It was a strange contrast to the weird silence that prevailed at the homes figuring in the case.

Informed that Winnie would return to Phoenix Tuesday, October 20, on an early morning train, peace officers, reporters and numerous spectators created a scene out of the Keystone Cops. Chief of Police Brisbois, County Attorney Andrews, half a dozen detectives and a dozen newspapermen met the Southern Pacific Argonaut at 6:30 A.M. They searched the train to no avail. The next train due, the Golden State Limited, was searched its entire length shortly after it left Los Angeles and again at Yuma and Buckeye. A railroad detective rode outside Car No. 10, reportedly carrying Mrs. Judd. The stateroom believed to be hers was found to be occupied by two men. The crowd then dashed to Sky Harbor Airport to meet the 10 A.M. flight from Los Angeles. It arrived without Winnie. Back to Union Station went the crowd to greet another train, the Phoenix. When no Winnie showed this time the crowd drifted away, worn out by the wild chase.

5. IN A FUNERAL PARLOR

COUNTY ATTORNEY LLOYD ANDREWS and investigator John L. Brinkerhoff left by airplane for Los Angeles at 3 P.M., October 20, to coordinate their investigation with that of L.A. authorities and to return the bodies to Phoenix.

Winnie's trail was now reported as reaching into Canada and Mexico. According to one lead, she had gone to New Jersey. Officers guarded all roads into Mexico. In Los Angeles, planes, trains and highways were searched for three days and two nights without results. Police at first promised a speedy capture, then began to describe Mrs. Judd as a "clever, ingenious woman with no nerves."

A woman fitting Mrs. Judd's description was sought in the area of Renton, Washington, fifteen miles south of Seattle. Night Sheriff Allingham said the woman was "positively identified" by the many persons who had seen newspaper photos of Mrs. Judd. The woman had asked about a bus schedule; when she failed to appear in time to take the bus, the police suspected "a ruse" and that she might be headed for Canada. At the same time, police in northern California were searching for a woman hitchhiker who looked like Mrs. Judd, according to five persons who had given the woman a ride. She told them she had been a resident of Phoenix.

Maricopa County Sheriff J. R. McFadden announced in Phoenix that there were convincing clues Mrs. Judd had an accomplice. Deputy Attorney Rodgers shared the sheriff's belief, but nothing further was revealed. Detectives had discovered new evidence suggesting that Miss Samuelson's body had been dismembered at the scene of the murder, 2929 North Second Street. Purported bloodstains were discovered in the bathroom and on a mop handle found in the garbage. Officers suggested that the mop was burned after Miss Samuelson's body had been dismembered in the bathtub.

Soon crowds of the curious began to visit the setting of the crime. Roger Thorpe, owner of the duplex, hired a man to stay in the house; M. G. Koller, Winnie's landlord, kept her apartment locked.

It was revealed that nine tablets of poison were missing from a phial found in a medicine case belonging to Dr. Judd at 1130 East Brill Street.

Winnie's brother, Jason, was questioned again October 22 in Los Angeles. County Attorney Andrews said, "I am not satisfied with his story. I am not through with him."

Winnie's brother was reported as knowing the whereabouts of his sister. He said, "I am certain I can get a message to her. I couldn't, however, get any cash to her. And I believe she would reply to my message. There may be a message waiting for me now, but I couldn't get it." He refused to clarify these statements. Police said he was not under surveillance, but newspapers reported that he was.

Jason said, "My sister is clever, and she has more nerve and self-control than any woman I know. If she met a policeman right now she could look him straight in the eye and not give anything away."

She was rumored to have done just that. One story held that she had been hiding in a sanitarium near Los Angeles during the first four days, while over two thousand officers throughout the West searched for her. Two policemen were said to have entered the sanitarium and questioned her while her injured hand was being dressed. But she had outwitted them and escaped, according to the story.

Dr. Judd feared that Winnie's body would be found in the ocean. Nevertheless, he made a plea through the Los Angeles morning newspapers to his wife to surrender. The *Los Angeles Times* offered $1,500 and the *Los Angeles Examiner* $1,000 for exclusive information leading to Mrs. Judd's arrest. Dr. Judd announced that he had retained Richard Cantillon, Milan Medigovich and former Judge Louis P. Russell as attorneys.

"I earnestly beg and implore her to come to me or these attorneys," Dr. Judd pleaded publicly. "I know that she had not a violent temper. If she has committed the crime with which she is charged, it means that it was done in a period of irresponsibility and in an irrational state or condition. I want to assure her that if this comes to her attention, she will have every support and assistance I am able to give her."

Responding to her husband's appeal, Winnie telephoned attorney Cantillon. She later talked to Judge Russell but refused to go to his office. During her fifth phone call, he suggested meeting her at the funeral parlor of Alvarez and Moore at Court and Olive streets. She agreed. "I think that will be all right. Send someone to meet me at Fifth and Olive streets, in front of the Biltmore Hotel." This was on October 23.

James Carey, special correspondent of the *Arizona State Democrat*, filed this report of the bizarre arrangements in Los Angeles:

Edward Mallory, of the undertaking firm, was given a car and entrusted with the errand. He found her waiting on the sidewalk in view of hundreds of pedestrians and a number of policemen.

"I'm a little nervous," she said apologetically, as she entered the car. "And my hand is hurting dreadfully."

Then she exhibited the bandage—the lone mark by which

officers hoped to trace her and identify her as the wanted woman.

They drove back to the undertaking parlor. Russell had also "invited" Sheriff Traeger, Taylor and Undersheriff Eugene Biscaiius to be present.

Mrs. Judd entered through a side door, and was taken to a bedroom upstairs.

Down on the ground floor, a wake was in progress, and the party trod lightly, conversing in whispers, so that the mourners would not be disturbed.

Dr. Judd and the fugitive's brother, who was with her when she attempted to obtain the trunks containing the bodies at the Central baggage station last Monday, entered the room with her.

Their arrival plunged the mortuary into a maelstrom. Upstairs, Inspector of Detectives David Davidson and Detective Frank Ryan attempted to enter the room in which Mrs. Judd was being questioned.

Mallory, unaware that they had been leading the search, blocked their path, and Ryan sent him sprawling. A gun flashed, and was hastily holstered.

Sobs came through the transom, as Dr. Judd embraced his wife. Then her sister [in-law] Pearl Ines, entered the room, and another outburst of weeping ensued.

Down in the huge reception room, a formidable semicircle of cameras had been established.

At 6:40 o'clock, Alvarez appeared at the head of the wide, winding staircase and gave the signal that "she's coming."

Outside, flashlights popped prematurely and the acrid odor of powder mingled with the sickly sweet scent of tuberoses.

The stage was set.

From behind a newel post, Cantillon and Russell appeared, walking very slowly. Between them they supported an unusually tall, attractive woman. She carried her head sidewise and her straggling yellow hair hung over her eyes. A black cloth coat, with yellow fur trim, was thrown over her shoulders. Beneath it was a white blouse and a green skirt. She wore no stockings, no hat, and carried no handbag.

Her left hand was held upon her breast, an ungainly white bandage covered the flesh to a point above the wrist. Funeral lights overhead made her face very pale, but seemed to magnify the size of the large and smoldering eyes.

Attorney Russell issued this statement, attributed to Mrs. Judd:

I had gone to the girls' home to remonstrate with Miss Samuelson for some nasty things she had said about Mrs. LeRoi. Miss Samuelson got hold of a gun and shot me in the left hand. I struggled with her and the gun fell. Mrs. LeRoi grabbed an ironing board and started to strike me over the head with it. In the struggle, I got hold of the gun and Sammy got shot. Mrs. LeRoi was still coming at me with the ironing board, and I had to shoot her. Then I ran from the place—."

Mrs. Judd's condition would not permit her to continue with the story.

County Attorney Andrews and Deputy Harry Johnson of Phoenix joined the Los Angeles officers in questioning Winnie before she was taken to the Georgia Street Receiving Hospital for treatment of her wound. She would not reveal where she had hid out. Andrews said, "We may as well have been questioning the Sphinx insofar as getting information on the case was concerned."

About five hundred onlookers had gathered at the hospital to get a glimpse of Winnie, and she attracted the attention of patients as well. A .25-caliber bullet was removed from the base of her middle finger, close to the point where it joined with her fractured index finger.

While under the influence of anesthetic, she made disordered and rambling remarks, punctuated with silence and screams:

"Oh, Doctor—I fought—I fought so hard. You'd have fought, too. . . .

"Doctor, kiss me—I've been so mean. . . .

"I wish I had a Catholic priest here. . . .

"I always wanted to be a nurse, but I couldn't. I wasn't strong enough. I loved the clinic. . . .

"Oh, don't hurt my hand. I've been asked all those questions, and I answered them. They're pinching my hand. It hurts. Oh, Doctor, just hit them once for me. . . .

"Don't let them ask me any more questions—make them stop squeezing my poor hand. . . .

"I've told them everything. I've told them the truth."

The police surgeon said "home remedies" had been applied to the wound and that it did not appear to have been treated by a physician. Dr. J. E. Kirkpatrick, who removed the bullet, said there were contusions over much of Mrs. Judd's body. He gave the bullet to Lieutenant Frank Ryan and L.A. police ballistics expert Spencer Moxley later received it for comparison with the bullets that had killed Mrs. LeRoi and Miss Samuelson.

Mrs. Judd was to have been kept under observation at the hospital but when she said she was hungry, a trip to a downtown café was arranged. According to County Attorney Andrews, Mrs. Judd laughed and joked with her husband and the others in the group. Andrews said, "She told us she had been in Los Angeles since her arrival Monday. She told us that she had had only occasional food."

Winnie was next taken to the L.A. county jail, booked on suspicion of murder and questioned in the detectives' room in the presence of her attorneys and Dr. Judd. When defense attorney Cantillon objected to certain questions, Dr. Judd and the attorneys were ordered to leave the room. As he left, Cantillon told Winnie, "Don't talk." Once outside, Dr. Judd slipped a note under the door informing the officers that he or the attorneys must be present at the interrogation. Dr. Judd was again allowed to enter the room. After intensive questioning, a special guard was assigned to Mrs. Judd for the night.

Despite a statement by Detective Chief Taylor that Mrs. Judd had confessed to the crime, Winnie's attorneys said she had made no statement of "legal standing." They said she would not make a statement until the trial.

6. THE "DRAIN PIPE LETTER"

On October 24, one day after Winnie Ruth Judd surrendered to police in the funeral parlor, a plumber in the Broadway Department Store in Los Angeles reported finding a scrap of paper bearing the name Judd on a rest room floor. Police probed the toilet drains. One of them produced ten water-soaked telegraph blanks, upon which were written a letter. Deciphering of the letter, almost pulp when retrieved, was a delicate and laborious task. It was addressed to Dr. W. C. Judd of Santa Monica, California, and apparently written by Mrs. Judd while hiding overnight in the draperies department of the store.

Police also recovered a partially obliterated note to a Los Angeles physician asking him to deliver the letter to Dr. Judd:

Dear Doctor Moore:

I am being sought for by the police and can't get any message to my darling precious husband Dr. Judd. I've got to tell him . . . so will you deliver this let . . . to it and deliver the messa . . . be kind to my poor hus . . . I do love him

. . . I'm crazy . . . I . . . mes . . . when I get tired in . . .
worried mentally and sick mind & b . . . then finding me for
my crime . . . a . . . tell Dr. Judd forgive him . . . tell him
. . . to please not die of grief . . . I love him and hope he
wont hate me for being wicked.

Thank you and Mrs. Moore for having been so good and
sweet to me in the past. One of my hands is about shot off
so I can scarcely write. Do me this favor to let Dr. Judd know
what happened . . . I cant. I love him but through . . . nobody but my dear husband a . . . ter and parents believing
me. I'm . . . ng away from the police . . . best regards and
hoping you do this. . . .

Police authorities said the letter constituted a confession
by Mrs. Judd of the killing of her former close friends and
shipping their bodies in the trunks. She denied writing the
letter or attempting to destroy any. The authorities declared
the handwriting was precisely that of Mrs. Judd, and that it
contained information which could not possibly be known to
any other person.

The postal telegraph blanks she intended Dr. Moore to deliver to her husband became known as the "drain pipe letter":

Darling:

A confession I've kept from you for life because I was
so happy with you and loved you so why tell you. I am crazy
only when I am very angry or to [sic] tired physically my
brain goes wrong. One obsession I've always had is wanted
or saying I had a baby. 1st when I was seven years old I
wanted a baby at our house so bad I told at school that
mother had one and for days told the neighbors we had one
and such cute anticks it did far beyond an infants ability.
Then when I was 16 on my birthday a fellow I was going
with and I had a split up. I was furious my girl friend was
the cause curiously I liked her just as well we chummed together, but this boys cousin antagonized me by crowing that
some one could take him from me. I had taken her boy friend

months before from her. The man's name was Fred Jensen
he wished to be friends but liked my chum Laura Walters.
It was O K until j-y Burns I hate her always will crowed (I
had taken a fellow Ronald Carpenter from her later they
married) I told Fred Jensen about it and asked him not to
go with Laura. I loved Laura, but I hated Joy her crowing
Fred thought I was doing it for meanness etc. and so finally
as so many unmarried girls in that part of the woods were
having babys I conceived of stating I was and would make
Fred marry me if necessary. I was 16. He was 26. Fred Jensen
never touched me. I had never had intercourse with him or
with any man until I met you. Fred I believe is honest. He
cried and cried and told daddy he'd never touch me. He used
to tell me I was crazy. I said well quit going with Laura or I'll
send you to the Pen. I won't be tormented by Joy Burns. I
was going pretty good at school then my teachers loved me.
I was good in English class my stories were published in the
school paper and in the city paper I made up in my 90 Botany
zoology. The teachers all like me and I did splendid in Modern History my class mates like me and I them but I got so
worked up I quit school and said I was pregnant and
swore out warrants against Fred made darling dresses all
kinds of dainty things I later gave for little girls dolls. Fred
would walk home from church with me and tell me I was
crazy. I said I knew it, but if I started this thing I would
finish it. I wanted him to go away until I went back to college then go with Laura, but please not then that I had an
insane temper. So finally after about ten months I decided
I'd have to confess a lie or do something drastic so I pre-
ceeded to hop out of my window one night in cold October
in my gown and I grabbed a few gunny sacks and overshoes
and run away and say I'd been kidnapped. First I wrote a
letter that I had a baby girl (Why I don't know) then I ran
away was going to get some clothes at my home sixteen miles
from there and be gone awhile and my Fred had had me kidnapped and I got away. I brought suits against him and assumed a [as soon as] Joy moved I dropped charges and that

was the end. This is the first time I have ever told this my parents believe Fred wicked. I did it all myself and never have told it to anyone until now. I've always wanted to tell Fred I was sorry He was a good boy He thought it was funny until I had him arrested for rape and kidnapping etc. I'm sorry to tell you this doctor. Here is a confession I should have carried to my death if I had been intimate with any man I would have told you but I didn't tell you anything to hurt you I've wanted your respect confidence and love. There in Mazatlan or rather Tyoltita I was sick a couple of days so as Mrs. Heinz had been so thrilled over being pregnant I decided Id say I was. I had hoped for three weeks I might be until I came unwell so when you moved I wrote I had had a miscarriage. Then again I told Mrs. . . . and Mrs. Aster I was where you saw I was menstruating the very week we left there. I don't know what possessed me to tell that I had a little boy. I even showed pictures of you with a baby and showed Dyers baby pictures as my baby who was with Mama so I'm crazy on that line. And aside from that and occasionally a rage I get into I seem quite bright. I was working so hard at Phoenix when you went to Bisbee then something went wrong in my head and I registered under an assumed name and called you up gave a fictitious address just to hear your voice and see you then cried all night for doing it. Got a car next morning to sooth my nerves at the garage below the Hotel and drove to Warren. Then finally wanted you to soothe me and told you I was there. You know how I cried and cried. I was crazy You said I was at the time, I came back and Mr. H. came out the next evening he had been on the coast and he said what's the matter you look terrible you look crazy. My two doctors said I looked terrible. I've written you for a month how my nerves were doing. Then Thursday Mr. H. bought the girls a new radio Mr. Adams had let them have his but they didn't like him so hated to use his radio. Mr. H. wanted me to get some other girl and go with him out to the house I knew a pretty little nurse who is taking Salvarsan but she has nothing contagious now. I

certainly am not expecting them to do wrong, anyhow, so
saw no harm she's pretty and can be interesting so we went
out to the girls house. Dr. Brinckerhoff and a couple
Mr. H. friends were there. The girls didn't like to it so Mr.
H. asked us to have dinner with them I refused so he got
dinner and came over to the house. The first time he has ever
done it but it was a nice clean evening I truly didn't even
take a drink you can ask. The remains of their drinks are in
the ice box. Next day Ann came over and we had lunch together the remains of the dinner the night before. She
wanted me to go home with her that night. Denise Reynolds
was going. I had some histories to do and couldn't, I said
if I get through in time I'll come over and play bridge, but
I stayed all night. The next morning all three of us were
yet in our pajamas when the quarrel began I was going hunting. They said if I did they would tell Mr. H. I had introduced him to a nurse who had syphillis. I said Ann you've
no right to tell things from the office you know that only
because you saw me get distilled water and syringes ready
and she hasn't it contageoush the doctor lets her work nursing. Well Ann said I asked Denise and she thinks I should
tell Mr. H. too. And he certainly won't think much of you
for doing such a thing. You've been trying to make him like
you and Mr. D. too getting him to move you and when I
tell them you associated with and introduce them to girls
who have syphillis they won't have a thing to do with you.
And when we tell Mr. P. about it he won't take you hunting
either. I said Sammy I'll shoot you if tell that we were in
the kitchen just starting breakfast she came in with my gun
and said she would shoot me if I went hunting with this
friend. I threw my hand over the mouth of the gun and
grabbed the bread knife she shot I jumped on her with all
my weight and knocked her down in the dining room Ann
yelled at us I fired twice I think and since Ann was going to
black mail me too if I went hunting by telling them this patient of Dr. Curtis' was syphillitic and would hand me over to
the police I fired at her. There was no harm introducing

this nurse who is very pretty to the men. One doesn't get it from contact but they were going to kill me for introducing this her initials are D. E. St. Josephs to their men friends Ann said before Sammy got the gun Ruth I could kill you for introducing that girl to . . . and if you go hunting I will tell them and they won't think your so darn nice anymore. I don't want to bring Mr. H. into this he has been kind to me when I was lonesome at the 1st place I worked and has trusted me with many secrets of all he did for the girls such as caring for Ann giving her extra money and the radio and he's been a decent fellow. It would separate he and his wife and he's been too decent. Mr. D. kept Ann in an apartment here in L.A. for several days then got her state room to Ph and she was mad enough to kill me when he helped move me over. Part of my things are still in the girls 3 hats, thermos bottle, black dress cook book, green scarf you got me in Mexico and a number of things. Doctor dear Im so sorry Sammy shot me whether it was the pain or what I got the gun and killed her. It was horrible to pack things as I did. I kept saying I've got to I've got to or I'll be hung I've got to or I'll be hung. I'm wild with cold hunger pain and fear now. Doctor darling if I hadn't got the gun from Sammy she would have shot me again. Forgive me not forget me. Live to take care of . . . sick. Doctor, but I'm true to you. . . . The thots of being away from . . . it me crazy. Shall I give up to . . . don't think so the police will hang me. It was as much a battle as Germany & the U.S. I killed in defense. Love me yet doctor.

7. THE CROWD WAITS

ON SATURDAY, OCTOBER 24, extradition papers were sent by special plane to Arizona Governor George W. P. Hunt at Tucson for his signature. When they arrived, Sheriff McFadden immediately flew the same morning to present the papers to Governor James Rolph, Jr., in Sacramento, California. The sheriff was accompanied by a matron, Mrs. Lon Jordan.

During Mrs. Judd's questioning by detectives that day, she indicated her willingness to return to Arizona. But Winnie's husband told his wife, "You know we are going to fight extradition to Arizona."

"We are?" she asked. "Why?"

"We think you'll be better off here," Dr. Judd said.

"Why, I like Arizona," she said. "It's the only place for me." Nevertheless, one of Winnie's attorneys obtained from Superior Court Judge Charles Burnell a writ of habeas corpus, prohibiting her extradition until after a hearing scheduled for November 3.

Rival Los Angeles papers were soon at work printing various life stories and personal accounts by Mrs. Judd, Dr. Judd and

Mrs. Judd's brother, Jason. Reporters from two newspapers, six men in one group and five in the other, finally confronted one another at the door of the county jail hospital. The six-man contingent was prepared to offer Mrs. Judd one of the largest sums ever paid a criminal for a personal story, but arrived late.

The others, just leaving a meeting inside with Dr. Judd, who had already begun his own draft, accused their opponents. One shouted, "And you're the smart guys who got out that warrant for Doc Judd for practicing medicine without a license, eh?" Blows were exchanged while notes were passed inside to Mrs. Judd. She had already been interviewed by one paper, for a fee, and now said that only if Dr. Judd agreed would she sell her story a second time. The Doctor had already left. Temporarily stymied, one reporter from each paper remained to watch the competition.

On Tuesday, extradition papers were approved in Sacramento by the California deputy attorney and Sheriff McFadden left for San Francisco in a state automobile driven by the governor's chauffeur. Governor Rolph, who was ill, was being cared for there at St. Francis Hospital. When McFadden got the governor's signature, he proceeded back to Los Angeles.

Mrs. Judd, now convinced that she should remain in California, wept hysterically when she learned Governor Rolph had signed the extradition papers. "They can't do that! I have tuberculosis! My hand is hurting terribly. I can't be moved."

Winnie's attorneys announced they would fight extradition by forcing an examination of the papers. Defense Attorney Louis P. Russell said, "The reason we seek to delay her return is not because we have any desire to hinder justice. We are reliably informed, however, that in Phoenix the feeling against our client is high, and we believe this hysteria should subside before Mrs. Judd can be assured a fair and impartial trial."

Sheriff McFadden was not concerned. "She'll go back in a few days," he announced. "She knows me. We became acquainted when she helped nurse my wife once. I told her

I'd see that she was cared for properly on the trip back. I don't think she wants to kill time."

At the jail hospital on Wednesday, Mrs. Judd said, "I am not afraid of returning to Arizona for trial. I think that the jury will believe I had to fire in self-defense. In addition, I have received word from a man who will be the star witness in this case that he will back me up."

By Thursday, Winnie had changed attorneys and dropped any effort to fight extradition. Her new attorney, Paul Schenck, and Dr. Judd conferred with her as she prepared to leave for Phoenix.

Winnie's hair was waved by Daisy DeVoe, who was Clara Bow's secretary before she began serving an eighteen-month term in the county jail for theft from Miss Bow. Miss DeVoe advised Winnie to be sparing with makeup during the trial.

Late Thursday night, October 29, Winnie left for Phoenix in a van of cars, in the custody of Sheriff McFadden, County Attorney Andrews and jail matron Mrs. Jordan. Mrs. Judd appeared to be in good spirits, having discovered that Dr. Judd was riding in one of the accompanying cars. She did not know that Dr. Judd left Los Angeles, where he was under bond for practicing medicine without a license.

On first seeing her husband at a car stop that night, Mrs. Judd said, "Doctor! Doctor! I'm so glad to see you. Oh, kiss me, dear."

Dr. Judd had been told to stay away from his wife, but Sheriff McFadden allowed this brief encounter.

At Yuma, the group stopped for breakfast. Cameras flashed, while Yumans struggled to catch sight of Winnie. She remained alone while Dr. Judd ate with Andrews and newspapermen.

At Gila Bend, Winnie learned that a crowd of about a thousand people awaited her arrival at the courthouse.

"Oh, God, no!" she said. "Oh, Sheriff . . . isn't there . . . can't we . . . ?"

About twenty miles outside of Phoenix, the cars were met by a police escort, arranged by the police chief and a deputy sheriff to clear traffic. Mrs. Judd grew increasingly despondent as the cavalcade of cars approached their destination, where a crowd of the curious had been gathering since early morning. The caravan arrived in the early afternoon, and Winnie was ringed by photographers as she was given a bouquet of flowers by three women who forced their way through the crowd. Newsmen waited inside the sheriff's office. Inmates in the women's section of the jail had decorated the window bars with paper flowers. Closely guarded, Winnie was escorted to the county jailer's office.

"Please, Sheriff," she said, referring to the reporters, "don't let them come in here now. I can't face any more of those flashlights and cameras."

Newsmen and photographers were nevertheless allowed a half-hour session with Mrs. Judd. She had nothing sensational to reveal but posed for photographers, who were making her for the moment the most photographed woman in America. Winnie was asked by a reporter to pose with a telegraph form from a Los Angeles newspaper which was supposedly to publish her story.

"Shall I read the telegram?" she asked.

"Go ahead," the reporter told her.

"It says, 'Don't spend so much on long-distance calls when you can telegraph.'"

One photographer attempted to get a closeup of the murderess and the bench on which she was sitting.

"Hey, you can't do that!" shouted Sheriff McFadden. The sheriff jumped in front of the bench, which had been carved with an inscription by a former inmate: "This is a Hell of a place, and how!"

"We haven't painted it over yet," said the sheriff.

After spending Friday with four other women prisoners, Mrs. Judd was given a cell to herself. Acting as an associate of Paul Schenck of Los Angeles, Phoenix attorney Samuel Franks conferred with Winnie during the weekend. Other visitors were denied access. Mrs. Judd had begun receiving "fan mail," both good and bad, in Los Angeles, and over three hundred strangers tried unsuccessfully to visit her during the first four days of her confinement in Phoenix.

There was speculation Mrs. Judd might seek a change of

venue, which could be granted by the judge presiding over her arraignment. It was also rumored that Winnie might plead insanity rather than self-defense, as she had previously announced.

"I don't believe Mrs. Judd will succeed with an insanity defense," Andrews said. "I am convinced that she was perfectly sane when she killed Agnes LeRoi and Hedvig Samuelson, and I am sure I can convince an Arizona jury of it."

Previously, Arizona had convicted only two women of first degree murder. Only one, Mrs. Eva Dugan, was hanged, in February, 1930. She was decapitated by the rope, and as a result of this incident, the Arizona legislature passed a bill replacing the gallows with lethal gas. However, this effort was frustrated by the attorney general, who ruled that any change in the state's method of execution would have to be approved by popular vote.

Those who were superstitious began to believe that Friday, the customary day for hanging at the state penitentiary, was an unlucky day for Winnie. Friday, October 16, was the date of the murder, according to state prosecutors. Mrs. Judd had surrendered in Los Angeles on a Friday, and it was on a Friday that she was returned to Phoenix.

Popular superstitions about Mrs. Judd's fate were enhanced by Count Louis Hamon, an internationally famous psychoanalyst, astrologer and author who visited Phoenix to observe Winnie and cast her horoscope. In his opinion, she was fully capable of committing the murders or of accepting vicarious guilt, "even to the limit of fanatical glory of martyrdom in going to her own doom."

Known professionally as "Cheiro," Count Hamon had analyzed British Lord Kitchener's life at the request of the British Admiralty and had predicted in 1900 that Mata Hari would be shot at dawn seventeen years later. The count said that adverse influences in Mrs. Judd's life climaxed on October 16 or 17. "She would be likely to commit crime, under suggestion, hypnotism or narcotic of any kind, or easily be deluded into the idea that she had committed crime," he said.

"Without going into technicalities," continued the count, "it is an unfortunate horoscope from the start, indicating financial uncertainty with great difficulties, trials, adversity, mental unbalance, and a brain that never was normal after the age of puberty had passed. Further, the intensity of her love nature is so apparent that she would shield anyone she loved at this period of her life. This woman is an actress in every sense of the word. Had conditions been more fortunate, there are indications she would have succeeded in a dramatic career."

On November 3, Winnie appeared before Justice Clarence E. Ice of the East Phoenix Precinct, where she was charged with murdering Mrs. LeRoi and Miss Samuelson. A large crowd had filled the county building when Mrs. Judd arrived. Wearing black and no makeup, she appeared pale and nervous. When Justice Ice took the bench, attorney Franks said, "She is not very well," and she was excused from standing. The charges were read. Franks then asked for a hearing, and County Attorney Andrews said that November 16 had been agreed upon as the time.

Some exchanges between the prosecution and counsel for the defense were not so agreeable. In an interview in Los Angeles, Schenck had said, "Statements in newspapers credited to County Attorney Lloyd Andrews of Phoenix and Sheriff J. R. McFadden of Maricopa County considered by me to be true, flatly show these two officials to have broken promises made personally to myself and client while she was confined in the Los Angeles County Jail.

"I was given to understand [by Andrews] she would not be made the target of lengthy questioning, nor unnecessarily harassed. Now I find from reports that they expect to question my client for sixty hours or until they break down her self-defense story . . . that might possibly be proper in the presence of her attorney and where she would be advised as to her legal rights.

"They [officials in Phoenix] likewise told me they would place Mrs. Judd in confinement and that she would not be molested, except for the usual routine of questioning, until

I could be with her. I want to know, and I shall find out, just why all this has been forgotten and the Arizona authorities are rushing headlong into a most drastic investigation and attempting to drag my client along with them.

"The days of the Inquisition and such methods are gone, and I intend to see justice is meted out in this case. She will not be harried and worried with continual visits from newspapermen and forced to tell and retell again the story of the slayings and her attempt to do away with the bodies. This harrowing experience has been related by this woman twice already to my knowledge."

County Attorney Andrews reacted sharply, particularly on the subject of harassment by newsmen. "Mrs. Judd has been advised both by myself, and by all others in Phoenix who have questioned her, as to her constitutional rights," he said. "This is always done by ethical prosecutors.

"I made no trade with Schenck or anyone else. I did agree, however, that her preliminary hearing would be delayed a reasonable length of time. This has been done and will be done. Mrs. Judd has not been made the target of lengthy questioning by my officers or others since her arrival. In fact, she has been allowed the first rest she has received since her arrest. Neither has she been subjected to unnecessary harassment. The statement that she has been or will be questioned for sixty hours is so ridiculous as to be merely noise by any person in his right mind.

"I am at a loss to understand what can be meant by 'she would not be molested except for the usual routine in questioning.' She has not been 'molested,' if it can be called that, even by the 'usual routine of questioning.' She was too exhausted after her fourteen-hour trip from Los Angeles, and we allowed her two and one-half days to rest. The longest session of questioning, since her arrival here, occurred today when her attorney . . . conferred with her for four hours. However, just because Mrs. Judd was arrested in Los Angeles and is represented by Paul Schenck does not mean that she is to be treated any different from any other person charged with murder in Maricopa County.

"Since her arrival in Phoenix, newspapermen have been barred from her cell. The 'harrowing experience' of telling and retelling her story of the killing referred to by Mr. Schenck was an experience through which, according to the press, Mrs. Judd received thousands of dollars. It was her own story—one for which she was paid real money. And the only story she has told has been voluntarily made to newspapermen. I have yet to see one of her purported 'confessions' made to the constituted authorities.

"Any questioning Mrs. Judd may be subjected to in Phoenix will not be for the purpose of lining her pocketbook, but to determine how women were killed in violation of the law of Arizona. It seems to me that the real purpose of the general charges of harassment and molestation and breaking of promises can be for no other reason but to work up public sympathy for this confessed killer."

On Thursday, the sparring between the prosecution and counsel for the defense once again shifted from verbal to legal grounds. Mrs. Judd's attorney Samuel Franks was forced to obtain a court order permitting him to visit the house where the murders took place. "I am trying to check up on her story as she has told it to the newspapers," said Franks. Deputy County Attorney Robert McMurchie argued the motion to set aside the order.

McMurchie said, "Your honor, you might just as well have ordered the county attorney to divulge all the evidence against the defendant to her attorney."

"That is not a proper comparison," snapped the judge. "Thousands of persons have inspected the house at 2929 North Second Street, and now the county attorney refuses defense counsel to visit it for the purpose of preparing his case in justice court." In fact, over two thousand persons had paid ten cents admission each to tour the murder house.

After McMurchie had concluded his remarks, Franks began his argument, which Judge Phelps interrupted. "If you have any authorities, cite them," he said. "At the time I issued the order I did not look into the law—it was a matter of common sense." He subsequently refused to quash the order, and County Attorney Andrews further contested his decision.

Sometime after this hearing, Winnie was transferred from her private cell to the women's "tank." Sheriff McFadden said, "We put her back with the other women prisoners because it will save the county money. She is in good health, eats the regular jail food without complaint, and there is no reason to pamper her at the expense of the county."

Although Mrs. Judd had supposedly recovered from her Los Angeles to Phoenix trip, most requests for visits with her were denied. "She has talked with her husband, her attorneys and myself nearly every day, but no one else sees her," said the sheriff.

Winnie appeared once again before Justice Ice on Monday, November 9, escorted by sheriff's deputies and jail matron Mrs. Jordan. Winnie, without a trace of makeup, dressed in an ankle-length dress of black chiffon, was greeted by crowds composed largely of women gathered throughout the courthouse. One woman fainted and, with great difficulty, was carried outside, where another crowd stood on the sidewalk.

The courtroom held only two dozen newsmen and photographers and about sixty spectators. The coming and going of newsmen seeking the telephone was something of a problem, with some of the reporters forced to remain outside between recesses. Occasionally, fights broke out between sheriff's deputies and those who wanted admission. During this hearing, Mrs. Judd sat at a corner of the counsel table between the matron and Joseph B. Zaversack, an associate of Franks.

Eleven witnesses testified for the state, and two cast considerable doubt upon Mrs. Judd's version of the killings. In her previous statements she had asserted that she was shot in the hand during a struggle in which Miss Samuelson was killed, and that she had shot from a prone position as Mrs. LeRoi attacked with an ironing board. Dr. J. D. Mauldin, Maricopa County physician, testified that both women were killed by bullets ranging downward through the brain and that powder burns were noticeable. John W. Pritchett, the employee of Lightning Delivery Company, testified that Mrs. Judd's hand was not injured or bandaged when he picked up the trunk at 2929 North Second Street.

Pritchett said, "I saw Mrs. Judd's hand clearly. She held her purse in it. It was not bandaged, and had no wrapping of any kind. Her right hand had none either. She paid me with that one."

At Winnie's suggestion, Franks asked, "Did she tip you for your work?"

"She promised to twice, but she never did," returned Pritchett.

Mrs. Judd laughed and turned to her husband, who napped through most of the five-hour session.

The hearing was concluded at 4:05 P.M.—"Defendant held to answer without bond."

After the excitement of her preliminary hearing, Winnie spent a quiet Tuesday in her cell. She visited with her husband and conferred with attorney Franks, who conferred as well with Lloyd Andrews and his deputies. Meanwhile, Winnie's parents were traveling from Darlington, Indiana, to be with their daughter during the ordeal of her trial. Church members and neighbors donated the money necessary for the elderly couple to make the trip to Phoenix.

The Rev. and Mrs. H. J. McKinnell arrived by train on Friday the 13th. They were met by Franks and Rev. J. G. Fritz, a Phoenix Free Methodist minister. Anxious to see Winnie, the McKinnells rose early the next day and waited for word from the sheriff. "Don't be impatient," the elderly clergyman told his wife. "He will soon be here. He is a busy man, you know."

McFadden conferred with them in private in his office and then took them to a fifth-floor cell. No newsmen or photographers were allowed up. "I don't want these old people to go through more than they may have to," the sheriff said. "Let's leave them alone as much as possible until they get used to conditions."

Rev. McKinnell reassured his wife as they waited in the cell for Winnie. "Be brave, Mamma, be brave. Don't worry, Mamma; all this is going to come out all right. I don't believe anyone knows all in this matter. Have faith in our girl. Be glad to see her. Be brave."

Finally, Mrs. Judd arrived with the matron as McFadden called out, "Come here; your mother and father are here to see you." Except for the matron, they were left alone to talk.

An hour later, Rev. McKinnell left the cell. "It is more important that Mamma should be with Ruth," he told reporters. "I will have a lot of running around to do. Dr. Fritz wants Mrs. McKinnell and me to stay with them, but I can't do that. We must look for a boarding place—a moderately priced one, too, for you know we ministers are notorious for being poor."

Asked how he found his daughter, the Reverend answered, "I can't say. We were so glad to see her, and she was glad to see us. Ruth looks like she is being well cared for, and Mr. Mc-Fadden surely is a splendid man. I would not have been surprised had he searched me to find saws and other things, but he didn't. He treated us like we were his friends, and he is going to let Mamma and me see her every day. Mamma may stay with her for two hours if she wants to, so he said, and he said that I would be given ample time with her, too.

"Everybody wants to do something for us. I don't know how I am going to return all these kindnesses. We are in deep trouble, indeed, but how much lighter has our burden been made by kindness. I feel certain that Ruth will be treated fairly. You can't imagine how grateful we are to find friends instead of enemies. The horror of it all has disappeared much since last night. You know, I have never been so far away from home, and today we are in a strange land. But everything appears so bright here—the sun is brighter and the people are kind."

He acknowledged that Winnie was "not herself," but added, "Maybe we are not ourselves." One point he made strongly: "I want my daughter to tell the truth. No matter what happens, she must tell everything truthfully."

8. TO TELL EVERYTHING

CROWDS FILLED THE corridors and the courtroom as Winnie Ruth Judd was escorted to Division No. 3, Superior Court, for her November 16 arraignment before Justice Howard C. Speakman. She was accompanied by Dr. Judd, Sheriff McFadden and the matron, and on her way to the counsel table, she was greeted with a kiss by her elderly father.

Judge Speakman announced, "Case No. 11340—the State of Arizona against Winnie Ruth Judd." Winnie stood as William Choisser, court clerk, read the first information charging her with the murder of Agnes Anne LeRoi. Franks said, "We enter a plea of not guilty with the stipulation that we may be granted the privilege of filing a demurrer or any dilatory pleas or to withdraw the plea." Judge Speakman allowed ten days for any changes in the plea.

"How long will it take to try this case?" asked the court.

"Not very long as far as the state is concerned," said Andrews.

"Probably a week," said Franks. "We won't be ready for more

than a month," he added. "We must obtain depositions from the East."

"This is not different from any other homicide," said Andrews.

Judge Speakman asked if defense would be ready by December 15.

"No, your honor," said Franks.

"We will set it for December 15," said the judge, "and if the defense is not ready, it may make a showing for its postponement."

"You'll never bring her to trial on that date," was Franks' reply.

The second complaint, charging Winnie with the murder of Hedvig Samuelson, was read and the plea of not guilty entered. The trial date in the second case was also set for December 15.

"May the records show that we object to the trial date?" asked Franks. The objection was noted and the hearing concluded.

In Los Angeles, Paul Schenck said that he and Dr. Edward Huntington Williams would leave for Phoenix to examine Mrs. Judd. Franks had said a local doctor would also be called in as a consultant. On Saturday, November 28, Mrs. Judd received physical and mental examinations. Dr. Williams interviewed Winnie for three hours. Later, in the afternoon, the state's psychiatrist, Dr. Joseph Catton of San Francisco, talked with her for two and one-half hours.

A week later, Catton revealed that Winnie had concealed many details of the crime. "Mrs. Judd told me she could reveal a great deal more about what happened than was generally known," he said. "But she claimed she had not decided whether she would tell it. I also asked her about the confession found in a Los Angeles drain pipe and she replied she 'didn't know whether she was going to say she wrote it or not.'"

Franks' contention that Winnie would not be brought to trial on December 15 proved correct. Judge Speakman granted a continuance to January 19. The defense asked for the delay to permit the taking of depositions in the East. "We are taking depositions of relatives and friends of Mrs. Judd and from hospitals of the insane in Ohio, Indiana and Illinois, where relatives of Mrs. Judd have been patients," said Franks. He had earlier announced the defense would include a plea of insanity and said the depositions would be read into the trial.

Meanwhile, Winnie waited. She had finally been fingerprinted, her hand having healed. To the State Bureau of Criminal Identification, she became No. 16,212. She was also identified by these statistics—"Index finger and middle fingers badly wounded by bullet: 26 years old: blue eyes: golden brown hair: 65 inches tall: 109 pounds in weight: fair complexion."

To Sheriff McFadden during this time, she was a model prisoner. "She hasn't given us any trouble," he said. "I gave her to understand when we returned here from Los Angeles that she couldn't expect any special favors or any better treatment than that given other women prisoners. Of course, she has a temper, and has let it get the best of her several times. But she's been under a terrific strain and she's bearing up well. Withal, she's been a good prisoner and hasn't asked any special consideration. She hasn't said a thing about the slayings. I tried a number of times to get her to tell me certain details, but she has been tight-lipped. I told her if she would talk, we might be able to help her, but she refused, so I've abandoned the idea of encouraging her to tell all."

More than a week before the trial, Judge Speakman announced that there would be no "passes" or reserved seats assuring admission to the Judd trial. He had received letters from people and the press throughout the country seeking admission. The courtroom would hold only about two hundred persons, and according to the judge, it would be strictly "first come, first served."

Newsmen referred to Mrs. Judd in many ways. She was reported as "winsome Winnie," and as "the blond butcher." She became widely known as "the trunk slayer" and the "Tiger Woman." Newsmen described her as a vicious predator and wrote of the ferocity of her crimes with headlines such as "Tiger Woman to Appear in Court" and "Tigress Awaits Fate."

Newspapers were promising new developments in the case. Under the sub-headline "Sensations Promised," this story was filed by Kelly Turner, staff writer for the *Phoenix Gazette:*

Startling developments of a case that already has stirred the nation and gained world-wide attention are freely predicted for the trial. Almost unparalleled in gruesomeness and remarkable features as was the double killing—the trial is expected to rival the event itself in its new disclosures.

A blood-hued web of fact, speculation and mystery is woven around Mrs. Judd. Lines of this amazing tangle apparently are entwined around the lives of individuals here and in other cities.

County Attorney Andrews' task will be to unravel these threads of evidence and analyze them so that a jury may determine whether or not the state is correct in its contention that Agnes Anne LeRoi and Hedvig Samuelson were victims of premeditated murder.

Mrs. Judd must give a jury her answer to these accusations. Upon this answer rests her chance of escaping a penalty—possibly the hangman's noose.

Speculation of further sensations grew from the discovery that Winnie, allegedly by her own admission, had been kidnapped and seduced when she was a youth in the area of Calhoun, Illinois. According to records, she later retracted the story and admitted that it was false.

Dr. Catton, who had returned to San Francisco, revealed on January 17 details of his examination of Mrs. Judd. He hinted that a second person might have been involved in the crime. "From all aspects of the case as I know them," he said, "almost anything may develop." He quoted Mrs. Judd as saying, "If things don't go the way they tell me, and don't go the way they are planned, believe me, I'll get up and tell everything." In response to questions about the crime, Catton said she told him, "I have never even cut up a chicken in my life, Doctor."

Catton said, "Mrs. Judd told me there had been no man in her life until Dr. Judd, her husband, came into it, and no other man until about one year ago. She has admitted association with this other man up until the time of the murders. She refused to discuss whether she had seen him after the killing, and was tight-lipped about the events of the murder day. She also told me that statements she made about quarreling with Mrs. LeRoi and Samuelson were true." Mrs. Judd claimed to be the mother of a boy then living in Mexico, according to Catton. He said that she was sane and that her intelligence was about normal for her age.

Dr. Sidney Freid of Los Angeles, another psychoanalyst for the state, had previously examined Winnie and announced that she was sane. Two of the five physicians retained by defense counsel, who were not identified, judged Winnie insane.

By the eve of the trial, the state had subpoenaed over sixty witnesses and the defense about a dozen. Attorneys for both sides were reluctant to discuss the testimony they would present, the defense refusing to declare whether Mrs. Judd would take the stand. Assisting County Attorney Andrews in the case would be Deputy Attorneys G. A. Rodgers, Harry Johnson and Robert McMurchie. F. A. Hickernell and John Brinkerhoff had been investigating the case for the county attorney's office. Mrs. Judd would be tried first for the murder of Mrs. LeRoi, and if she escaped punishment on that charge, she would be tried for the slaying of Hedvig Samuelson.

The trial began on January 19, and the first two days were devoted to the selection of a jury. The prospective jurors were asked a number of similar questions concerning their religion, occupation and family status as well as matters more directly relevant to the case. With the very first candidate, Franks began probing possible reactions to pleas of self-defense and insanity.

"And if there should be evidence in this case that human life was taken by the defendant, and that evidence should convince you that the human life was taken in self-defense, as that defense is defined by the court in his instructions, would you hesitate, if you believed that self-defense was properly applied in this case under the court's instructions, and the facts, hesitate to vote not guilty?"

"No, sir."

"You believe in the law of self-defense as applied in a proper case?"

"Yes, sir."

"You believe that that is as good a law as the other laws on the statute books?"

"Yes, sir."

"Should you be convinced from the evidence in this case that human life has been taken by the defendant and that the facts do not show self-defense as that defense is analyzed and given to you in the court's instructions by the court, but that the defendant at the time of the commission of the act, if you believe she did commit it, was not of sound mind, was not capable of knowing right from wrong, as the court defines the question of mental state to you, would you, if you believed that beyond a reasonable doubt, hesitate to vote not guilty?"

"No, sir."

The question of where the burden of proof rested in a plea of insanity soon became a subject of contention between prosecution and defense. During the questioning of another prospective juror, Judge Speakman resolved the problem by asking, "Aren't we trying to cross a bridge before we get to it? In other words, the question of burden of proof is not included in the question and doesn't pertain to the question propounded to the juror.

"Mr. Juror," he concluded, "the court instructs you that after the close of this case, if after and when this case is submitted to you, if you then entertain a reasonable doubt as to the sanity of this defendant as defined by the court, then I instruct you that it is the duty of the jury to return a verdict of not guilty.

In view of that instruction, what is your answer to the question?"

"If it is your instructions, I would abide by your instructions."

Franks further questioned the juror regarding any preconceived opinions he might have:

". . . you wouldn't rely on newspaper stories that you have read or discussion that you have heard to tie her to the other facts to find a verdict of guilty, would you?"

"Absolutely not."

Most jury candidates had read of the case and discussed it, but few of them claimed to have any firm opinions as a result of the considerable pre-trial publicity. One was an exception. He was asked, "But you did form an opinion as to the guilt or innocence of the defendant from reading these articles and discussing them?"

"Yes, sir."

He was challenged by Franks and, despite Rodgers' objections, excused by the court from jury service.

Another candidate had firm opinions of his own, which were apparently not derived from news accounts of any kind. Neither did they, he testified, result from his personal acquaintance with Carl Harris, the friend of Winnie and the two murdered women. Most of the prospective jurors were questioned concerning their business dealings or acquaintance with Harris.

"In your business, did you do business, transact business with the Harris Lumber Company?" asked Franks.

"No, I never have."

"Or with Carl Harris?"

"Yes, I do."

"You know him personally?"

"Yes."

"Known him a long time?"

"Oh, six or seven years."

"It is a fact you saw his name mentioned in the newspapers you read concerning this case?"

"Yes, I have."

"And it is because of that that you do not feel that you can sit as a fair and impartial juror in this case with the idea that he might or might not be mentioned, is that it?"

"It is not at all."

The prospective juror finally responded that there were some "unconscious things" that might influence his verdict.

"Well, are these unconscious things—probably I have asked you before but I want to ask you again—things that you know about the matter, things that you believe because of the persons who have told them to you or friendships with people who it is alleged were connected with it, are they any of those three?"

"The things I believe, yes."

"From someone who has told you?" asked Franks.

"No."

"From reading the newspapers?"

"No."

"Couldn't evidence eradicate that belief?"

"It might."

"Whoever has that belief to eradicate from your mind starts, in a way, with a handicap so far as you are concerned?"

"Yes."

"We challenge for cause," announced Franks.

"Do I understand you to say," asked the court, "you did or did not have an opinion as to the guilt or innocence of the defendant?"

"No opinion as to the guilt or innocence."

"Is there any reason," continued Speakman, "that may be known to you alone why you could not sit as a fair and impartial juror if you were selected?"

"Yes."

"There is a reason that is known to you alone?"

"Yes."

"Do you resist the challenge?" Speakman asked Rodgers. "We do not," he answered.

"Stand aside," said Speakman. "Call the next juror."

Other prospective jurors were excused for a number of reasons. Several had reservations about capital punishment. A father of sixteen children was excused due to back trouble, on the advice of his physician. One candidate who was accepted later became the center of controversy surrounding the jury's decision. Defense attorneys would allege that he had been initially biased and had swayed other jury members to vote for the death penalty in an effort to get Mrs. Judd to talk. Nothing out of order, however, appeared in his responses to many of the same questions asked of other jury members by both prosecution and defense.

Prior to the recesses, Judge Speakman was careful to admonish the jury candidates regarding publicity about the case. He warned them not to read newspaper accounts of the case and on one occasion asked them to "not listen to any radio concerning this case."

On January 21, 1932, the twelve male jurors and one alternate were selected and sworn in. They were G. A. Jordan, clerk; Wallace Dooley, dairyman; Ed Jorgensen, farmer; Henry Lacey, locomotive machinist; LeRoy Prentice, watchmaker; A. L. Radtke, rancher; Myron S. Butler, salesman; Herbert Alston, farmer; Peter Christman, farmer; E. R. Levine, rancher; Ernest Majors, grovekeeper; Oscar Mitchell, one of the Salt River Valley's most prominent pioneers; and Clayton L. Trenton, the alternate juror.

The people of Phoenix held "varying opinions" as to the punishment Mrs. Judd should receive, according to her father. Rev. McKinnell had expressed this view in a letter to a friend in Muncie, Indiana. He added, "It seems that Ruth has made up her mind to suffer death rather than tell all she knows.

"We pray with her to encourage her to seek salvation. We also try to tell her there is still a possibility for her to lead a life of usefulness. She generally seems cheerful but I doubt whether she knows how serious her case is. In fact, it is hardly possible that we, her parents, fully realize or comprehend the terrible ordeal that is ahead of us."

9. THE BEST SHOW IN TOWN

WINNIE'S AIR OF indifference suddenly changed to a display of anger Thursday morning when Dr. Joseph Catton, psychoanalyst for the state, walked into the courtroom.

"Good morning, Mrs. Judd," he said.

She jumped up and shouted, "Get away from me! Get out of here!" Turning to her attorneys, she demanded, "Make him get out!" Then she told Catton, "I don't want you near me. You said you wouldn't talk about me, and you've been talking about me in all the poolrooms!"

Catton merely continued on his way.

The court clerk read an information charging that Winnie Ruth Judd did "willfully, unlawfully, feloniously and of her deliberate and premeditated malice aforethought, kill and murder one Agnes Anne LeRoi, a human being." Winnie was not charged with murdering Hedvig Samuelson.

"To which information, gentlemen of the jury, the defendant has entered a plea of not guilty," announced the clerk.

Carl Harris appeared with other state's witnesses to be sworn in. Judge Speakman explained that they must leave the courtroom to await their call, adding, "I am pretty easy to get along with, but I get kind of out of patience sometimes when we have to go out on the lawn or someplace to find the witnesses."

The county attorney soon made his opening statement, accusing Mrs. Judd of the crime and telling what the evidence presented by the state would show. Then the assistant county engineer, E. A. Woodworth, the first witness, was asked to identify a map he had drawn of the duplex at 2929 North Second Street.

Just before the jury members were excused for recess, the judge suggested they arrange with bailiff for any personal articles they might need. "I don't know how long it will take to try this case," he said, "but I would suggest that you not overlook the razor, because if it takes as long to try this case as counsel says, you will look either like Santa Claus or Rip Van Winkle."

Following the recess, Denise Reynolds, an employee of the Grunow Clinic, described her quiet evening with the victims on October 16, the night of the murder. She testified that a grocery boy was the only other visitor before her departure for a 10 P.M. appointment.

Mrs. Beverly Fox, an employee of the clinic, was the final witness of the morning session. She told of her telephone conversations with Mrs. Judd on the morning of October 17 about coming in to work. In the cross-examination, Franks asked, "She told you about her child, did she not?"

"Now, we object to that as not being proper cross-examination or within the purview of the direct examination," announced Rodgers.

The objection was sustained.

The afternoon session opened with very brief testimony by Dr. Laurence Dunn of the Grunow Clinic. He said he was Mrs. LeRoi's employer, and she had not made arrangements to be absent Saturday morning, October 17.

During most of the afternoon the witnesses were men who had taken the baggage from Mrs. Judd's apartment.

Wrangling over the admissibility of evidence marked Friday's session, as Phoenix and Los Angeles railway employees testified. Schenck argued that the suitcase should not be admitted because it contained parts of the body of Hedvig Samuelson and, as such, was an item of evidence which should be separated from the case on trial. Judge Speakman overruled the objection.

Sheriff McFadden and his deputies had made new arrangements for handling the largest crowd yet, mostly women. Winnie, in a new brown crepe dress, appeared unconcerned, but she continued to twist and crush her handkerchief in rapid, methodical movements throughout the day.

In the afternoon, movie newsreel film was taken of prosecution, defense and Judge Speakman on the south walk of the county building grounds. The attorneys relaxed and, in a good-natured spirit, exchanged barbs.

"Where do I collect for this?" Franks asked.

"I thought you had already been paid off," Andrews replied.

"When you take Lloyd's picture," said Franks, "don't have any film in your cameras."

"Don't worry, you will break them before you get to me," said the county attorney.

Attorneys Schenck and Andrews were wearing their "modified ten-gallon Western hats." "I'm glad you wore a big hat, too," said Schenck. "It will show our friends in the effete East that other men in the West wear hats like mine."

On Saturday, Andrews called Detective Lieutenant Frank Ryan of the Los Angeles Police Department to the stand. He was asked about his examination of the larger trunk and replied that he had found in it two women's purses.

"What did they contain, if anything?" asked Andrews.

"One purse contained a temperature thermometer and, in addition, there were two empty shells of .25 caliber and one lead bullet. In the other purse there was one empty shell. I believe that is the way they were."

"And what did you do with these shells and this bullet, if anything?"

"I turned them over to Mr. Moxley, our ballistics man."

After further questioning, Ryan was asked, "Now can you describe the position of the body which was in the larger trunk?"

"It was laying sort of on the side, it would be laying on the left side, the head up in the corner of the trunk. The body then, the knees were drawn up and the seat down in the opposite corner, in the lower—in the bottom of the trunk."

"Was that body intact?"

"It was."

"Now with reference to the smaller trunk, you were present there when it was unpacked?" Andrews asked.

"I was."

"And what was found in that trunk?"

"There was several—quite a number of sheets of blank paper. A light cotton blanket was tucked around over the articles underneath. When that was pulled back there was found to be two bundles wrapped up in some articles of woman's clothing; and when these were unwrapped, they proved to be the feet and legs up to the knees of a human being. There were— right under them was the head and shoulders and body down as far as the navel, of a woman. This was lying in the small trunk on its back with the hands folded across. Each one of the feet then were laid up alongside the head."

"And those were the only portions of that body which were in that trunk?"

"They were."

Asked whether he knew if arrangements had been made with his department for the surrender of the defendant, he said, "No, I do not."

Next, Ray Pinker, forensic chemist for the Los Angeles Police Department, testified. He said he was called to the county morgue on October 19, where the baggage had been taken.

"I opened the hatbox," he said, "and in the hatbox, I found some surgical dressings, miscellaneous cosmetics, a blue dress, I believe, and a small kit of surgeon's tools, scalpels, and a .25 Colt's automatic pistol."

The deputy coroner from Los Angeles, R. R. Creasey, testified concerning his examination of the trunks. Andrews asked, "Now, which one of the trunks did you open first?"

"We opened the larger trunk."

"And what was disclosed when the trunk was opened?"

"Well, without delving into the contents, the head of the body of Mrs. LeRoi was disclosed first." He confirmed Detective Ryan's statement that the body was intact and folded into the trunk.

"Now, with reference to the other—the rest of the contents of the trunk, what else was in the trunk other than the body?"

"Soiled bedding, several articles of clothing, a piece of rug that looked as though it had been cut from a larger rug, a pair of ice skates attached to boots."

"What did the smaller trunk contain?"

"It contained parts of the body of Miss Samuelson."

"Will you state just what portions of the body it contained?"

"The head, arms, upper part of the trunk and just the lower limbs from the knees down."

"Were you present when the missing portion of the body was brought in?"

"Yes, sir."

"Do you recall who brought it in?"

"I recall one of the officers, I think it was Mr. Pinker."

"Mr. Pinker. And what was the missing portion of the body brought in?"

"It was the pelvis and the thighs and upper legs."

"Now, what was this portion of the body contained in?"

"A brown leather suitcase."

Andrews asked the Los Angeles County autopsy surgeon, Dr. A. F. Wagner, about the nature of the bullet wound in the head of the body removed from the larger trunk.

"It was my opinion the gun was up against the head," said Wagner.

"And was there any evidence of powder burns on the temple at the point of entrance of the bullet?"

"There was a dark smudge which appeared to me to be

powder—I mean the carbon of unconsumed powder, gun-powder."

Andrews next asked about the direction that the bullet had likely traveled.

"The direction was downward?"

"Downward and backward."

The surgeon further testified concerning the wounds and lacerations on the body taken from the smaller trunk. He said it was quite possible the two women had been killed at the same time and that the dismembered body had been severed relatively soon after death.

In questioning the Los Angeles Police Department ballistics expert, Spencer B. Moxley, Andrews accepted a suggestion by defense attorney Schenck.

Andrews had asked, "And in your opinion was this gun fired from the gun or not?"

"It was," answered Moxley.

"You have 'a gun fired from a gun,'" said Schenck. The record was corrected, changing the first "gun" to "bullet."

Moxley testified that the three shells and the bullet turned over to him had been fired from the .25-caliber gun in evidence. Schenck attacked Moxley's qualifications as an expert and moved that his testimony be stricken. The motion was denied. While the jury was examining shells introduced in evidence, Judge Speakman asked whether the state could finish its case that day. Andrews said it could not.

"I realize most of the lawyers consider it contrary to lawyers' constitutional rights to try a lawsuit on Saturday afternoon," said Speakman.

"Not in Arizona," said Franks. "We are used to it."

Testimony continued as Dan Lucey, Phoenix detective, was called. Lucey was asked about his examination of Mrs. Judd's apartment at 1130 East Brill. Andrews said the state was attempting to prove that a shell found in Winnie's apartment on October 20, four days after the murders, had come from the gun found in her baggage. Defense renewed its objections that the apartment had not been shown to be in the same condition as when Mrs. Judd left. Then, Judge Speakman called a recess until Monday morning.

In excusing the jury, he said, "Now I have a very bad cold, and if you gentlemen have, we have a county physician who is paid by the month. If it is necessary for you to have a physician, just you advise the bailiff, and he will call the county physician. Between now and Monday morning I will do my best to get rid of this cold. Of course, I mean by the modern way of hot lemonade and not the old-fashioned way."

10. FAMILY SKELETONS

THE SECOND WEEK of the trial opened to a courtroom so crowded that one woman fainted and had to be carried out through jammed corridors. Mrs. Judd, in the ankle-length, black crepe dress which she had worn at her preliminary hearing, appeared pale. She seemed unconcerned with the proceedings, as the prosecution introduced into evidence the critical empty pistol shell which might damage her story of self-defense.

Phoenix detective Dan Lucey testified that the .25-caliber automatic shell had been found on October 20 in Mrs. Judd's apartment at 1130 East Brill. Asked by Attorney Andrews precisely where the shell had been found, he replied, "In the southwest corner of the bedroom under a chair." This shell, and the first three in evidence, were fired from the same automatic pistol, according to ballistics expert Moxley. Over defense objections, Judge Speakman allowed the shell to be put in evidence. The jury was left to determine whether this might have been the shell that held the bullet that injured Winnie's hand, which the state indicated was fired after the murders.

County Attorney Andrews had called his investigator, John

Brinkerhoff, to the stand to establish the identification of the bodies and their return to Phoenix. Andrews also recalled Mrs. Judd's landlord, Koller, in an attempt to fulfill defense counsel's demand that it be established that the apartment was unoccupied from the time Mrs. Judd left on Sunday, October 18, until the time that detectives began their investigation.

"Was the apartment in the same condition apparently?" asked Andrews.

"As near as I know, yes," replied Koller.

On cross-examination, Franks asked, ". . . on the day you were in there, this Sunday that the trunks were moved, you said all you did was go in and pick up the trunks and go out?"

"Yes, sir."

"You didn't look around?"

"I didn't observe things."

"Then you weren't back in the place until the day you went with the officers, is that correct?"

"Yes, sir."

"You weren't in there at any other time between those two days?"

"Yes, sir."

"Then how do you know that the things were in the same condition?"

"I said as far as I knew."

"You haven't any knowledge of it at all, have you?"

"Only in a general way, no, just by observing things in order is all."

Phoenix detective McCord Harrison later told of his investigations the evening of the day the bodies were discovered in Los Angeles. As soon as Andrews asked about his examination of the murder scene, Franks objected.

"We object to it until the proper foundation is laid that the matters and things investigated were in the same condition as at the time of the alleged offense," he said. His objection was overruled, but he soon renewed it.

"If this is going in," said Franks, referring to Harrison's testimony, "I want to show the court some newspaper items and things in those items."

"Newspaper items?" said Andrews.

"Yes, advertisements at ten cents a head," said Franks. The jury was excused before Judge Speakman asked, "Can the state show whether or not this house was locked?"

"No, we can't show that," said Andrews. He then said he would show that the examination of the murder scene was made before the crowds began their tour of the duplex at ten cents a head. The jury was recalled to the courtroom.

Phoenix police officers George P. Larrison and M. S. Frazier, and Orville Bechtol, superintendent of the Bureau of Identification, testified concerning their examination of the duplex on Monday, October 19.

Frazier said the back door was unlocked when he arrived and that some newspapermen and neighbors came by, about "half a dozen people."

Franks asked Larrison, "Did you have to tell the reporters, these newspapermen, to put back anything that they had touched or attempted to touch anything there?"

"I told them not to touch anything, and any time I saw anyone molesting anything at all, I told them to leave it alone."

"By that you mean that they would pick up something and you would tell them to put it down?"

"I don't recall seeing anyone pick up anything to carry it away."

"Not to carry away, but to look at it. Did you see them with anything in their hands and tell them to put it back and they followed your order?"

"I saw one of them over in the fireplace messing around where some stuff appeared to have been burned, and I told them to leave it alone."

"Whatever was in that fireplace, this man did disturb?"

"He probably messed around with his hand and stirred it up. There was just ashes there, as far as I could see."

"And nothing else that they touched?"

"I didn't see them touch nothing else. There were papers on a table, and I told them to leave that alone. I recall in the kitchen there was someone looking around . . . and I told them to leave that stuff alone until the fingerprint man got there."

Larrison was recalled and testified concerning blood spots he found "close to the head of the bed" and elsewhere in the house.

County Attorney Andrews asked, "You say that you examined the beds there in that room?"

"Yes, sir," he replied.

"What was the—just describe what was on each bed and the condition of the same when you made your examination."

"The bed on the north next to the north wall was a small light pad, not a full-sized mattress. And I think there were one or two pieces of bed clothing on that cot, and the other bed was made up entirely of quilts and a pair of sheets, I think."

"Then, I understand there was a pad on the bed on the north side of the room?"

"Yes."

"But there was not a pad on the bed on the south side of the room?"

"That is right."

"Was there any mattress in addition to this pad on either one of the beds?"

"No, sir."

Dr. H. L. Goss of Phoenix was questioned about the laboratory tests he performed on blood samples from the duplex.

Assistant Prosecutor Rodgers asked, "Calling your attention to such examination as you made at that time, where did you find the blood spots that you examined?"

"We found certain spots throughout the entire house, with perhaps the exception of the front or living room, the reception room. We made, we took samples of purported blood from the bedroom and from the bathroom, from the dining room and the kitchen, I think a little breakfast room. Some of these were blood and some were not."

"Now, I wish you would explain to the jury as a result of your examination of blood spots as you have detailed, just what you did determine to be blood spots and what were not blood spots, and the location of the various ones to which you refer?"

"The spots in the bedroom on the floor and the floor board we found to be blood, at one spot in the dining room, the kitchen, rather, the linoleum, those were the only spots which gave a positive test for blood. The others were all negative."

"Referring to the spot again that you said was out in the kitchen, were you able to determine from your analysis and investigation whether that was human blood or otherwise?"

"No, I was not. It was given a simple test for blood, but there was not enough to do a qualitative test to differentiate from other forms of blood."

Mrs. Roger Thorpe, who with her husband owned the duplex, had identified the piece of blood-stained carpet found in the trunk as having been taken from the "east bedroom."

The Monday afternoon session began with Dr. Samuels, who had been Mrs. LeRoi's dentist in Phoenix. By an examination of dental work, he identified Mrs. LeRoi's body at A. L. Moore and Sons Mortuary. A second doctor identified Miss Samuelson's body.

Another former landlord of Winnie's testified that he last saw her on Friday, October 16, at his home between 5:30 and 6 in the evening. She asked him about the value of a building at Twelfth Street and McDowell, where she could live with her parents. She also asked to use his car on Saturday so that she and two other girls could visit friends in a subdivision.

The next witnesses were a former housekeeper for Mrs. Le-Roi and Miss Samuelson, and Earl Riley, the Los Angeles Broadway Department Store engineer who removed the postal telegraph blanks known as the "drain pipe letter" from the store's clogged plumbing.

Mrs. Judd's jail fingerprint card was offered in evidence, and the defense immediately objected. Franks asked B. O. Smith, county fingerprint expert, "Mr. Smith, at the time you obtained the data on this card for identification, this party was under arrest?"

"Yes, sir."

"Did she have a lawyer present?"

"No, sir."

"Was she told of her constitutional rights?"

"No, sir."

"You just took her hand, put ink on it and rolled them on the card?"

"Yes, sir."

Following a discussion of whether the accused's constitutional rights had been violated by the procedure, Judge Speakman asked, "Mr. Witness, at the time you say Mrs. Judd signed the card, was there any force used by you or anyone present?"

"No, sir. In fact, she volunteered to do that several times before it was done."

The objection was subsequently overruled.

Then, Sheriff McFadden identified a booking slip signed by Mrs. Judd. The Maricopa County jailer had identified a piece of paper as the signed receipt for a Christmas gift of pajamas. The receipt was used by J. Clark Sellers in identifying the handwriting on the "drain pipe letter." He concluded that the handwriting was the same. Copies of photographs used in his examination were distributed to jurors, counsel and the court. When Franks and Schenck asked to study them overnight, the court was adjourned for the day.

On Tuesday, the prosecution called its last witnesses, Doris Easton, a registered nurse, and Mrs. Oscar Lewis, wife of a boxer recently sentenced to prison for murder. Miss Easton had met Mrs. Judd about the first of September, 1930, and Anne LeRoi in April of the next year.

Assistant Prosecutor Rodgers asked Miss Easton about her activities the day before the murders: "And calling your attention to Thursday evening, that being the 15th day of last October, did you see the defendant, Mrs. Judd, on that evening?"

"Yes, I saw her that evening."

"Where did you first meet her that evening, Miss Easton?"

"She came to my home after me about seven o'clock in the evening."

"Who, if anybody, accompanied her there at that time?"

"Carl Harris."

Rodgers asked her to recall the conversation that took place in a car on the way to 2929 North Second Street.

"When we started out to the apartment of Miss Samuelson and Mrs. LeRoi, Mrs. Judd asked Mr. Harris to remember that he had promised her if we went out there that they were not to know that she was in the car, that she was there at all, and he said he would remember."

"Now, Miss Easton, when you arrived out there at the apartment of Miss Samuelson and Mrs. LeRoi, what is the fact as to whether or not you or Mrs. Judd went into the house?"

"Neither one of us went into the house. We both stayed in the car."

"Calling your attention to Carl Harris, did he go in the house when you arrived there?"

"Yes, sir."

"And where did you and Mrs. Judd stay during the time that he was in the house?"

"We remained in the car that was parked in the driveway."

"Now, as you were sitting there in the car at that time, did you have any conversation with Mrs. Judd, Miss Easton?"

"Yes. When we drove up to the house, Mrs. Judd asked me if I knew who lived there. I said, 'No.' She answered then, 'Well, I won't tell you then.' I said all right, that if she didn't want me to know why that was her affair. Just after that, Anne came to the window and stooped down in front of the window and picked up something, I believe. Mrs. Judd looked at me and said, 'Now, you know who lives here.' I said, 'Yes.' A little bit later, she said, 'What do you think of Carl?' I said, 'He seems very nice.' Mrs. Judd answered, 'He is nicer than that; he is perfectly grand.' She said, 'Anne and Sammy think so, too. You know I used to live here with Anne and Sammy, but we had a little difference and I moved away.' She said, 'In fact, that is what I moved over—our difference was about Carl.'"

Mrs. Lewis next took the stand and was asked about a conversation she had with Mrs. Judd in August at the Grunow Clinic.

"Well, the conversation was in regard to Mrs. Judd and a boyfriend's name that was Carl," she said. "The last name I do not know, whether it was Carl Harris or Carl anybody."

Her remarks about the "anybody" were stricken from the record before she was allowed to proceed.

"And she made a remark that Carl was going to Los Angeles and that he was coming back for a day and then going on to the East and stay two weeks. And she was indeed glad that he was gone because she thought Sammy was trying to take Carl away from her. Who Sammy was I do not know.

"And Mrs. Judd said that Sammy's boyfriend was here, and that perhaps he would stay here, would be here when Carl came back. And she said that she got so angry at times about Carl and Sammy that she could, the remark she made was, 'either go crazy or die,' or something like that, something to that effect."

Following Mrs. Lewis's testimony, the exhibits in evidence were shown to the jurors, and the prosecution rested its case, with the implication that jealousy was Mrs. Judd's motive for the slayings.

Franks began the defense with a number of minor witnesses. Among them, Phillip Peterson of Wickenberg and his daughter Grace told of noticing on October 17 at the Grunow Clinic that Mrs. Judd's left hand was bandaged. (The baggageman had already testified seeing her without a wound that evening.) Peterson said Winnie told him that her hand had been burned. George E. Reese, a real estate man, said Mrs. Judd had asked him to find a house big enough for her family and two women friends. He last saw her on the night of October 15, and they selected a house in the 1200 block on East McDowell.

The first major witness to be called for the defense was Winnie's sixty-six-year-old mother, Mrs. Carrie B. McKinnell. Franks asked about an incident relating to a baby that had occurred when Winnie was seven years of age.

"Well," said Mrs. McKinnell, "she told some of her schoolmates and some of our neighbors that we had a baby at our house."

"Who had the baby?"

"I."

"Yes. . . ."

"And the neighbors came in to see it and told us they came to see the baby, and I could not imagine what they meant. They said, 'Why, Ruth said you had a baby,' and there was none."

"There was no truth in that matter then?"

"Not a bit."

"About that time what were her habits insofar as being able to control herself in bed-wetting?"

"Well, she had that habit for about twelve years."

"From infancy up to twelve years of age?"

"Yes, sir."

Franks then asked about any other unusual incidents in Winnie's childhood.

"When she was ten years of age," said Mrs. McKinnell, "she took a notion she would make her own living and started to run away to Chicago. She went to one of the members of the church . . . to tell her goodbye, and she told her where she was going to go, to Chicago. Well, she started and they let us know about it. Mr. McKinnell went to get her and he traced her through the cornfields. She would go back and forth like it was in her mind, like she did not know whether to go on or come back. She would start one way and then start back. He looked around and followed her tracks as near as he could. . . . He went back to the house where this girlfriend of hers lived, and she was there. Of course, he brought her home with him."

"How long was she gone that time?"

"Oh, it wasn't very many hours; they let us know immediately."

"Did anything occur when she was sixteen?"

"Well, yes."

"What was it?"

"She went with a young man, and we think that he was indiscreet."

"What was his name?"

"Fred Jensen."

"Fred Jensen. How old was Ruth then?"

"Sixteen."

"And how old was this young man?"

"He was twenty—about twenty-four."

"Where were you living?"

"We were at Olney, Illinois."

"Tell us about the incident."

"She was going to school in Greenville, Illinois. School was out in June, and she came home. This young man, when he saw her at church, wanted to bring her home. She says, 'No,' she says, 'I have company, and I have got to go home with the one I came with.' She said he asked her the third time right while she was with the other young man for her company, and she wouldn't go with him. He says, 'Well, maybe then some other time.' Then he made it a point to try to go with her. He would come and go with her to church sometimes, and sometimes he would take her to shows, and sometimes go out car riding. Mr. McKinnell followed him out to the car one night and said, 'Fred, be good to my little girl; she is all the little girl I have.' He took her car riding and went way off, quite a distance, and came to a turn-off place that led into the woods. He stopped and asked her to get out. Well, she wouldn't do it. He took ahold of her and tried to pull her out. She held to the car, and she said she just asked God to let some car come along that would start them on so that he would let her alone.

". . . I don't think she said that he had what he desired. I don't think that took place then. I don't remember what she said about that. I don't think it did, but when he got in, he said, 'Ruth, you are an angel, and I am a devil,' and he cried or pretended to cry . . . and so he brought her home. I don't know when that, when this took place, but anyway she thought that he ought to marry her.

"And the reason why I thought there must be something wrong, I found her making clothes for a baby."

Mrs. McKinnell then said she took Winnie to see a Dr. Weber at the sanitarium in Olney. He examined her and said he thought she was not pregnant.

"What, if anything else, happened?" asked Franks.

"One night we went to bed, and the next morning when I woke up Ruth was gone."

"How old was she then?"

"She was about seventeen."

"And what month was it?"

"I think it was October."

"When did you next first locate her; how long after that did you locate her?"

"She was gone all that day and the following night and the next day. We were looking for her all the time, had people out looking for her. She came home that evening, the second evening."

"By herself or someone bring her?"

"She came by herself to our house, but she was brought from Calhoun by the Methodist preacher there."

"When she came home, where did she tell you she had been, or what if anything had happened to her?"

"She said she had been kidnapped, and these people had taken her to a house in Brown Station and put her in there. She said she stayed there all that day."

"Go ahead."

"At night, she heard some voices, some men's voices talking to a woman where they put her—put her in a house where there was two women. She heard some voices of some men there. She went to a window and opened it and tore off the mosquito bar. That wasn't wire screen; it was just a screen—tore it off and slipped out. She said she just asked the Lord to direct her the way home, and she started the right way. She said she came down the railroad until she got to Calhoun. That was just about morning then, just about light. She said she went and got up into a loft of a garage so that she would not be seen in her nightclothes, and a gunny sack that she had cut holes out to put her head and arms through. . . . She stayed there all day, or nearly all day. This preacher had occasion to be down there to the garage, and he clumb up in there. She had been asleep. When she saw him, she said, 'You get away from here,' and he said, 'I am not going to hurt you.' He said, 'Why are you here?' She said that he tried to find out why she was there, and he saw that she had a gunny sack on. . . . He got clothes for her and brought her home. . . ."

"What, if anything, did your daughter do concerning Fred Jensen?"

"I hardly know how to answer that . . . she swore out a warrant for him to have him arrested."

"Your daughter did that?"

"Yes."

"Do you know if he was arrested?"

"Well, he wasn't there. I think he caught on to it that he was going to be arrested, and he skipped."

Mrs. McKinnell said she had Winnie examined for pregnancy once more, and the doctor said, "I don't think she has ever—that she has ever been pregnant."

"Mrs. McKinnell, to your knowledge has your daughter ever had a child?"

"No, sir, not to my knowledge."

When Franks finished his examination of Mrs. McKinnell, Judge Speakman asked whether cross-examination of the witness would be long. Rodgers said that it would, and County Attorney Andrews read to the jury the postal telegraph blanks that had become known as the "drain pipe letter."

Speakman, evidently weary from his cold, adjourned court early that day. "I notice the law provided for an alternate juror, but it doesn't provide for an alternate judge," he remarked laconically, "so gentlemen, we will take a recess until tomorrow morning at nine o'clock."

Before Wednesday's session, Mrs. Judd appeared relaxed

and embraced her parents before a movie newsreel camera in the courtroom corridor. But Winnie became increasingly nervous when Mrs. McKinnell was cross-examined. Winnie's mother repeated most of the testimony she had given before but emphasized that Winnie was "very fond of dolls."

". . . when she broke one of her dolls," said Mrs. McKinnell, "she cried so hard—I never saw a mother weep more bitterly over losing her baby than she did over that doll being broken."

Rev. McKinnell, in frock coat and clerical collar, took the stand and confirmed much of his wife's testimony.

"When your daughter was a child," questioned Rodgers, "and during her young womanhood, Rev. McKinnell, she had good manners and behaved herself well, did she not?"

"Yes, sir, generally. She manifested a hot temper, angry, and then she would be over it quickly."

"In other words, she became angry about in the way people ordinarily do about things, did she?"

"I think so."

"She was usually, outside of the little incident to which you have referred in your testimony, obedient to her parents, wasn't she?"

"Fairly so; yes, sir."

"She seemed to have a fair sense of right and wrong, did she not?"

"Well, except when she would get mad; then she did not have."

Winnie's father cited several instances of alleged insanity in the family history. These were his father's mother, his father's brother, his sister's son who committed suicide in Bisbee at age twenty-seven. Both Rev. and Mrs. McKinnell mentioned two second cousins of Winnie, one who had died in an insane asylum in Peoria, Illinois, and another the family considered to be mentally deficient.

During Rev. McKinnell's testimony, Andrews renewed the objections he had made earlier concerning the admissibility of testimony about hereditary insanity. Schenck finally maintained that the defendant would be shown to be suffering from transmissible or hereditary insanity. Later, counsel for the defense began introducing a series of depositions from witnesses in the East to show insanity in Mrs. Judd's family history.

A recess was called early in the afternoon so that a physician could examine a juror, G. A. Jordan, who had a bad cold. Court was recessed until 1 P.M. Thursday, but Jordan's physician ordered him to bed shortly after noon that day. Another juror, Clayton L. Trenton, also became ill from a cold. The crowd of spectators, which had been gathering since 10 A.M., was disappointed to learn there would be no trial that day.

When Mrs. Judd was brought to court Friday morning, she was met with birthday greetings from her parents for her twenty-seventh birthday. When, because of the illnesses, Judge Speakman announced a postponement of the trial until the following Monday, Sheriff McFadden said, "Birthdays are the same as other days in jail." But he relaxed the visiting rules to permit Rev. and Mrs. McKinnell to visit with Winnie on Friday afternoon.

11. THE "GOOD DOCTOR"

MONDAY MORNING, Mrs. Judd claimed illness, with pains in her side. An examination by the county physician, Dr. J. D. Mauldin, revealed that her temperature was normal. When Winnie was still not ready by 8:30 A.M., she was told she would be handcuffed and taken to court in a wheelchair. Shortly after 9 A.M., she and the jail matron walked into court.

The defense presented another deposition to establish insanity in the McKinnell family and then, in a surprise move, called Dr. Judd to the stand.

The Doctor testified that, during his twenty-two years of medical practice, he had been in charge of or on the staff of mental institutions in Oregon, Minnesota and Indiana. He spoke of Winnie's unusual behavior in Mexico and several peculiar incidents that occurred after their return to the States.

"I took her to Mexico," said Dr. Judd, "to an ideal location for her, a high, dry altitude. She had a perfectly open dwelling upon a mountain, and the finest water and trees surrounding there. I tried to give her, as well as I could, just the treatment

I would give a patient in an institution. I had two girls take care of her."

"For tuberculosis?" asked Franks.

"For tuberculosis," said Dr. Judd.

Franks asked the condition of Winnie's health at the time of her marriage to the Doctor.

"She was tubercular at that time," replied Dr. Judd. "She was coughing continually. She was having night sweats and had been for some time losing weight, having lost, I believe in the last year, about twenty pounds." He said her health improved for a brief time after their marriage.

"It did not continue," he added. "In the summer of 1925, a little more than a year after our marriage, she became pregnant, and at once her health began to fail again."

"And the pregnancy, did it continue to the time of the birth of the child? What happened, if anything?"

"After about three months of pregnancy, her condition, mental and physical, had become so serious that I called another American physician from the Smelter Hospital, a few miles away, in consultation. After studying her case for some time, we thought we were justified in performing an abortion, which was done.

"She suffered very severely from the nausea of pregnancy so that she could retain almost no food whatever, and was growing very weak. She was able to see that herself. She consented to having the abortion performed because she could see that she was failing too fast, that she could not stand it the coming months."

"Now, as to her mental condition?"

"Yes. She was in an hysterical state a great deal of the time. She would have periods of weeping, sobbing with no reason that one could know. She would have periods of laughing and dancing around, waving her hands, snapping her fingers as though in a state of exhilaration with nothing to cause any such outburst of pleasure or celebration. She showed some delusions. For instance, she spoke a number of times of the baby as though it had been already born, spoke of it as though it was now in existence. I remember one time we had an Airedale dog around. One morning, she told me that the baby had gotten out of his coop and had caught the dog by his hair, and the dog dragged him all around the room. At that time, I thought she was just kidding me and teasing me. I didn't realize that she believed that thing. Then she would dwell upon the future of her baby, and in a most unreasonable way, wondering whether she should call him Moses or Caesar or Napoleon, whether she ought to make a military leader out of him or a great teacher.

"She had several spells, I suppose I might say to put it plainly, when she would be frightened by something which would be in her mind. In the night, she would spring out of bed, run clear out of the bedroom, hide in a closet. I could usually bring her out of this by taking her out and walking up and down the room. Several times she remarked to me, 'I know I am dreaming.' She would go on with her sobbing, 'I know I am dreaming.' It would be several minutes before she could escape from this fear.

"Altogether with her rapidly diminishing weight, her growing weakness, her recurrence of temperature, this mental condition was so serious so early in the pregnancy, we thought we were warranted in terminating the pregnancy, which we did."

"And then, Doctor, during the rest of your married life did pregnancy occur at any other time?"

"Yes."

"When, Doctor?"

"1929."

"And where were you living then?"

"At Tayalto, Durango, Mexico."

"Was there anything about her getting in that condition that was unusual, Doctor, because of the circumstances of your married life?"

"Yes."

"Will you tell the jury what it was?"

"Because of her physical condition and because I was in no position, being uncertain as to my future as to where I would live or what I would do, to have a child, I had refused to permit her to become pregnant from the first day of our marriage. She had continually beseeched me, begged me to permit her to have a child. I told her that as soon as we could possibly do so she should have one, but the time was not yet. I could reason with her; she would admit that what I said was true, was right, but then at the end of our conversation, she would come again to, 'Oh, I want a baby.' She would dwell upon what she would do with the baby, that she must have this baby. At the time she became pregnant, I had prepared for her to use an antiseptic douche, and the way it was used was a fairly sure prophylactic. After she had become pregnant, I found that she had deceived me in that she had not used the douche. She would go to the bathroom, running the douche water down through the toilet bowl, never using it at all. Of course, she told me this only afterwards. I knew nothing about it at the time she was doing it."

"And you say she did become pregnant again. In what month was it—do you remember, 1929?"

"I should say in early May."

"And did she have a child to that condition—was a child born or did something happen to it?"

"I did not know. I never knew she was pregnant. As soon as she found that she was pregnant, she said nothing whatever about it but asked me to let her go out to California to visit my sister and aunt there and revisit the LaVinia Sanitarium where she had been some six months as a patient, a tubercular. I did not know this until long afterwards. She went out to California. I let her go, and there in Santa Monica, while visiting with my aunt and sister, she had an uninduced abortion. Of this she told me nothing until long afterwards."

"Do you know how far along she was at that time?"

"No, I don't."

"Now, will you explain to the jury what the term 'uninduced abortion' means."

"One that was not caused by any operation."

"Commonly called a miscarriage?"

"Yes."

"That happened about what month in 1929, if you recall?"

"July or early August, I would say."

"Doctor, during your married life, was there ever a child born to the marriage?"

"No."

"Did your wife or yourself bring in the home a child to live with you and raise as your own?"

"No."

"Did you ever during the married life have a child living with you, a small child?"

"No."

"You have not gone through any adoption proceedings for a child?"

"No."

"Nor your wife to your knowledge?"

"No."

"Nor had the care of one for such a length of time or in such a way as to have it in the home with you for any length of time?"

"No."

"And your wife has not done that to your knowledge?"

"No."

"Now, you lived in Mexico, and you and your wife were there. Under what circumstances did your wife come to Phoenix, Arizona?"

"We were at Agua Aita, Coahuila, Mexico. We came out together to the Port, a border town, Eagle Pass; and I bought her a ticket for Indianapolis, Indiana, with her pullman ticket. I boarded the train with her, and we went to Spoffard, Texas, a junction point for the railroad. She went on the train to Indianapolis. I took the next train going west to El Paso where I had the promise of another position.

"About two weeks afterwards, I was staying at the Del Norte Hotel, and she appeared there to see me. I had been wondering why I had not heard from her from Indianapolis, or from her home rather, in Indiana, Darlington. She told me she had taken the train to San Antonio and left the train, come to a hotel, stayed all night, the next morning gone to the station, the ticket office, cashed in her ticket to Indianapolis, and bought a ticket to Mexico City. When she reached Eagle Pass on her return, she found that she did not have money enough to allow her to continue her trip to Mexico City. So she had left the train then at Eagle Pass, just before reentering Mexico, and had sold her ticket to Mexico City, and now had come from Eagle Pass to El Paso in an automobile with a woman who wanted to drive from Eagle Pass to Los Angeles. I tried to get her to explain why she was going to Mexico City, why she had bought a ticket to Mexico City, and for the first time she showed a species of confusion, and could give no explanation, saying she did not know herself. She had no friends in Mexico City, had a cousin living out of Mexico City in a mining town; but I don't believe Mrs. Judd ever knew where she was. Apparently the reason she didn't go—she had only sixteen dollars and some cents left in her pocket. It wouldn't even buy her a pullman ticket to Mexico City. Well, the two women left the next day, starting on for Los Angeles. The next thing I heard of Mrs. Judd, she wrote me from Phoenix. They had reached Phoenix and started for Los Angeles. Something about the car broke down. She came back to town, and she said she had got herself a job here. She was going to work here in Phoenix for a while. That is the story of her coming to Phoenix."

"At the time she left you and boarded the train going to Indiana, you may state whether or not the relationship between yourself and your wife was congenial?"

"Absolutely. We had never had a serious quarrel in all the times we were together—a statement I hate to make, because few women believe it, but it is true."

Franks asked about Dr. and Mrs. Judd's residence at the 2929 North Second Street duplex. "And how long were you neighbors, you and your wife and Miss Samuelson and Mrs. LeRoi?"

"Six weeks, I should say."

"During that six weeks' time, state whether or not you were visiting back and forth, your wife and yourself?"

"Very frequently."

"And the two women?"

"We spent many evenings there, and the girls were back and forth, Sammy not so much—she spent most of the time in bed, Miss Samuelson. Mrs. LeRoi was back and forth, and Mrs. Judd and I were in and out of their place frequently. We frequently went over there for dinner, and the girls came over and had dinner with us."

"For how long a period of time to your knowledge did the relationship of Mrs. Judd and these two ladies continue?"

"From January up until August 8th, 1931."

"And then you left Phoenix, did you?"

"Then I left Phoenix."

"Now, when you left, where did you go?"

"Bisbee, Arizona."

"And from Bisbee did you come back to Phoenix?"

"No, I did not."

"Where did you go from Bisbee?"

"To Los Angeles."

"And at the time of going from Bisbee to Los Angeles, did you notify Mrs. Judd of your leaving?"

"Yes."

"And was the relationship between you and your wife still continuing as friendly?"

"Perfectly so."

"And you remained, as I understand, in California, and were there during the time this is alleged to have occurred in October?"

"Yes."

Franks asked Dr. Judd to describe an incident which occurred while he was living temporarily at the Copper Queen Hotel in Bisbee, seeking a permanent position at the hospital. Mrs. Judd had called him there just before lunch on Sunday, August 16, 1931.

"I thought at first that she was calling me in Bisbee from Phoenix. I asked her what was the matter. She said, 'No, I am not in Phoenix; I am in Bisbee.' "

" 'Well, where is your room?'

" 'It is Room 27.'

" 'Well, 27 where?'

" 'At the same hotel, your hotel, Copper Queen Hotel.'

"Well, the thought struck me was, she must have come down with a party from Phoenix, or something, and that was how she happened to be in this room. So I went down to the desk and took a look to see who was at 27. It was a single room, and the name there registered at Room 27 was Lucy Rider. But it was in Ruth's handwriting. I knew it was."

"And did you or did you not have any conversation with her about the registration at the hotel?" inquired Franks.

"Well, as soon as she opened the door and I stepped in, she threw herself into my arms. She threw her arms around my neck, and went into a paroxysm of sobbing and crying, as though she was in the deepest distress one could possibly be. She was almost hysterical. She was sobbing so loudly that I knew the other guests of the hotel would hear her. I drew her over to the bed and laid her down, on the bed, while I closed the transom, and went over and sat down beside her. I tried to get her to explain to me what was the matter. She was entirely incoherent. About the only words I could understand was, 'I don't know what is the matter; I don't know what is the matter; I don't know what is the matter with me.'

"I think it was half an hour before I attempted to hold any conversation with her at all, and then I thought I might shift her mind from her trouble, whatever it was, for a few moments, by changing her environment, getting her out of that room. So I persuaded her to leave that room and come on up to my room. Then I tried to talk with her, did talk with her, and tried to get her to explain how she happened to be in Phoenix or Bisbee, and why she came down. Her only answer was, 'I don't know, I don't know what is the matter. I guess there is something the matter with me.' Finally, she told me that she had come down the night before. When she told me that she had come there a little after ten o'clock the previous evening, had spent the night in that hotel there with me, not one hundred feet away from me, and had never called or communicated with me until noon the following day, I told her, 'Well, Ruth, I guess you are right, I guess you are crazy.' I thought that might irritate her enough that she would give me some explanation, but it didn't.

"She spent the afternoon with me there. Several times I reverted to the subject, 'Now, Ruth, come on and tell me what it is, what is the matter, why did you come down here and stay this night there, and all this forenoon, and never communicate with me.' She didn't know why. The only explanation she could give was that on the way down, in some way, there was a fire started in the bus. She went down on one of these Greyhound buses. There was a fire started in the bus, and she was asleep. Somebody shouted in her ear and wakened her. She sprang up and jumped out of the bus, fell down and soiled her dress. She ran down the road a ways in fright, and she said as she went into the hotel, the lights of the hotel showed her how soiled her dress was.

"She just hated to register there as my wife, so she thought she would register under another name at the hotel and then call me up. Then, she didn't know what was the matter. She just never could force herself to go to see me or to notify me that she was there in the hotel, but she did call me twice by phone. She disguised her voice so that I did not know who it was until afterwards. Once she called me, and said nothing except, 'Who is this, who is speaking?' until I lost my temper and hung the receiver up. The second time she called up and gave me a fictitious call to answer. She said she just wanted to see me go out of the hotel."

Franks then asked about Mrs. Judd's arrest.

"Now, I will ask you if you were not called at the time of the arresting of Mrs. Judd?"

"Yes, I was."

"You were in court when Officer Ryan testified that he arrested Mrs. Judd; mentioning the street, I forgot just where he said it was, did you hear that testimony?"

"Yes."

"I will ask you if you were familiar with the circumstances leading to her arrest on that day at that time?"

"Yes, I am."

"And will you state whether or not to your knowledge any arrangements were made for her being delivered into the custody of the officers, arrangements in advance, prior to her arrest?"

"I cannot say definitely what arrangements were made. I had my arrangements with Mrs. Judd, and she met me when I went up to the Alvarez Undertaking Parlors. Several hours afterwards, the county officials, police and deputies were there. Just at what time Mr. Cantillon and Judge Russell notified them to come I do not know."

12. INSANITY

MONDAY AFTERNOON BEGAN the complex, and often sensational, testimony of the psychiatrists. The defense first called Dr. George W. Stephens, superintendent of the Arizona State Hospital. Schenck questioned Dr. Stephens concerning his extensive background in neuro-psychiatry. He asked how many times Stephens had visited Mrs. Judd at the County Jail.

". . . oh, twenty or twenty-five," said Stephens.

Asked whether Mrs. Judd knew right from wrong on October 16, if she had committed the act charged, Stephens replied, "She did not know the nature of the act and was irresponsible." He admitted that, at the beginning of the trial, he felt he could not make a positive diagnosis, but said he had seen enough during the trial to convince him that he "need not have hesitated a moment."

Dr. Stephens recounted some of the incidents that occurred during his examinations of Mrs. Judd. On one occasion, Winnie had asked, "You haven't seen my baby, have you, Doctor?" He replied, "No, have you a child?" She said, "Yes, I want you to help me get that child." Winnie claimed that her child had been taken from her by an unidentified woman and kept at a house at 364 East Thomas Road.

"You want to see a picture of my baby?" she had continued. "Yes, I would like to see it," replied Stephens. Winnie had then shown him a picture pinned to the mattress above her lower bunk. Stephens also noticed at that time pictures of the murder victims pinned to the same mattress. "I thought it was rather a queer place to have this picture gallery," he said.

He cited other instances of what he considered to be delusions, including Winnie's alleged mistreatment by county officials.

Schenck asked, "And what particular classification did you give to the form of insanity you deem here present?"

"Dementia praecox," he said. "I first came to the conclusion that it was a psychosis with psychopathic personality."

Asked if there was a "paranoiac strain or trend," Stephens replied, "Yes, sir, I think there is." He continued, "Yet there are other trends and other things that go to make up dementia praecox, schizophrenia; we call it schizophrenia."

"What does dementia praecox mean?" asked Schenck.

"Dementia praecox is a definite disease or insanity which is an insidious one coming along about the time of adolescence —usually between the ages of fifteen and twenty-five, has definite characteristics which fix it as that type of disease. There are a number of types of insanity or psychosis, and psychosis and insanity is the same thing."

"May I ask you, Doctor—the two terms, dementia praecox, what particular significance has the word 'dementia' there?"

"The word 'dementia' is deterioration of the mind."

"Actual physical deterioration of the mind, is it not?"

"Yes, sir."

"And the 'praecox' means youth?"

"Yes, sir."

"Now, then, you said schizophrenia was but another name of dementia praecox. Will you split that word up if you can, and tell us what that means?"

"Well, that means—as far as I can define it—it means rather

an ego eccentric existence, living within one's self, or rather, I don't know exactly how I could express it to the jury."

"May I ask you, does not the word 'schizo' mean to split?"

"Yes, split personality."

"I don't want to lead the witness," said Schenck, "but maybe we can get it reduced to language that we may understand."

Prosecution soon objected to Schenck's attempts to simplify what he called "these great long jawbreaking names."

"We are willing for the counsel and witness to do that," said Andrews, "but let the witness boil it down and not the counsel."

"All right," said Speakman, "you boil it."

"You do the boiling and the splitting," Schenck told Stephens. "Let's go on. You say you made a definite diagnosis of dementia praecox?"

"Yes, sir, and I didn't say definitely paranoia dementia praecox. I think it is a mixed type, and I haven't definitely decided."

"Tell us what you base it on, everything you recall to mind, everything you did base it on."

"I based this deterioration of this young woman almost from infancy to the present time and particularly deterioration that has come about in the last two years," said Stephens. Referring to Mrs. Judd's stereotyped movements in the courtroom, he said, "She folded that handkerchief, I counted one minute four times, which would make about, I think, 1640 to the day's work." Recalling her emotions during recess, he said, "The emotions jumped from blazing anger, you might say, to mirth; and that is not normal." He concluded, "She has no connected train of thought."

Schenck asked whether Mrs. Judd's delusions were hereditary.

"They certainly are," said Stephens, "certainly come from hereditary taints that are handed down, if you want to call them taints." The doctor also said he had found many cases of dementia praecox associated with tuberculosis.

Rodgers opened his cross-examination of Dr. Stephens by attacking his qualifications. Questioned about the political nature of his position, Stephens confirmed that he had been replaced by one of his assistants for a period of two years.

"And so then, you came back at the beginning of the year 1931, when the political complexion changed again in the state?" asked Rodgers.

"That is correct," snapped Stephens.

Rodgers continually requestioned Stephens about his diagnosis. Exasperated, the doctor finally retorted, ". . . I have talked pretty thoroughly on it; and, of course, the counsel doesn't seem to get it."

"Don't worry about me; you just take care of yourself," said Rodgers.

"I am going to," Stephens assured him.

On Tuesday, Dr. Edward Huntington Williams, Los Angeles physician and surgeon, was called as a witness for the defense. Schenck questioned him regarding his specialty, "nervous and mental diseases." Williams had examined Mrs. Judd once in jail and testified that, if she had committed the act charged, she would not have known the difference between right and wrong. His diagnosis was similar to that of Stephens, but he added a reference to the endocrine glands. The lawyers believed this to be the first criminal case in which endocrine glands were advanced as a causative factor in an insanity plea.

In particular, Williams discussed the thyroid glands, the reproductive glands and others. He said the use of thyroid for curing insanity "happened to be a most important event in psychiatry." Citing the number of cases cured in mental institutions, he said, ". . . they have cleaned out all the back halls because they have given this treatment." He added that the reproductive glands "play a very important part in most cases, at least a high percentage of cases of dementia praecox.

"Now, in this defendant," continued Williams, "she is an undeveloped—she is not a fully developed woman in this sense, that there has not been a sufficient action of her—of the ovarian secretion so as to produce a person who is entirely normal in physical makeup. That is, she is what we call a eunuchoid, a eunuch being a person with no organs of reproduction, and

The trunks in which the bodies were shipped, just after being opened for the first time in the Los Angeles baggage room. The body of Mrs. LeRoi and parts of Miss Samuelson's body were found in the large trunk. Most of the rest of the latter's body was packed in the smaller trunk to the right (open lid showing). Mrs. Judd also carried some parts of the body in a handgrip at her seat on the train from Phoenix to Los Angeles.

Here are the most recent photographs of Miss Hedvig Samuelson, left, and Mrs. Agnes LeRoi, right, both of Phoenix, Ariz., the victims in the Los Angeles trunk murder mystery in which police have been carrying on a nation-wide hunt for Mrs. Ruth Judd, doctor's wife, who is a suspect in the killings. Inset are the gun and surgical instruments which were found in a hat box carried by Mrs. Judd and which are believed to have been used in the slaying and in the dismemberment of one of the bodies.

Arizona police "mug shots" of Mrs. Judd taken after her apprehension in Los Angeles and extradition to Arizona in January, 1931.

The two murder victims, in a news photo of October 26, 1931, before Mrs. Judd was apprehended. The caption reads: "Murder Victims Shot in Bed, Officers Claim After Probe."

The thirteen murder trial jurors (including the alternate). No women jurors were allowed at that time in Arizona. Some of their names have been changed in the text of this book for legal reasons.

Detective Dan Lucey following witness Carl Harris out of the courtroom during the murder trial. Harris, never called to the stand, was later accused of being the lover of both victims and Mrs. Judd, and of arranging the dismemberment of Miss Samuelson's body.

Courtroom scene. Mrs. Judd is indicated by arrow. On her right is Sheriff J. R. McFadden; on her left, a matron. Mrs. McKinnell, Winnie's mother, sitting. Judge Howard C. Speakman is leaning forward at the bench.

Dr. George W. Stephens, superintendent of Arizona State Hospital, listens to Mrs. Judd during a recess of her murder trial. Dr. Stephens testified that Mrs. Judd was insane, suffering from "dementia praecox." Photography was then permitted in a courtroom.

Mrs. Judd, right, at the counsel table with her defense attorneys, Paul Schenck and Joseph Zaversack.

Dr. William Judd, Winnie's middle-aged husband, bends to kiss the "Tiger Woman," following the reading of the verdict guilty at the end of the murder trial. Her mother stands to the left, back to the camera. The calendar above dates the trial ending—February, 1932.

Winnie with her new chief counsel, O. V. Willson, during her insanity trial in Florence, Arizona, in 1933.

Mrs. Judd, slouched down in the front seat but acting happy, after her successful trial for insanity in April, 1933. She is being taken from the penitentiary to the Arizona State Hospital by the deputy and two matrons in the rear seat.

Mrs. Judd Tells Story Of Slaying Two Girls

"It was a blunt end knife, and I grabbed the knife, and as I grabbed for the gun and the knife—I don't know at the same time or not,—but I grabbed them right there, and as I grabbed towards the gun, she had it pointed towards my heart.

Shot Through Hand

"She shot me through the hand this way (indicating). I had the bread knife this way (indicating), and I stabbed her twice in the shoulder. At that Anne came yelling out into the kitchen, and I said, 'Give me that gun to Sammy. Give me that gun.

"And Anne yelled, "Shoot, Sammy, shoot!"

"The bread knife bent double like that. It was a green-handled knife, and it bent completely double. I then grabbed with this hand (indicating) toward the gun. This hand was shot (indicating), and I grabbed toward the gun with this hand (indicating) and only with the back of my arm tried to get the gun out of her hand, and twisted like this the gun in her hand, and this finger was torn and this finger torn wrenching for the gun.

"Her finger was yet on the trigger when that shot went through her chest; the shot that went through her chest. Anne grabbed up the ironing board that was behind the water heater there, and when Sammy and I fell on the floor, when that shot went through her chest we fell on the floor.

Fell To Floor

"I don't know how it was we tripped, but we fell on the floor, and Anne came over and beat me with the ironing board and yelled at Sammy. 'Shoot, Sammy, shoot!'

"And I said, 'Sammy, give me that gun. Give me that gun!'

"And Anne yelled, 'Shoot, Sammy,' and she beat me over the head and she beat me and beat me with the ironing board as we rolled there back and forth in the doorway there fighting for the gun. We rolled back and forth in the doorway and fought.

"I fought for my life. I fought for every ounce of strength that I had for that gun there in the doorway and rolled back and forth, and

Article excerpts from the *Arizona Republic,* Phoenix, Arizona, dated January 19, and April 23, 1933. The second trial of 1933 created great interest in her story of the murders told before her first trial in 1931.

Trunk Slayer Found Insane

Tonight the fact that death on the gallows once more had passed her by—this time perhaps for ever —made no apparent impression on her consciousness or emotions.

She did not betray by the flicker of an eyelash, any understanding of the jury's verdict which had set a crowded courtroom off to a tumult

Uncomprehending Eyes

Her features were blank and her eyes uncomprehending as she walked for the last time from the old-fashioned Pinal county courthouse, where for seven days she had sat fidgeting in her chair, sometimes in hysterics, as lawyers wrangled over her life.

Warden A. G. Walker of the Arizona state prison, smiling, his features stamped with relief, sought a way ˮ her through the vociferous crowd. Women sought to grasp her hand, to pat her on the shoulder. She paid no attention to them.

Icily Aloof

Pale and icily aloof—she had received indifferently and failed to return caresses showered on her by her aged parents, the Rev. and Mrs. H. J. McKinnell of Darlington, Ind.—she went back to her little adobe cellhouse in the women's ward of the state prison, sat down on her cot, and made ready to allow the matrons to prepare her for bed, saying not a word.

The jury deliberated one hour and 57 minutes, asking for instructions once, and taking five ████.

The first ballot resulted in a vote of 10 to 2 for insanity, but two of the jurors withdrew before signing the verdict. Four more then were necessary to win to the side of insanity, the ninth juror necessary eunuchoid being one with those not acting enough, the arms being too long, legs too long and the pelvis too narrow. She is underdeveloped."

Dr. Williams maintained that dementia praecox usually begins in puberty, and said, "She has a history of beginning menstruation at thirteen and then she skipped for almost a year, and then another period, and then skipped again for a year; and that shows a faulty development during the time that she was in this episode about the young man and the supposed pregnancy, when I believe she did not menstruate."

"What particular sphere of mental activity," asked Schenck, "is first affected by this disease—volitional, emotional or intellectual?"

"Well, it is the emotional. It is the judgment and so forth, not the intellect. That is, many of these people can remember, many of them continue to be very smart, continue to be very intelligent, but it is the emotions, their feelings, the emotional sphere, as we call it, in distinction from the intellect."

Williams said people suffering from dementia praecox show, as a rule, a lack of emotion or feeling. At other times "they will laugh, silly laughter about nothing, or have crying spells about something."

Rodgers cross-examined him, citing a book entitled *Insanity Plea*, which Williams had written. Williams acknowledged that, as he had written in his book, he did not feel expert witnesses should be questioned by a person who does not know as much about insanity as a doctor, "My theory being, which I believe is held by every intelligent and honest physician, that these cases should not be brought before a jury of laymen because it is unjust, and that the doctors should make their reports, come to their conclusions as they please, be appointed not by either side but by the magistrate himself and make their reports to him."

Asked whether experts in insanity have ever been fooled by malingerers, Williams answered, "I suppose they have," then added, ". . . but when we find malingering, we know the majority of the malingerers are insane."

Asked again whether the defendant knew right from wrong, Williams said, "She did not know right from wrong, not anything like in a normal sense. If she had, she would have certainly in this case, if she did this, she would have certainly taken a more intelligent means of getting rid of the bodies. She had every opportunity in the world to have it made out that it was a case of suicide and murder. She took, if she did it, the most absolute asinine way to get rid of the bodies imaginable."

Rodgers concluded his cross-examination by referring back to Williams' view, expressed in *Insanity Plea*, that because under the present law physicians had to testify before a jury of laymen, they would be justified in tailoring their testimony to fit the legal definition of insanity if in their opinion the accused was medically insane. "In other words, you do believe that in certain contingencies a, what you term in your book, a slight bending of the truth is warranted?"

"I have said so in the book. I must believe it," replied Williams.

On redirect examination, Schenck asked Williams whether he had read a book entitled *Manual of Psychiatry*, by Dr. Sidney Freid. At this point the jury was excused from the room, and Judge Speakman had a few words of caution for counsel. He said, "Don't go adrift into the realms of mysteries so far as we laymen are concerned, except upon the questions involved in this case."

Schenck finally asked Williams, ". . . you would consider Freudian theories of repressed desires as an exploded theory, would you not?"

"I think so," said Williams. "He had a lot of words that are good, but I consider the general theory as exploded."

The defense rested its case with the testimony of the next witness, Dr. Clifford A. Wright, a Los Angeles physician. He said that he and Dr. Williams had started the Psycho-endocrine Clinic, then a department of the Los Angeles General Hospital. Dr. Wright, who said he had specialized in endocrinology for about fifteen years, confirmed much of the earlier testimony by Stephens and Williams.

He added, "This girl was born in a religious family, was repressed. She says the earliest recollections are being taken to protracted religious meetings, revival meetings, kept up until ten and eleven o'clock. It was made quite a feature in her family. Very early, she worried about the meaning of the religious songs as pertaining to herself.

"Now, she has delusions surrounding recent events," he continued. "She feels that the District Attorney, Mr. Andrews, and Mr. Harris are in league against her. She says they play golf together and put up a job to have her hanged. She says that Mr. Harris would kill her on the streets if he could.

"Now, she has the delusion that there are men on the roof of the jail. They come over there nearly every night, call her by name, 'Ruth'; and a few nights ago, they had a flashlight there. At first, she thought these people were friends. Now, she feels they are there to kill her."

The state began its rebuttal testimony with half a dozen witnesses called to confirm the state's contention that Mrs. Judd was sane during the months preceding the crime. Dr. Sidney Freid followed them to the stand, and his testimony so infuriated Winnie that she attacked him after court had adjourned for the day. Walking in the hallway, Winnie grabbed a jail matron's arm and shoved her at Freid, who was knocked into the wall. Mrs. Judd then turned and kicked at Sheriff McFadden as she threatened, "My husband will get you!"

After he had qualified as an expert in psychiatry, Dr. Freid told the jury that Mrs. Judd was sane on October 16, and capable of knowing right from wrong. He had given Winnie a neurological and a mental examination.

"I asked her if she was happy or sad, or indifferent or elated," said Freid. "Her answer was, in substance, 'Why talk about that. Nobody likes to be in jail. I am here on a serious charge. I wish my husband was here. I don't like to talk when he is not around.'

"When she wanted to answer questions directly, her answers were always to the point and correct. At no time was her conversation incoherent, irrelevant or absurd.

"She said that she had sex relations with her husband when he was well and had experienced orgasms when her husband was well, that she wished to become pregnant. She was wild about children. Said she was anxious to have a baby by Mr. Harris, that she had sexual relations with him for a number of months, that sex relations with him were satisfactory. Says she felt that she loved her husband, but she loved him in a maternalistic way, that he had been sick. She said she felt differently toward Mr. Harris, a romantic feeling toward him. Said she worried about the fact that she told Dr. Judd about the sexual relations. She grieved because this information hurt him, and she was sorry for that."

Freid continued, "I inquired of her if it was right to steal, to lie, to commit burglary, to commit adultery, to kill. She said it was wrong to lie, to steal, but in self-defense one might be excused for killing. Said she didn't care to talk about adultery; and if one were really in love with a person, that adultery was not so wrong as it might seem.

"She was asked what her defense was going to be, in other words, 'What story are you going to tell?' She said, 'That depends on the kind of a break I get. I may tell everything that I know. I will just have to wait and see. Mr. Harris will help me, but he is not in a position to do so. They would have him arrested if he came around here.' "

Before the trial, Harris had issued a formal statement to the effect that he was "innocent but perhaps indiscreet."

"I asked her," continued Freid, "if she ever had any homosexual relations, and she vehemently answered, 'No, I never had; I am not that kind of a girl. Sammy and Anne may have had those kind of relations. They seemed to have loved one another more than usual, but I won't say they did have. I won't talk about them like that.' "

On Wednesday, Freid and Schenck waged a verbal battle for almost six hours, as each attacked the other's point of view on scientific questions. Discussing various definitions of insanity, Freid said, "I am not a Freudian, and neither do I agree with

White. I don't agree with any author, particularly in all his entirety."

"Let us go back," said Schenck. "We will be over in Germany in a minute."

"Stay in Arizona," said Judge Speakman.

Freid was hostile and sarcastic during much of his cross-examination. At one point, Schenck asked about Mrs. Judd's skeletal structure. "I don't think she was ever very fat," he said.

"The bones, the bones are always slim. I never saw any fat bones," answered Freid.

"If you meant to be facetious, we will try that," replied Schenck.

Asked whether he agreed with the author of a book titled *Dementia Praecox*, Freid said, "Inasmuch as it agrees with my own personal experience. I accept no authority as absolute other than God Almighty. . . ."

Freid had said that he thought Winnie was malingering, or faking insanity. Probing, Schenck asked, "She punched you in the back yesterday?"

"Yes, I think she did. She punched me quite vigorously, with a little purpose."

"You think that was malingering also?"

"Her foot slipped accidentally on purpose, kind of gave me a real good bump, so I knew she was around."

Schenck spent a good deal of Wednesday at the blackboard illustrating Mendel's theory of heredity and Winnie's family tree, to establish that she suffered from inherited insanity. Prosecution continually objected, and Freid said he could not make any judgments from Schenck's charts because they did not conform to Mendel's law. Judge Speakman attempted to arbitrate the confusion as Schenck drew one series of diagrams after another.

In redirect examination, Rodgers asked, ". . . does this Mendelian hypothesis to which you have referred mean anything whatever to you in connection with this case?"

Freid concluded that "even though there is a defect in this

case, the defendant might have been one of the lucky ones that was normal under the descent of the Mendelian hypothesis."

Dr. J. D. Mauldin, county physician, expressed his belief that Mrs. Judd was sane and malingering.

Dr. Joseph Catton, an assistant professor at Stanford Medical School, said he specialized in "nervous and mental disorders." His testimony created a sensation in the courtroom Thursday as he discussed his examination of Mrs. Judd. He recalled asking her, "Did you drink anything at the girls' house that night?"

"No," she had answered.

"Did anybody drink there or was anybody drinking there that night?" he asked. "She said, 'The only one who drank was Carl Harris,' and then she quickly put her hand over her mouth and said nothing further."

Dr. Catton spent most of the day on the witness stand, taking four hours to answer a seventeen-word question put to him during the morning session.

"It is my opinion that she was sane," he said, "so that she was able to comprehend the rightness and wrongness of the act if she committed it."

During his first conversation with Mrs. Judd, the sheriff had said, "Oh, Mrs. Judd, Jack Dempsey is in town and has expressed a desire to come over and see you."

"Oh, is that so?" replied Winnie.

"Her face lighted up, and she had the normal reaction of a woman with that sort of information," said Catton. "Mrs. Judd proceeded with me in the course of my examination in exactly the same way as any normal average person I have ever seen."

He had given Mrs. Judd a physical as well as mental examination. "As a matter of fact," he said, "I believe if Mrs. Judd had about fifteen pounds more weight, that she would make a very good model for a woman of her particular height and size in some dress establishment. In addition to looking over her body for various defects and about those endocrine glands, let me tell you this under oath—I would be the most ridiculous ass if I said this girl was a eunuch or eunuchoid.

"Mrs. Judd gave me absolutely a clear bill of health regarding hallucinations. Never had them in her whole life. . . .

"I found this girl to be a little tiny more than average modest. She kept covering her shoulder if this thing would drop down when I was examining her. She had that little refined business of putting her skirt down a little further when I examined her, and I found her emotions showed her related to modesty."

He said Winnie's emotions were characterized by modesty, sympathy and pity.

"She showed revulsion, that means horrible reaction feelings, to the fact that the girl was cut up. She showed average normal feelings of bitterness over the reactions toward her of the two girls who had been killed, telling me that these girls didn't treat her squarely. That in spite of the fact that she used to wait on these girls when they were sick—she used to shampoo their hair, rub their scalps, do this and that for them—there was no reciprocation. As a matter of fact, they treated her meanly rather than by reward. She showed bitterness in that connection. She showed scorn, scorn for C.H., telling me that this C.H. had come into her life and, just like the rest of men, wouldn't raise a finger to help her even though she may be hanged.

"She showed average jealous reaction concerning her work at the clinic with the other girls, and the moment I touched jealousy, Mrs. Judd hesitated. She appeared to be in deep thought. Then speaking rather rapidly, she said, 'I am not a jealous woman. I have never been jealous in my life. Why, Dr. Judd used to have mistresses before he was married. I insisted— I not only allowed it, but I insisted—that he write to those people now. I want to tell you that C.H., while I love him with my whole heart and soul and more passionately than I ever loved my husband, I have not been jealous of him. . . .'

"She says that she never violated her marriage vows until December 24, 1930. Ruth Judd says that night she slept with C.H. and sex relations took place. She says from that time on, up until the time that these crimes were committed, if they were committed, that even including ten of the fourteen days preceding October 16, this love life continued."

Catton said he asked, "Mrs. Judd, is it ever right to take a human life?"

"Yes, in self-defense," she had answered.

"Is it ever right under any other conditions?"

"No," she said.

Catton had asked her about the "drain pipe letter."

"Now, just a minute, Doctor," she had said, "I have never admitted that I wrote that letter. I don't know whether I am going to say I wrote it or not. Some of the lawyers in Los Angeles told me I wrote it, and Mr. Cantillon told me I didn't. Mr. Franks says I didn't. And I don't know whether I am going to say I wrote it or I didn't."

Mrs. Judd had reportedly received $5,000 for writing an article for one of the Los Angeles papers. Catton had questioned her about the article.

"I asked her," he said, "if she had written this article for the paper, and she informed me that she had not written it. I told her she had previously told me that she had written the article, but that in some places she had been misquoted, and she said, 'I did not write that article.' I asked her if it were true that she had received $5,000 for writing that article, and she said 'Yes.'

"I asked her if she had any other source of finances to help her in her trial, and she closed her lips tightly and turned away. She said, 'I will not answer that.' I asked her specifically if Carl Harris or any other person was putting up money, and she said she would not answer that."

Catton asked her about the article's reference to Mrs. LeRoi and Miss Samuelson.

"She states at this point that some doctors at the hospital wanted her to stay away from those girls, because they were homosexual perverts, and she knows they were. She has seen them sleeping together and making rather excessive love, one with the other."

Catton told of a January examination of Mrs. Judd, when he discovered that she had not lost her sense of humor. Winnie was informed that the doctor had arrived. She said, "I know doctors; they always keep us waiting, so now they can wait for me."

"She didn't cry at all on the second examination," said Catton, "not a tear, unless she cried when I was out of the room. She did smile, and at one time when we were talking about revival meetings, she quoted some little song. I don't remember all of it, but she included something about wanting to go to heaven on roller skates. Then she volunteered, 'Do you know, I used to imagine out and act out all of those songs.'" Recalling that she was forced to attend revival meetings with her parents, Winnie told Catton, "I used to picture myself doing the things and being in the places they were talking about."

During his second examination of Mrs. Judd, Catton had asked again about her defense. He had said, "Mrs. Judd, as a matter of fact, you have never cut a human being in your life."

She had replied, "I am going to say that I did."

"Please answer the question," he said. "Have you ever in your whole life cut a human being under any condition?"

"Dr. Catton," she had replied, "I have never even cut a chicken."

"Won't you tell, or aren't you going to tell, the complete facts of this case?" he had asked.

"If things do not go the way they are planned," she had said, "believe me, I will get up there and tell them everything."

Thursday's session was adjourned until Saturday, February 6, because Friday was Arbor Day, then a legal holiday. Judge Speakman said, "If there was a way in the world to hold court tomorrow, I would gladly ignore the holiday and do it, but I don't see any way that we can legally hold court tomorrow. I assure you that all day Saturday we will saw wood. We won't waste any time, so you may be excused, gentlemen, until Saturday morning."

Barbed remarks were exchanged Saturday as Schenck cross-examined Catton. Schenck asked whether the doctor had been given a chair, meaning a professorship, at the University of California. Catton replied, "They didn't give me a chair; they gave

me a stool." Schenck reminded him that this was no occasion
for facetiousness. After lengthy discussion, Catton acknowledged "that it is entirely possible that any symptom of insanity may be more or less apparent at one time and not so
apparent at another time." Schenck was not so successful in attacking the doctor's other testimony.

Testimony was concluded at 4:32 P.M., when a night session
began to seem likely. Judge Speakman had announced that he
would hold night sessions "till midnight if necessary," so that
Schenck could finish his cross-examination of Dr. Catton.
Court was recessed until 9 A.M. February 8, when counsel
would present their final arguments and Judge Speakman
would instruct the jury.

13. BEGINNING OF THE END

In the morning, Assistant Prosecutor Rodgers opened arguments. They continued to 4:40 P.M., with the only interruption occurring when a gray-haired woman spectator fainted and was carried from the packed courtroom.

Rodgers attacked the defense plea of insanity as an "excuse for the crime. I don't criticize the attorneys for their attempt. It was to be expected. There is nothing else they can do. But that doesn't mean you gentlemen must swallow it, that you should free this defendant on opinions here expressed on her insanity. When all other defenses fail, look ever and anon for the claim of insanity. Subterfuges, however, are neither here nor there when measured by the standard of human justice which says: 'Thou shalt not kill.' I shall not presume to tell you men what you should or should not do, but it occurs to me if you desire to protect and secure the lives of your own loved ones, you must not let this crime pass."

Attorneys Franks and Schenck followed with lengthy arguments for the defense. In conclusion, Schenck said, "I believe the court will instruct you and that the state then will take this defendant in hand, not as a felon, but as an ill person and will keep her in custody as long as she remains insane." He compared Mrs. Judd's condition with that of someone suffering from a physical disease. "Smallpox patients are not hanged, they are isolated. This woman is suffering from mental illness. Why hang her if the smallpox patient is spared?"

County Attorney Andrews closed the arguments, calling the claim of insanity "just bunk." Leaning close to the jury, he concluded, "Arizona statutes provide for infliction of the death penalty in a proper case. If this case does not deserve it, I have never seen one that did. It is in your hands."

Judge Speakman immediately began his instructions to the jurors. He offered them a choice of six verdicts—guilty of murder in the first degree with punishment fixed at death; guilty of murder in the first degree with punishment fixed at life imprisonment; guilty of murder in the second degree with the sentence to be determined by the court; guilty of manslaughter with the court determining the sentence; not guilty; and not guilty by reason of insanity.

The all-male jury began deliberations at 5:15 P.M. Myron S. Butler, a twenty-six-year-old salesman and one of the youngest members of the jury, was elected foreman. Not counting a break for dinner, deliberations took two hours and forty minutes.

It was 9:21 P.M. before Judge Speakman, court officers, Mrs. Judd and the jury were gathered in the courtroom for reading of the verdict.

Without formality, Judge Speakman addressed the jurors. "Gentlemen of the jury, have you arrived at a verdict?" Foreman Butler silently handed the folded verdict slip to Bailiff W. A. McNabb, who passed it to the bench. Judge Speakman glanced down at the slip of paper, then admonished the spectators, "Before this verdict is read, I want you to know there will be no demonstration in this courtroom, regardless of what this verdict may be."

Total silence gripped the crowded courtroom as the verdict slip was given to William Choisser, clerk of the court, for the reading. He asked the jurors, "So say you all?" They nodded, and he began reading. Dr. Judd, sitting beside his wife, became noticeably tense. As Choisser read, ". . . find the defendant guilty of the crime of murder in the first degree," Dr. Judd slipped his arm around Winnie's shoulders. When he continued, ". . . and fix the punishment at death," Dr. Judd's left hand tightened convulsively on her shoulder, his fingers jerking spasmodically. Defense counsel appeared stunned.

But Winnie Ruth Judd stared straight ahead, methodically twisting a handkerchief about her hand. A *Phoenix Gazette* dispatch was to say that:

Even the nerve-hardened newspapermen cringed. But not Ruth Judd.

Nerves, a rage, a frenzy, a scene? Nothing like that. Ruth Judd was easily the most indifferent person in the courtroom.

Why? Has she something hidden away in the secret recesses of her mind that she knows will save her life if she only says the word?

If not, Ruth Judd is made of things as hard as steel. She may outdo the iron men that have faced death on the gallows without a flinch.

But maybe she does not realize the appalling significance of her act. Regardless of what she was when she killed Agnes Anne LeRoi in the trunk double murder, Ruth Judd is an enigma woman now.

She appears more like some little girl that is watching wide-eyed, that doesn't know what it is all about. She may be acting. But if she is, what acting in the face of death. Only an omniscient God can tell.

Within minutes after the verdict was read, Judge Speakman set Tuesday afternoon, February 23, as the date when he would pronounce the death penalty, fix the date for execution and hear a defense counsel motion for a new trial.

Mrs. Judd's trial had spanned three weeks, the longest criminal trial to that date in Maricopa County. It closed without testimony from Carl Harris or Winnie herself. He had appeared on the first day of the trial under subpoena to be sworn in as a state's witness. But Prosecutor Andrews never called him to the stand. At one point during the trial, Andrews reportedly told a newsman that Harris had come to him long before the trial, making himself available as a prosecution witness.

During the next several days, a number of letters were received by Governor George W. P. Hunt, requesting that he intervene and prevent the hanging of Mrs. Judd. A mysterious unsigned radiogram, sent from Prague, Czechoslovakia, said, "Stay your hand. Winnie's sacrifice not necessary. Await information. Innocent."

On February 23, in Judge Speakman's court, defense produced a bundle of affidavits charging that Juror Oscar Mitchell had been biased and prejudiced against Mrs. Judd prior to and during her trial. And on the following day, the prosecution countered with affidavits denying defense allegations.

Judge Speakman disposed of all defense charges and denied the motion for a new trial by Wednesday evening. A heated exchange with Mrs. Judd preceded his setting of May 11, 1932, as the execution date. It was to be on a Wednesday, a departure from the long-standing Arizona custom of scheduling executions for Friday. Judge Speakman set a precedent to avoid a Friday the 13th hanging. He said, "The superstition surrounding Friday the 13th is a relic of barbarism. It has been my aim in this trial to guard against anything spectacular, any show of any kind. For that reason I selected a day unassociated in the public mind with superstition."

Superstitions aside, the fixing of an execution date seemed to mark the end of Winnie Ruth Judd.

14. DEATH ROW

At 8:04 p.m., soon after Judge Speakman's courtroom had been cleared, Winnie Ruth Judd began the sixty-seven-mile journey to the Arizona State Prison at Florence. The trip was made in a sheriff's office car driven by Sheriff McFadden, within the car were matron Mrs. Lon Jordan and others. Mrs. Judd joined in singing popular Mexican songs. She particularly enjoyed singing "Quatro Landes" ("The Four Ranches"), a doleful folk song.

During the leisurely drive, McFadden asked Winnie about certain details of the crime for which she had just been convicted. She declined to answer most of the questions; however, in reply to the query, "Did you have an accomplice?" she said, "Yes, I had an accomplice."

Prison officials, including Warden William Delbridge, met the party upon arrival inside the twenty-foot walls of the institution. Prisoner No. 8811 was the designation assigned to Mrs. Judd, and she was taken to the prison hospital for a thorough physical examination. Prison physician H. B. Steward reported her in good health, although "her heart was pounding from the effects of her emotions." He said she was visibly shaken.

At midnight, contrary to the previously announced plans that Winnie would be put in the women's ward, she was taken directly to Death Row. She shuddered. "I visited a lot of dark caves when I lived in Mexico and wasn't afraid, but this dark place scares me to death." Death Row consisted of four cells, dimly lit, with gray walls. The cells were in a small building which housed the gallows. Only a few steps from the narrow corridor fronting the cells were the thirteen steps leading up to the hangman's noose awaiting Mrs. Judd.

After she was settled in her cell, Sheriff McFadden and the others who had brought her from Phoenix bid her goodbye. Warden Delbridge then suggested she turn out the light and get some sleep. "I want to do anything you say," Mrs. Judd said.

The next morning she was officially "registered." Her fingerprints and photographs were taken and the history of her case recorded in prison files. Winnie's money—a dollar bill, a quarter and five pennies—was checked in at the warden's office.

That day in Phoenix, Governor George W. P. Hunt revealed he had received four appeals in the mail that he intervene in the execution of Mrs. Judd. The appeals came from Houston, Texas; and Los Angeles, San Jose and Redwood City, California. He had previously received scores of appeals on behalf of Winnie. Attorneys pointed out that the governor had no authority in the case unless he received a recommendation for commutation of sentence from the Arizona Board of Pardons and Paroles.

On the night of February 25, Winnie received her first visitors. "Oh! I'm so glad to see you," she sobbed as her father and mother appeared at her cell door. It was a surprise visit. All three broke into tears, and Warden Delbridge ordered a guard to unlock the door. Mrs. McKinnell embraced Winnie, then her father took her in his arms and said, "Don't worry, daughter, God is with you. He'll take care of you." Delbridge let the McKinnells stay in the cell for a half hour, and told them they could visit Winnie "for an hour or so" each Sunday. Rev. McKinnell said he and his wife would move to Florence within a few days. At the end of the visit, the McKinnells knelt with their daughter and prayed. Both parents offered prayers, Winnie quietly repeating the words.

During the next few days, while she adjusted to life on Death Row, Winnie's attorneys, Samuel Franks and Joseph B. Zaversack, began preparing their briefs for an appeal to the state Supreme Court for a new trial. This was a move designed, at best, to gain a retrial; at worst, to gain a stay of execution.

Despite the virtually complete isolation of Winnie's cell from the rest of the "big house," the prison's grapevine hummed continually with news and rumors about the star boarder. The inmates of the prison, more than six hundred, showed the same curiosity about the "Tiger Woman" as those on the outside. They gave her a cat and a bird as pets.

Being a Death Row boarder, Winnie partook of such delicacies foreign to regular prison fare as milk and cream, vegetables, steaks and other choice meats. Arizona's condemned ate well, and Mrs. Judd soon showed interest in the variety of her menu. However, Warden Delbridge reported she was fascinated much more by the steadily increasing volume of fan mail. Letters addressed simply to Mrs. Judd, Arizona Prison, were delivered as promptly as those with complete addresses. The warden said she spent a great deal of her time writing. "We haven't asked her what it is about and she hasn't volunteered any information. She hasn't sent any of the writing out in the mail."

But Winnie was by no means the only person continuing to receive mail regarding her case. Lin B. Orme, Sr., chairman of the Arizona Board of Pardons and Paroles, reported receiving a lengthy plea for clemency on behalf of Mrs. Judd from a resident of Los Angeles. The letter, written in longhand, was barely legible. Orme filed it, since there had been no application for commutation of the death penalty before the board, and there could not be until Winnie's case had been disposed of by the state Supreme Court.

Governor George W. P. Hunt received two out-of-state applications for the privilege of hanging Arizona's most famous prisoner. They were sent by G. Phil Hanna, the "humane" hangman of Illinois, and F. P. Griggs of Iowa. Both offered to come out of retirement as executioners and hang Winnie at no cost to the taxpayers of Arizona. Hanna was by far the more distinguished hangman. He had "retired" four years earlier after officiating at the execution of Charles Birger, notorious Illinois gang leader. Although admitting "I never hung a woman before," Hanna counted on Mrs. Judd being the sixty-second person to hang "painlessly" at his hands. He told Governor Hunt he had followed his strange calling for humane reasons. He ascribed the bungled job of hanging Eva Dugan at the Arizona State Prison as due to nervousness on the part of the hangman, and said she would not have been decapitated had proper procedures been followed. Hanna said he believed the ugliness had been removed from hangings over which he had presided inasmuch as the condemned went to their deaths without physical pain. He used a rope woven by hand of soft fibers; it cost $65, and Hanna kept it in a moisture-proof box wrapped in absorbent paper to prevent decay. His executioner's gear included three stout straps, a black hood and a pair of handcuffs. The hands were fastened in front by the handcuffs, and the longest strap encircled the arms above the elbows, buckling in the center of the back, thus functioning like a strait-jacket in rendering the hands and arms immovable. Another strap was wrapped around the ankles and a third placed above the knees. The black hood was placed over the head and pulled down over the shoulders. Hanna then threw the noose around the head, drew the rope tight with the slip side of the knot against the victim's left jawbone, and stepped back, signaling for the gallows trap to fall.

Neither hangman's application could be accepted, since, according to Arizona statutes, the prison warden was charged with officiating at executions at the penitentiary's gallows. But on March 2, 1932, the warden's responsibility, at least temporarily, was lifted, for on that day, attorneys Franks and Zaversack filed notice of an appeal to the Arizona Supreme Court with the clerk of Maricopa County Superior Court. The very brief notice stated that Mrs. Judd was appealing the judgment, conviction and order denying a motion for a new trial. This action caused an automatic stay of execution. So May 11 would not be Winnie's death day. Winnie's counsel now filed an affidavit by Mrs. Judd that she was "without means and wholly unable to pay" for appeal records. This new angle in the case precipitated a hearing. The affidavit made it necessary for the court clerk to assemble documents, and Clerk Wilson said they were ready except for the current transcript of the murder trial. The transcript, because it was 2,587 pages long, would require a month to copy. Thus it would be at least late fall or early winter before the formal appeal would actually be considered. Attorneys Franks and Zaversack announced their client had gained perhaps a year of additional life because of their efforts. Winnie took the stay of execution calmly. She had expected it.

Warden Delbridge, despite the stay, said Mrs. Judd would not be taken off Death Row. He explained it was easier to take care of the condemned woman there, and that she was "better off" alone.

On March 9, seven days after Winnie's signed affidavit had been filed, Maricopa County Attorney Lloyd J. Andrews launched an effort on behalf of the State of Arizona to determine her financial status. Andrews filed a petition in Superior Court asking that Mrs. Judd "be examined touching the matters stated in her affidavit, wherein it is claimed that she is without means." In discussing the petition with newsmen, Andrews said, "It has been rumored that Mrs. Judd received large sums of money from newspapers and other sources for her stories. If such is true, we are at a loss to understand how these funds have been dissipated. If it is a fact that Mrs. Judd did receive a large sum of money, taxpayers of Maricopa County should not be forced to carry the extra burden of her appeal." There was also speculation that Winnie had been paid off to hush up evidence that might incriminate others.

Monday, March 21, 1:30 P.M., was the time set for Winnie to give testimony in Speakman's court concerning her finances. Reporters assumed she would be asked where she had obtained funds to pay for her defense in the twenty-one-day trial; the amounts she received and what she did with them; and whether or not she had any money left. Speculation was about evenly divided as to whether Winnie would use the hearing as an opportunity to carry out her long-promised threat to "tell all."

Meanwhile, on March 10, in Los Angeles, the trial of Dr. Judd on charges of practicing medicine in California without a license was postponed pending the Doctor's progress as a patient at the Fort Whipple Veterans' Hospital near Prescott, Arizona. Los Angeles Municipal Court Judge Clement Nye was told by attorney Paul Schenck that Dr. Judd had suffered a nervous breakdown caused by the strain of sitting through his wife's murder trial. On March 18, inmates of the Veterans' Hospital attempted to help Dr. Judd obtain dismissal of charges pending against him. Believing him to be neither physically nor financially able to go to Los Angeles to stand trial, the veterans hoped to get a suspended sentence without Dr. Judd's appearing in court.

Despite his patient status, Dr. Judd was subpoenaed March 19 to appear at his wife's financial hearing two days later in Phoenix. The action was hailed as the most important move made by County Attorney Andrews since he started action to investigate Mrs. Judd's finances. Dr. Judd had reportedly handled all of his wife's finances after her arrest. Rumors arose that large sums of money had been paid by Coast newspapers and national magazines for the "confessions" of Mrs. Judd and her life story, with Dr. Judd handling the financial arrangements. Another of Andrews' objectives was to find out if the Judds held any "community property." Under Arizona law, if there was any property held by Dr. Judd that must be shared by man and wife, that property must be used in paying costs of the death conviction appeal to the state Supreme Court.

Attorney Andrews subpoenaed tellers of all Phoenix banks, including the First National Bank of Arizona, Valley Bank &

Trust Company, Phoenix National Bank and Arizona Bank, to determine if any deposits had been made in Mrs. Judd's name.

Warden Delbridge and two prison guards escorted Mrs. Judd to Phoenix for her Monday afternoon hearing. They arrived at the Maricopa County Courthouse just before noon. Over her protests, Winnie was taken directly to a cell in the county jail, which occupied the upper floors of the courthouse building. She had wanted to go straight to the courtroom. Passing Sheriff McFadden on the way to the cell, she said, "I don't want to go up there. They tried to poison me there, and I don't want to be poisoned again."

A throng estimated to number one thousand swarmed in and around the courthouse to get a glimpse of the "Tiger Woman." Rev. and Mrs. McKinnell, meanwhile, sat quietly in the same seats they had occupied during their daughter's murder trial. Dr. Judd sat near the defense counsel table. Attorneys Franks and Zaversack sat at the table. When Winnie walked briskly into the courtroom, Dr. Judd stood up, smiling to greet her. She said, loudly, "Well, hello, I haven't seen you in a long time." They struck up a conversation that was easily heard all over the courtroom. Judge Speakman pounded with his gavel and told them to be quiet. They talked in whispers after that. As during her trial, Winnie continually twisted a handkerchief around her left hand.

County Attorney Andrews opened the hearing with an explanation of why he had brought such action. He said the county should not be forced to pay out money on Winnie's behalf if she and her husband could afford the costs. Franks then objected to the proceedings on the basis that Andrews had not brought the action within the five-day limit he said was required by law. Judge Speakman declared a ten-minute recess to consider the arguments.

During the recess, Dr. Judd told reporters it was untrue that he wanted to stay away from the financial hearing. "I haven't any money," he said. "Why in hell would I be in a government hospital if I had any money?"

Upon reconvening court, Speakman abruptly upheld Franks' argument that Andrews had waited too long before taking action, and the hearing was over. But Winnie had only just begun. Within moments she churned the courtroom into an uproar with a sensational tantrum. She shrieked with all her might, screaming accusations at Andrews and shouting almost incoherent denials of her guilt. Dr. Judd slapped her across the mouth in an attempt to hush her outcries. Finally, Sheriff Mc-Fadden, with help from a deputy, carried Winnie from the courtroom. She continued screaming in the midst of a milling mob in the hallway. "You're trying to protect a political friend!" she shouted at Andrews. "You're trying to hang me, and I won't have it! I didn't cut those bodies! I couldn't do it!" She told the sheriff in the jail elevator she was being "framed," that she was being denied an opportunity to talk.

County Attorney Andrews didn't take Winnie's outburst lightly. He immediately announced plans to conduct a press conference in Winnie's cell. Less than an hour later, eight persons, including several newspapermen and two shorthand reporters, faced Winnie.

"You said you wanted to talk and now we're going to give you an opportunity," Andrews said.

"When I talk, I'll talk at my second trial," Mrs. Judd interrupted, "or else in the courtroom before people."

"That won't make a bit of difference if you give us the facts. They are taking them down in shorthand," Andrews said, pointing to the shorthand reporters.

"What do you want them for? You want them to go out here and try to hang somebody else," Winnie snapped.

"I'm not concerned with you personally. If anybody else is involved in this case, I want to know who it is. I've been trying for six months to learn who it is. Now will you tell me who it is?" the county attorney asked.

"No. I will not. You know," she replied. Winnie suddenly began to storm about the cell, gesturing wildly and talking incoherently much of the time. She verbally attacked Andrews for the testimony she asserted he produced or failed to produce at her trial. She claimed state's witnesses "lied" to convict her, and said Judge Speakman had been "unfair."

"You say the shooting was at 10:30. Well, I was at home, in my own home, until 11:30 and a man came over to my house and picked me up in a car. . . . He wants the glory of hanging another woman," she screamed. "Sammy shot me. You're trying to keep me from a new trial because I have no money. I've been a political football—that's all. It's a little bit of notoriety to hang a woman. They don't do that in most civilized states. You know good and well that I never cut up a body."

Deputy McMurchie, who had accompanied Andrews into the cell, then asked, "Are you willing to say anything that will help the county attorney?"

"My God, no!" Mrs. Judd screamed. "I will do anything to help myself. I'm not helping him."

The "Tiger Woman" stalked wildly about her cell. "Judge Speakman said, 'May God have mercy on your soul.' I haven't got a soul. My God, you can't do that anymore. They can't do that to me anymore. I said, 'My God, you leave me alone,' you can't do that anymore; you can't do that anymore!" she screamed, over and over, as attorneys, newspapermen and shorthand reporters walked away.

Hours later, Winnie Ruth Judd was back on Death Row, the only occupant of the four cells reserved for those condemned to a gallows death. There she remained until, during the early days of April, she became hysterical again. Prison authorities sent for her parents.

Winnie reportedly had placed several lines of string in her death cell, warning visitors to beware of the strings "as they are high-tension wires." It helped Winnie get off Death Row. Her words of two weeks earlier, when face to face with County Attorney Andrews, proved prophetic: "I will do anything to help myself."

She was quieted only after removal to the women's ward, a sturdy adobe structure outside the death house wall which housed twelve other women convicted of crimes ranging from a misdemeanor to murder.

15. "I'M GAME...IF YOU ARE"

SAMUEL FRANKS ANNOUNCED on April 5, 1932, that he and
his associates, Joseph Zaversack of Phoenix and Paul Schenck
of Los Angeles, had been dismissed as defense counsel by Dr.
and Mrs. Judd. No reasons for the dismissal were given. The
next day, an announcement was made that the new counsel for
Mrs. Judd were Edward J. Flanigan, former Supreme Court
justice of Arizona, and O. V. Willson. Both were Phoenix attorneys.

Flanigan and Willson made the official presentation of Winnie's appeal to the state Supreme Court on April 7. With the
appeal were five volumes of court reporters' transcripts totaling
2,587 pages, and a half-dozen affidavits, including the one from
Mrs. Judd asserting her inability to pay costs of the appeal.
Defense counsel had thirty days to file the briefs supporting
contentions for appealing. However, due to the change of counsel and with the Supreme Court scheduled for a summer recess, it was expected that counsel would be allowed to postpone
the filing until early fall.

In the event the Supreme Court affirmed Mrs. Judd's conviction, she would still have two avenues left to escape the gallows. She could appeal to the state Board of Pardons and Paroles for a commutation of the death penalty to life imprisonment, or be judged insane at a sanity trial in Pinal County, of which Florence was the county seat. But a sanity trial could be held only if the prison warden filed an affidavit stating he believed Mrs. Judd insane. A judgment of insanity would result in her being committed to the Arizona Hospital for the Insane in Phoenix. An appeal to the United States Supreme Court was a possible third avenue, but counsel indicated it was a very remote possibility at that time.

Mrs. Judd adapted quickly to the less restricted life in the women's ward. Warden Delbridge declared she had become quiet and was apparently more contented. But he said she had reverted to her courtroom habit of continuously winding and unwinding a handkerchief around her hand. She seemed appreciative of the weekly visits from her parents.

On April 26, Judge Howard C. Speakman received an unsigned letter purporting to give the solution to the Winnie Ruth Judd trunk murder mystery. It said, in part: "Just a few lines to tell you that Mrs. Winnie Ruth Judd is not guilty of the killing of Mrs. Agnes Ann LeRoi and Hedvig Samuelson. . . . The man who did the killing is on his way to Mexico. . . . So please let Mrs. Judd free." The letter, written with pencil on ruled note paper, was dated March 30, Phoenix. However, the cancellation stamp on the envelope showed it had been mailed April 23, in Kennedy, Texas. Judge Speakman filed the letter in a box along with more than two hundred others he had received since the Judd trial.

Five weeks later, on May 31, Judge Speakman was the subject of a motion filed by state counsel with the clerk of the Arizona Supreme Court. In the motion it was revealed that Judge Speakman had initialed several records in the Judd case. The motion was to correct those records by having the judge add his full signature. The motion was upheld, and the signatures added. The move was made by the state to prevent the possibility of a new trial for Mrs. Judd on technical grounds.

Apparently no attorney serving in a defense counsel capacity
for Mrs. Judd had noticed Judge Speakman's technical goof.
Now it was too late for the "Tiger Woman" to escape the gallows simply because the judge had used the initials "H. C. S."

With both Mrs. Judd and her legal counsel now playing a
"waiting game" until the state Supreme Court passed judgment
on her appeal, the condemned woman was becoming better
adjusted to prison life. In early August, Warden Delbridge said,
"She has become a model prisoner, but she has developed a
nervous condition. She doesn't cause any trouble, although at
times she gets into a wrangle with other inmates in the ward
when they talk about her." Two of her fellow inmates were
Zora Neal Ross, of Prescott, convicted of manslaughter in the
death of a military service veteran; and Jennie Rutledge, convicted in Phoenix for slaying her mother. Although Winnie was
not the only woman inmate serving time for murder or manslaughter, she was the only one condemned to die.

Delbridge reported that Winnie spent most of her time in
the "snakes" of the women's ward. The "snakes" was the small
cell used as solitary confinement when disciplinary action was
prescribed. The warden explained she was not placed there
for disciplinary reasons, but that the cell had been especially
fixed for her when she was transferred from Death Row. She
occasionally strolled out in the small courtyard for exercise or
to chat with one of the other eleven women convicts. Winnie
was often visited in the courtyard by her parents. But usually
she ran from other persons whose curiosity led them to seek
her there, retreating to her cage-like sanctuary in the "snakes."

There was a bench in the courtyard where Winnie often sat,
easily seen through a window in the nearby prison administration building. She was often observed biting her thumbs and
chewing on the ends of her fingers. She smiled occasionally,
and her blond hair was usually combed neatly as though she
were expecting a special visitor at any time. The women inmates did not have to wear special clothes as did the men just
over the wall behind the adobe women's ward. Winnie had a
choice of clothes, but more often than not she wore a simple,
clean white dress.

Warden Delbridge said moving Mrs. Judd into the women's ward had built up her morale. She enjoyed the freedom afforded by the courtyard, he said. But her nervous condition was gradually becoming worse, and she worried a lot about the outcome of her appeal to the state Supreme Court. Delbridge said she seemed hopeful her fight to escape the gallows would be successful. He added that she had no hope of escaping from the prison. The women's ward was surrounded on two sides by a high iron fence and the prison wall and the administration building on the others. The courtyard was always under watch.

Mrs. Judd often expressed a desire to see her husband. She had seen him only once since her trial, that occasion being in Judge Speakman's courtroom when he disallowed a hearing into her finances. Dr. Judd was still a patient at Whipple Veterans' Hospital near Prescott on August 31. On that day, he was granted another continuance by Los Angeles Municipal Court Judge Ambrose in his trial on charges of practicing medicine in California without a license.

On September 1, Winnie's counsel, now numbering six attorneys, filed the appellant's opening briefs for a rehearing in the Arizona Supreme Court. The three hundred pages of briefs alleged twelve errors by the Maricopa County Superior Court in the Judd murder trial. Two major points were presented. One dealt with the interpretation of the term "legal insanity" and the other with the failure of Judge Speakman to give an instruction to the jury on self-defense as an excuse for killing. It was claimed that this was the first time the state Supreme Court had been asked to define legal insanity. Mrs. Judd's counsel declared the story told by their client in the famous "drain pipe letter" to her husband, as read to the trial jury, was sufficient to constitute a reason for instructing the jury on self-defense, and that the trial court erred in failing to do so. In the letter, Mrs. Judd said she had killed in self-defense. The defense offered during the trial was insanity, and except for the story of a fight between Winnie and Mrs. LeRoi and Miss Samuelson in the "drain pipe letter," the record of the case showed no self-defense evidence. This was admitted by counsel in the briefs, but they held that the evidence in the letter introduced by the state was sufficient to warrant instruction on the point.

J. R. McDougall, Arizona assistant attorney general, was granted an extension to November 1, as the deadline for the prosecution to answer the defense counsel briefs.

On October 31, Dr. Judd received a Halloween surprise in a Los Angeles court where he was on trial. He was his own defense witness. He admitted working for $6 a day as a substitute physician, but said he did not write prescriptions and gave only first-aid treatment. Dr. Judd also admitted he did not have a California license. The jury deliberated less than an hour before it found him not guilty. He returned to Fort Whipple.

That day in Phoenix, McDougall filed his sixty-seven-page brief with the Arizona Supreme Court. The state claimed the trial court had not erred in failing to instruct Winnie's jury that it could give a self-defense verdict. The state declared there was no evidence in the "drain pipe letter" to show Mrs. Judd had shot Agnes Anne LeRoi in self-defense, but rather that the letter tended to show Mrs. Judd had fired at Mrs. LeRoi because she was going to "blackmail me, too, if I went hunting —and would hand me over to the police." The state said the Supreme Court had defined insanity many times before and there was no need to do it again. The state concluded its brief by asserting that every legal right had been extended to Mrs. Judd during her trial, and that the judgment should be affirmed.

Oral arguments on the briefs were conducted before the high tribunal on Wednesday, November 21. One attorney anxiously awaiting the decision, expected by mid-December, was Paul Schenck. Although he had been dismissed as a member of Mrs. Judd's counsel, he remained deeply interested in her case. In a law practice begun in 1899, he had saved from the gallows ninety men and women accused of murder. The Judd trial represented the first major defeat of his career. He retired shortly after it and died of a heart attack in his home at the edge of California's Mojave desert.

Meanwhile, Mrs. Judd kept busy weaving rugs and making

quilts. A Florence woman asked her to make a quilt which she wanted to purchase as a Christmas present for a little girl. Winnie liked doing things for children.

Late in the afternoon, December 12, Arizona's high tribunal announced its decision. Winnie Ruth Judd's conviction was affirmed, and Judge Speakman was upheld on every point challenged by defense counsel. The court ruled Mrs. Judd must die, and set February 17, 1933, as the execution date.

Warden Delbridge, known as the "little man of the prison" and called "Uncle Billy" by some convicts, went to Mrs. Judd. "I have unpleasant news for you and have come to inform you the state Supreme Court has denied your appeal for a new trial."

Winnie shouted, "Oh, Mr. Delbridge, I'm no murderer. I fought for my life when she came at me with the gun." She then turned to her mother, who had been summoned to comfort Winnie, and said: "Mother, I am a good woman. I have never associated with bad, low or degenerate people. I never cut up those bodies. I could not have done it." Her father then said, "Let us pray."

Delbridge did not tell Winnie about the new execution date. He said he would not do that until receiving official notification from the Supreme Court. The warden lived up to his "Uncle Billy" image by allowing Mrs. McKinnell to spend the night with her daughter. "I think her mother being with her will build up Mrs. Judd's morale," he said the next morning. "I told Mrs. McKinnell she could stay with her as long as she wants." He disclosed that recently Winnie had hysterically screamed in her cell, "I'll never hang!"

Following the Supreme Court's ruling, newspaper reports speculated whether the "Tiger Woman" would finally tell all and name her accomplice. Sheriff J. R. McFadden, who had talked with Mrs. Judd several times since her imprisonment, said he believed she might have an ace up her sleeve which she might play at the last possible moment. "I repeatedly told her that if she would only tell the truth she might benefit by it," McFadden said. County Attorney Lloyd J. Andrews felt differently. "No matter what she says, it will not mitigate the circumstances that she is a cold-blooded murderess," he declared. "She killed two women, she can't get away from that fact no matter what her story is."

Advised a day after the decision about the new execution date, Winnie continued to maintain she would never hang. One of her defense attorneys, Howard Richardson, assured her "there are a number of things we expect to do to save you." Defense counsel had fifteen days to file a petition for a rehearing before the state Supreme Court.

A three-hour private meeting, involving defense counsel, Dr. and Mrs. Judd, and the Rev. McKinnell, was held at the prison December 15. Dr. Judd had requested a special furlough from Whipple Veterans' Hospital in order to visit his wife and confer with her attorneys. The request was denied, but Dr. Judd went anyway. (The "Good Doctor's" action resulted in his being dropped from the hospital's roll of patients.)

Both Winnie and her husband had repeatedly hinted—Mrs. Judd in letters to her husband, and Dr. Judd in periodic statements from the Veterans' Hospital at Fort Whipple—at the involvement of another person either in the actual slayings or in the dismemberment of Miss Samuelson's body. Immediately upon learning of the Supreme Court's decision, Dr. Judd reportedly had said, "I am going to do now what I should have done months ago—which is to tell all the truth and the whole truth of this case—and when I do there will be another person in a prison cell and Ruth Judd will stand exonerated of this horrible crime of which she has been accused and convicted."

Warden Delbridge had allowed the meeting to be held in the matron's room, with guards and matrons out of hearing range. When the small group came out of the room, Mrs. Judd appeared highly nervous, unwrapping and wrapping a handkerchief jerkily about her left hand. She was talking excitedly to Dr. Judd. She was overheard to say to her husband that she was "game" if he was. What the remark implied no one would say.

16. THE "ACCOMPLICE"

ON DECEMBER 19, at Winnie's request, a private conference was held at the prison. Attorney Willson, Sheriff McFadden and Warden Delbridge were with the "Tiger Woman." Dr. Judd participated in the session by long-distance telephone. None of the participants would discuss what had transpired, but the sheriff admitted that he and Willson had been accompanied by a shorthand reporter, who took down all questions put to Mrs. Judd and her answers. Asked if Winnie had told a "new story," McFadden replied, "She didn't tell me anything about the case that I didn't know before."

During the last week of 1932, the Arizona Supreme Court denied the defense counsel petition for a rehearing. Then a "knight on a white charger" materialized—a subpoena requiring Winnie to testify before the Maricopa County Grand Jury on Wednesday, December 28, in Phoenix. This was her big opportunity to "tell all," and she made the most of it, telling a new "whole truth" story in a closed grand jury session.

Twenty grand jury members, Sheriff McFadden and County Attorney Lloyd J. Andrews heard Winnie's latest version of her alleged crime. She repeated her story of self-defense, then pointed an accusing finger at Carl Harris, charging that the prominent Phoenix businessman was an accomplice.

Winnie appeared in good spirits during a lunch break in the four-hour hearing. Asked if she was ready to go back to the prison, she said, "Oh, no. I'm not half through. I haven't had half a chance to tell what I want to say. I'm going back [into the hearing chambers] at one o'clock. One of the jurors was hungry, you see."

Later that day in Los Angeles, one of her Los Angeles attorneys, Arthur C. Verge, said, "I believe Winnie is telling a true story of what happened."

On Friday, the grand jury petitioned the state Board of Pardons and Paroles to grant Mrs. Judd an immediate commutation of her death sentence to life imprisonment. The jurymen stated that Mrs. Judd had convinced them she had killed Agnes Anne LeRoi in self-defense. Her testimony also convinced them that Carl Harris had been Winnie's accomplice. Therefore, the grand jury, as one of its last official acts of 1932, brought an indictment against Harris, charging him as an "accessory to the crime of murder."

The formal indictment charged that "on or about the 16th day of October, 1931, one Winnie Ruth Judd . . . did then and there willfully, unlawfully kill and murder one Agnes Anne LeRoi, a human being . . . and the said Carl Harris on or about the 16th day of October, and after the commission of the said crime of murder by one said Winnie Ruth Judd, well knowing the said Winnie Ruth Judd to have committed the said crime of murder and with full knowledge that a felony, to wit: murder, had been committed by the said Winnie Ruth Judd, did then and there willfully, unlawfully and feloniously conceal the commission of the said crime from the magistrate and did harbor and protect the person of said Winnie Ruth Judd, contrary to the form, force and effect of the statute in such cases made and provided and against the peace and dignity of the state of Arizona." Hedvig Samuelson was not mentioned in the indictment—Mrs. Judd had been tried only for the LeRoi slaying.

Harris was notified by phone of the indictment. Shortly after 11:30 A.M., he appeared with legal counsel in Superior Court. Judge Speakman set bond at $5,000. This was quickly reduced to $3,000, and the accused man posted bond with a cashier's check. Speakman set January 4 as the date for a preliminary hearing. In a statement released by his attorneys, Harris said, "There is no basis of truth in the charge, nor in any statement that produced it. That it is absolutely false and a grave injustice to me will be proved at the proper time."

Harris' attorneys were quick to point out what they termed a major flaw in the indictment. If the jury was convinced Mrs. Judd had killed in self-defense, then there could have been no murder. And if no murder had been committed, then Harris should not have been indicted as "an accessory to the crime." If there was no murder committed, then there was no crime, the attorneys said.

Warden Delbridge, just retired as superintendent of Arizona State Prison, said, "She had been afraid all the time she wouldn't get to tell her story. But now she is feeling much better." He said Winnie predicted her chances of avoiding execution were now greatly improved because she had been allowed to testify before the grand jury.

One of "Uncle Billy's" final acts as warden was to declare he would not request a sanity hearing for Winnie. Any hope for this avenue of escape from the gallows now rested with the new warden, A. G. Walker.

Warden Walker was one of several new faces suddenly involved in the case of Winnie Ruth Judd. With elections recently concluded, Benjamin Bakin Moeur became the new governor; Renz L. Jennings was the new Maricopa county attorney; and there were two new members on the three-member Board of Pardons and Paroles.

Jennings' first assignment as Maricopa county attorney was to represent the state during the hearing and attempt to bring Harris to trial. Before the grand jury, Harris repeated that Mrs.

Judd's statements contained "no basis of truth." Harris' chief defense counsel, Frank O. Smith, said his client wanted to get the matter settled at once, without delay.

The preliminary hearing began January 4 in Judge Howard C. Speakman's courtroom. Defense counsel filed a motion to quash the indictment, and County Attorney Jennings was granted a twenty-four-hour continuance to prepare his case. The next day, Judge Speakman blasted the recently recessed grand jury for publicly stating some of the events that had transpired during Mrs. Judd's "secret" testimony. He said the jurymen broke the law in so doing; then again blasted the jury for filing the indictment in Superior Court. Speakman held that the state Supreme Court had taken the Judd matter out of his hands when that high tribunal affirmed the court's actions during Mrs. Judd's murder trial. "The grand jury has a right to recommend to the Parole Board, but no right to return any such thing as that into this court because this court now has nothing to do with the case of Winnie Ruth Judd."

Attorney Smith filed a demurrer charging: "The indictment wholly fails to present a distinct issue for trial."

On Friday, despite lengthy argument by County Attorney Jennings, Judge Speakman ruled the indictment was defective but declined to quash the charge and ordered Jennings to resubmit the case to a Justice of the Peace Court. The judge ordered that the $3,000 bond Harris had posted December 30 remain in full force until the new complaint was settled.

While County Attorney Jennings was preparing the new complaint, former County Attorney Andrews, who had attended the grand jury proceedings, spoke out: "I don't believe her [Mrs. Judd's] story, and I wouldn't consider going before the Pardon Board in her behalf. Mrs. Judd has told too many stories—five or six in all, and there are discrepancies in each of them. There are too many things which would have to be explained before I could believe any of her stories. She first sold her 'true story' to the *Los Angeles Examiner* for $5,000. . . . This woman consistently has sought to commercialize this atrocious crime. Every story I've heard of the deaths of Agnes

LeRoi and Hedvig Samuelson—and each was reputed to come from Mrs. Judd—has been different.

"I tried to get Mrs. Judd to tell me what actually happened when I first saw her in the office of Chief of Detectives Joe Taylor in Los Angeles. She refused to talk on advice of counsel.

"I tried to get from her the real story when she was brought from the county jail to my office for a conference after our return to Phoenix. Her answer was the same.

"After she was convicted—in the presence of newspapermen —I gave her the chance to talk, for which she had been clamoring. She didn't tell the story then that she now tells, though the press was only too anxious to record it.

"Now that her avenues of escape are closing she comes forward with this story involving Harris. Before I believe her story, the location of the wounds in the women's heads must be reconciled. Blood spots on the window shade next to Mrs. LeRoi's bed and underneath her bed must be explained. The fact that Mrs. Judd's own gun was used in the slayings—the shell found in Mrs. Judd's apartment, and the clever acting in court of the blond woman slayer also need some explaining. Emphatically, no! I do not believe her story."

The new complaint against Harris was filed late Saturday afternoon in the West Phoenix Court of Justice Nat T. McKee. It charged Harris as an "accessory to the crime of murder" in that he "aided and assisted" Winnie Ruth Judd in disposing of, and concealing the body of, Agnes Anne LeRoi; advised and directed her "not to reveal or disclose that she had committed the crime of murder"; and further abetted her crime by "aiding, assisting and advising her" to escape from Maricopa County and Arizona to California.

On Monday, January 9, Jennings' office prepared an affidavit and court order directing that Mrs. Judd be brought to testify for the state at the preliminary hearing, scheduled to begin in two days. Mrs. Judd voiced a willingness to face Harris from the witness stand.

Also on Monday, Harris' defense counsel filed a motion in

Judge Speakman's court seeking a transcript of Mrs. Judd's grand jury testimony. The motion was denied.

By late Tuesday, it was believed the hearing might have to be postponed indefinitely because Justice McKee was ill. Physicians attending Justice McKee announced he had contracted pneumonia and Superior Court Judge J. C. Niles was substituted to serve in the capacity of magistrate.

On Monday, January 16, Judge Niles allowed Harris' attorney, Frank Smith, to subpoena the transcript of Winnie's grand jury testimony. This was acknowledged as a substantial victory for defense counsel on the eve of the preliminary hearing. Mrs. Judd would have to be extremely careful to avoid having her testimony impeached.

Two weeks of delays and hassling over legal technicalities ended on January 17 when the much-publicized Harris hearing finally began. For eight days (the longest preliminary hearing yet in Arizona), Winnie Ruth Judd, time after time, electrified the courtroom gallery of two hundred spectators with startling revelations, hysterical outbursts and verbal attacks on Carl Harris. And time and again many of her statements were ordered stricken from the official court record. On the witness stand her fireworks never stopped exploding.

The hearing began with considerable argument over whether Mrs. Judd should remain in custody of Sheriff McFadden, who also was subpoenaed as a witness. Judge Niles ruled he could remain in the courtroom as he was officially responsible for Winnie during the hearing.

McFadden was questioned vigorously by defense attorney Smith during a break in the three hours of opening-day testimony given by Mrs. Judd. Smith concentrated on quizzing the sheriff about the ironing board that Winnie alleged had been used in an attack upon her by Agnes LeRoi. The attorney wanted the ironing board introduced as an exhibit. McFadden testified he had brought the ironing board into the sheriff's office and had locked it in the "booze" vault, after his early visits to the murder cottage. Asked what was in the vault,

McFadden said, "Most everything you would look for—except the ironing board."

Asked how exhibits in certain cases were recorded when stored, McFadden replied, "I don't keep the records myself."

"There is no reason why you should?"

"No, sir!"

"But you would expect a deputy to do so?"

"Yes, sir. I don't bother with little things like that. I have too much else to do."

"You call that a little thing?"

"I mean the records. . . ."

"I'm taken completely by surprise here," Smith said. "I need this ironing board. It's an important piece of evidence."

Earlier, attorney Smith had elicited from McFadden the admission that he had once questioned Mrs. Judd for thirty hours in one stretch. Smith thus established that McFadden had obviously known something about the ironing board. Asked to describe the ironing board—how long it was—McFadden snapped, "I don't know. I never ironed."

McFadden's testimony proved a calm between Winnie's storms. Harris did little to help keep her calm. He smiled at times when Winnie became vehement, and laughed aloud when she screamed, "I'm not here for the purpose of clearing Carl Harris! He had an opportunity to clear me at my trial, but he didn't!" Another time, after accusing Harris of trying to signal answers to her, Winnie shouted, "I don't want him to talk to me! He's talked to me too much already! He told me not to tell anyone what had happened—not even my husband. He said to me, 'For God's sake, do you want to hang?' He bullied me that night, and now he is too big a coward to tell everything!"

During her stormy session on the witness stand, Winnie told this story of Carl Harris' alleged involvement as an accomplice:

"I saw him that night [Friday, October 16, 1931] about 11:15 o'clock. I can only make this time approximate. At 9 o'clock I went to the house of my friends, Agnes Anne LeRoi and Hedvig Samuelson. About 10:30 we had a fight. I was in my pajamas, my pink polka dot pajamas, ready for bed. My bed was made down in the living room. After the fight I took off my pajamas. They were covered with blood. I ran all the way home to my apartment at 1130 East Brill Street. It was about 11:30 o'clock. My purpose in going home was to get some money with which to call my husband, Dr. Judd, and tell him of the fight. As I was going out of the door of my apartment, Mr. Harris drove up in a car, and I told him what had happened. I told Carl that the fight had taken place."

When defense counsel objected to her testimony, Winnie screamed, "I expect Mr. Harris would be able to tell it more accurately!"

She continued her story. "I told him Anne and Sammy were lying on the floor. Carl said, 'What in the world is the matter with you?' I told him I was on my way to call my husband on long distance and tell him Anne and Sammy and I had had a fight. I told him I was shot. I told him Anne and Sammy were shot. I told him about the quarrel. Carl then dragged me out to the car and we drove back to the Second Street house. We went in through the kitchen door—Carl preceded me. When we got inside the door, he stopped and said, 'My God! Sammy!' And he ran over and stooped at the side of Sammy and . . . he stooped down and felt Sammy's pulse and examined her chest wound. He picked Sammy up and carried her into the bedroom and put her on Anne's bed—his hands were bloody—he reached over and pulled down the blind next to the bed with his hand. He then went to the kitchen and turned off the light. He came back into the hall and turned on that light. Then he came into the bedroom and felt Sammy's pulse, looked at her chest wound, and said he thought he would call a doctor. He dialed the phone several times. He told me he had enough on him to hang him.

"He then told me he would get a trunk and he walked past Anne's body and went out into the garage and pulled in a great, heavy trunk. He told me not to tell anyone. 'For God's sake don't tell anyone. Least of all don't call your husband. Do you know what this means to me and you?' There was only one other besides my husband I would talk to, and that was Carl Harris. Unfortunately, I talked to Carl Harris that night instead of talking to my husband. When Carl went out to get the trunk, he said he would get a truck and take it out on the desert. He picked up Anne and put her in the trunk. I was— his hands were yet bloody and I told him his fingerprints would be on that trunk. He picked up Anne—her body was lying on the kitchen floor—he picked her up—I didn't know that I had shot Sammy in the head.

"After he put Anne's body in the trunk, he told me to clean up as things looked terrible. I couldn't. I was all worn out. I was in terrible condition. I had been beaten until my body was black and blue. I had been through the worst fight a girl had ever been in. He mopped around a bit.

"When he took me to my house, Sammy was lying on Anne's bed and Anne was in the trunk. The apartment was not cleaned up completely when we left. Things were in a terrible condition. He took me back home because he was afraid I might become hysterical and rouse the neighbors. We arrived at my apartment at about 12:30 o'clock.

"Carl called me Saturday morning. I had told him to call on the lobby phone at the clinic. I hurried out to answer when he called and he asked me what I had done about my hand. I said, 'Nothing.' I asked him to let Doctor [Judd] dress it. He said that was perhaps the best idea after all for me to go over to the Coast and have Doctor take the bullet out of my hand."

Winnie said she met Harris Saturday night at the murder cottage. "I went to the house before he did. He drove around and around and didn't stop until 8:30. I was scared to death, as I didn't know but what I might be the next one killed. He drove into the alley and I went out to meet him. Then he drove into the garage. We went into the house through the back door. The house was cleaned up and the beds were made. The trunk was in the living room. He said both bodies were in the trunk and Sammy had been operated upon. He told me to go to Los Angeles and to call the Lightning Delivery to take the trunk with me as baggage. He told me to call at almost train time.

I did. He took his billfold out of his pocket and said he would have to go to his office to get more money for my transportation. He told me to meet him a block from the depot. He told me a Mr. Wilson would meet me Sunday morning when I arrived [in Los Angeles]. But I didn't get away until Sunday night. When I got to Los Angeles, I went all over the station looking for this man—I looked for him for two hours before I went to anyone else for help."

Mrs. Judd then related how the trunk had been too heavy to lift, and that it was taken to the Brill Street address. "I waited all Saturday night for Carl and I was in a terrible frame of mind—I do know this: when they carried the trunk out of the Second Street house I noticed something spilled on the porch. When they left the trunk at the Brill Street house I went back to the Second Street house and turned the hose on the porch. I took the last car [streetcar] out and caught the same car back."

The "Tiger Woman" testified she did not see Harris after their Saturday night meeting "until he came into the courtroom at my trial and raised his hand as a state witness." Asked by County Attorney Jennings if a mattress was missing that night from the bedroom of the murder house, Winnie said, "The beds were made up but Carl had taken the mattress off the bed."

Then Jennings asked Winnie about her first meeting with Harris Friday night, the 16th. She replied, "Thursday night he was at my house and told me he was coming over Friday night. Anne asked me to come over Friday night as Denise Reynolds would be there and we could play bridge. I said I couldn't because I had too many [case] histories to write. This was at noon. At 5 o'clock, Anne said I had better change my mind and come over. I said I had to do the histories. Dr. Franklin was there and took Anne home. About 5:30, after I had finished two histories, I decided I was tired and didn't know whether to go to Anne's or go home, as Carl said he would come to see me. I called his office and they said he was not in. If he doesn't come over I'm going over to the girls' house, I decided."

During cross-examination by attorney Smith, Winnie told about having worked at various times for Mrs. Leigh Ford and Dr. Charles Brown, now deceased. She told of going to work at the Grunow Clinic and meeting Anne and Sammy in January, 1931. At one point, after asking Mrs. Judd about how many times Harris had driven around the Second Street house on Saturday night, Smith leaped to his feet and demanded, "Whom are you watching and communicating with back there in the courtroom?"

"I'll turn then and face this way," she replied, turning toward newspapermen seated in the jury box.

After suggesting she turn back and face Judge Niles, attorney Smith declared, "He is the one who will decide whether or not you are telling the truth."

Winnie almost became hysterical when defense counsel demanded she state how she "knew Harris had disposed of the mattress." She shrieked, "Well, he's done some trick about that mattress. . . . You're trying to trick me now . . . I'm telling God's truth . . . I'm telling you what I intend to write when I commit suicide. . . ."

Moments later, after calming down considerably, Winnie said, "I am not accusing him [Harris] of murdering anyone but only of operating on Sammy or having her operated upon and obliterating the evidence—and there were some organs missing, too. I wish that mattress would be brought in here and it would show that no one was shot in bed and it would have cleared me at my trial."

Smith then asked, "How do you know an operation was performed?"

"He told me Sammy had been—I do know that when he is drunk he calls himself 'Doctor Buckley.'"

Defense counsel objected to further testimony on the ground that it was irrelevant and not responsible. Court was recessed until 10 A.M., Wednesday.

Forty minutes into her testimony the next morning, Winnie Ruth Judd began a dramatic recital that kept the overcrowded courtroom in deep silence. It was the first time she told in public about actual details of the double slaying. Defense attorney Frank Smith led her through careful questioning up to the fight that culminated in the deaths of Agnes Anne LeRoi and Hedvig Samuelson.

"You mean you want me to go into the quarrel?"

Smith nodded, and Winnie began.

"Anne asked me how Carl Harris ever met Doris Easton, and I told her that I introduced them. She asked me if I didn't know better than to introduce Carl to that girl and I said, 'Well, what difference if I—what is the difference to—what does it mean to you, anyhow?' And she said, 'Well, I told Denise Reynolds that Carl was out with Doris Easton last night, and that I thought that I should tell him what I know about Doris Easton.' And she said, 'Denise agreed with me, that she thought that I ought to tell him, too.' And I said, 'Anne, you know that you have got no right to tell anything of a professional secret. You have got no right to tell professional secrets out of the office and you only know this about Doris Easton because you happened to come into the office when she was taking an injection.'

"And she [Anne] said, 'Well, just the same I am going to tell Carl Harris—Carl—about Doris Easton.' And I said, 'Well, you certainly have no right, and what does it mean to you anyhow? What difference is it to you whether he goes with the girl or not?' And she said, 'Well, it ought to mean a lot to you.' She said, 'I know that he has been going over at your house nearly every night since you moved from here, and I don't think that you moved for any other purpose than so you could have Carl Harris over at your house every night.'

" 'No,' I said, 'there is not a word of truth in that, and you know that!' And she said, 'I wonder what the Doctor [Dr. Judd] would say if he knew that Carl had stayed over at your house nearly every night since you moved from here.' She said, 'You know I have a mind to tell the Doctor.' And I said, 'You have not got the mind to tell the Doctor anything about me, because I know plenty on you.'

"And I threw up to her—I threw up to her about her meeting—going to meet Carl in San Francisco at the Plaza Hotel. I think that was the name of the hotel. And I said—and I threw up to her all that I knew about her and . . . do I have to tell the names of everybody?—about her having an apartment over on the Coast with a prominent contractor."

Attorney Smith jumped up. "It is unfortunate that this testimony involves so many people. It is exceedingly unfortunate that the name of this nurse, and of other citizens, should be dragged into this, and I regret it deeply. I am perfectly willing to exclude the public from this hearing if it is desired."

County Attorney Jennings countered, saying he was "not responsible as county attorney for what her testimony may be."

Smith then asked, because of the importance of the testimony, that it be continued. He added that "Carl Harris is just as innocent of these charges as any man in this state."

"And he is not!" Mrs. Judd screamed. Women in the audience—and most of the audience were women—applauded. Judge Niles pounded his gavel for order, but Winnie shouted on. "He is responsible for the deaths of three girls in this state! Anne and Sammy are dead . . . and I have only four more weeks to live. . . ."

Order finally was restored, and Winnie's accusations were ordered stricken from the official court record.

Her composure regained, Mrs. Judd continued her story. "When she [Anne] told me that she had a mind—that she wondered what the Doctor would say if he knew that Carl Harris had been coming over to my house nearly every night since I had moved from there, and that she had a mind to tell him, I said, 'Anne, you haven't a mind to tell my husband anything about me, because I know too much about you. I know all about your going to meet Carl in San Francisco, your having an apartment over on the Coast with the prominent contractor, and his getting a drawing room for you and you coming to Phoenix. And besides that,' I said, 'if I ever started in telling things about you, there would be no end to it, and you know that.' I said, 'You know the time that you went up there to the clinic and turned the thing on the X-ray machine because you wanted to spite Dr. Lansfield?'

"I didn't tell everything at this time, but to tell you all that she did when I mentioned the X-ray machine—it would have caused someone to be burned—just to spite Dr. Lansfield. She didn't want anyone in the clinic to know that she did that, but I threw up to her that I would tell the doctors at the clinic that she had turned the thing on the X-ray machine, which would have burned someone. And I said, 'Besides that, Anne, you know that every doctor nearly in the clinic has quizzed me as to whether you two girls were in love with each other, and I have denied it every time. I said, Absolutely not! But I am through with you now and I am going to tell every one of them in there that it is true that you two girls are perverts.'

"At that time I went out and took my glass of milk [Mrs. Judd earlier had testified that she got the glass of milk from the icebox while looking for something to eat] and went on out into the kitchen and set it down in the sink.

"Sammy came running around through the hallway, through the living room, and back through into the breakfast room there. As I turned around she faced me with a gun. She said, 'If you dare to tell anything on Anne, I will kill you sure.'

"She had the gun in her hands. I grabbed the gun with this hand [indicating her left hand] and she shot, and as I grabbed the gun, I grabbed towards the knife. I grabbed the bread knife off the kitchen table there. It was a blunt-end knife, and I grabbed the knife, and as I grabbed for the gun and the knife —I don't know at the same time or not—but I grabbed them right there, and as I grabbed towards the gun, she had it pointed towards my heart.

"She shot me through the hand this way. I had the bread knife this way, and I stabbed her twice in the shoulder. At that, Anne came yelling out into the kitchen, and I said, 'Give me that gun' to Sammy, 'Give me that gun.'

"And Anne yelled, 'Shoot, Sammy, shoot!'

"The bread knife bent double like that. It was a green-handled knife and it bent completely double. I then grabbed with this hand toward the gun. This hand was shot [indicating her left hand], and I grabbed toward the gun with this hand [indicating her right hand] and only with the back of my arm tried to get the gun out of her hand, and twisted like this the gun in her hand, and this finger was torn and this finger torn wrenching for the gun.

"Her finger was yet on the trigger when that shot went through her chest; the shot that went through her chest. Anne grabbed up the ironing board that was behind the water heater there, and when Sammy and I fell on the floor, when that shot went through her chest as we fell on the floor.

"I don't know how it was we tripped, but we fell on the floor, and Anne came over and beat me with the ironing board and yelled at Sammy, 'Shoot, Sammy, shoot!'

"And I said, 'Sammy, give me that gun. Give me that gun!'

"And Anne yelled, 'Shoot, Sammy,' and she beat me over the head and she beat me with the ironing board as we rolled there back and forth in the doorway there fighting for the gun. We rolled back and forth in the doorway and fought.

"I fought for my life. I fought for every ounce of strength that I had for that gun there in the doorway and rolled back and forth, and Anne beat me with the ironing board all the time she was there, and said, 'Get her, Sammy! Get her, Sammy! Shoot! Shoot! Get her!'

"And I said, 'Sammy, give me that gun! Give me that! Let go of that gun! You give me that gun. . . .'"

Winnie became hysterical. She screamed: "If anyone thinks they are going to hang me for killing in self-defense, I'll write it all out and take it to God—he's the Supreme Judge—Carl just wants to play around. I am convicted of murder. There was no murder. I shot in self-defense. Carl Harris made me the goat for all this."

The references to Harris were ordered stricken from the record.

Mrs. Judd finally concluded her story. "Sammy and I were

struggling for the gun. Anne came in with the ironing board and beat me—we were rolling on the floor—I got the gun— Anne was braining me with the ironing board. Anne came toward me and I fired. As I shot, she hit me with the ironing board—she fell and I fell—there I was, between Anne and Sammy on the floor."

The "Tiger Woman," looking nothing like a vicious predator, broke down and sobbed. "He don't care that Anne is dead . . . or Sammy is dead . . . or that I'm going to die . . . he just sits and laughs about it," she screamed at Harris, who smiled.

"I hope you've suffered everything that I've suffered," she cried, "and I hope you suffer as my mother, and Anne's mother, and Sammy's mother have suffered!"

Winnie shrieked, "You want to set Carl Harris free and hang me for something that Carl Harris did—when I shot in self-defense—and he . . . I'm going to die in four weeks . . . I know that Sammy is dead and Anne is dead, and I'm going to be dead. . . ."

Mrs. Judd was ordered taken from the courtroom. It took Maricopa County jail matrons nearly two hours to calm her. She was then returned to Judge Niles' court.

17. "CONFESSION"

As ON THE first day of the hearing, Harris' defense counsel again sought unsuccessfully to have Sheriff McFadden banished from the courtroom during Mrs. Judd's testimony, because he was a witness. However, the sheriff was ordered to move to the west side of the courtroom, where he was out of Mrs. Judd's line of vision. Defense counsel had previously charged she was being coached by someone in the room.

State's witness Wilma Tarr, an acquaintance of Mrs. Judd's who lived in the apartment next door at 1126 East Brill Street, told of having seen Harris visit Mrs. Judd on the night before the killings. She also told of hearing voices in Winnie's apartment after 12:30 A.M. on October 16. Miss Tarr's testimony collapsed when she admitted under cross-examination by Attorney Smith that she didn't remember having recognized the voices.

An ironing board, allegedly the one mysteriously missing from Sheriff McFadden's "booze" vault, was produced by Smith. But when asked to identify the board as the same one used in the fight by Agnes Anne LeRoi, Mrs. Judd would say only that it was an ironing board "similar to that one."

During later testimony, Smith asked Winnie if she had requested permission from her attorneys to testify during her murder trial.

"Certainly," she replied.

"And you were refused permission?"

"No, I was led to believe I would be allowed to tell later on."

"That you would be allowed after your trial?"

"No, during the trial. I was led to believe I was to be allowed to take the stand after Carl Harris. I begged to take the witness stand and tell everything in my defense—I prayed that Carl Harris would take the stand and tell everything. . . ."

Following one of Winnie's outbursts during the second day of the hearing, Harris became angered and started to rise from the defense counsel table. He was restrained by his attorneys. It marked the first time in nearly two full days of testimony that the lumber dealer let his smiling composure deteriorate.

A surprise motion and some intricate legal footwork—by both defense counsel and Mrs. Judd—highlighted the third day, Thursday, January 19.

Defense attorney Smith made a motion after lengthy cross-examination of Mrs. Judd netted only a series of evasive answers. The motion challenged her competency as a witness and asked that all of her testimony be stricken. Judge Niles took the matter under advisement, indicating he would rule on it pending further developments during the hearing.

It was speculated that, if sustained, the motion would put an end to the hearing and result in dismissal of charges against Harris. Mrs. Judd had been the only one to incriminate him. If the motion were denied, it was believed Mrs. Judd might have difficulty winning an insanity hearing before the date of her execution, if she asked for one. If he denied the motion, Judge Niles, in effect, would be saying that Winnie was a competent witness and therefore sane.

While Smith's motion caught County Attorney Jennings by surprise, some of his legal maneuvers angered Mrs. Judd's

personal legal counsel. Prior to the hearing, Smith had subpoenaed all members of Mrs. Judd's counsel as witnesses. He
then successfully pressed for their exclusion from the courtroom under the witness rule. On Thursday morning, after the
"Tiger Woman" had been on the witness stand nearly two and
one-half days, Smith withdrew the citation that had excluded
them from the courtroom. But not until he had dumbfounded
spectators in the crowded room with the declaration, "I have
a duty to perform for Carl Harris. I am not representing her—
but God knows she needs counsel!" Smith charged that all of
Mrs. Judd's testimony was "under compulsion" and without
advice from her counsel as to her rights. This statement further
amazed spectators, now that they knew why Winnie's own attorneys were not present to advise her.

Jacob Morgan, a member of Winnie's counsel, upon being
allowed into the courtroom, angrily charged, "We were barred
for two days on fake subpoenas! We resent the pitfalls that
are being dug for us purposely—and these attempts to push us
into them."

"The subpoenas were issued under due process of law,"
Smith replied. "If anything was wrong with them, I do not
know it."

"I challenge the sincerity of them!" Morgan shouted.

Later in the day, still smarting from Smith's declarations
that she was "physically and mentally diseased to the extent
she is incompetent to testify," Winnie demonstrated she had
some legal savvy herself. When Smith urged her to relate in
detail how she had repacked the bodies in the two trunks in
her own apartment on the night following the killings, Winnie
flared, "Now listen, the other day you tried to stop me when I
tried to tell you what Harris did to Sammy, and now I don't
have to tell. . . ."

Judge Niles cut her short, directing her to give a responsive
answer to Smith's question. Winnie shot back, "May I then
ask for my constitutional rights to say nothing about another
case that may be incriminating to myself?" She explained that
she referred to the Samuelson murder complaint, for which

she had not been brought to trial. The court upheld Winnie, ruling she did not have to answer the question.

She proved herself to be an agile "defense attorney" once again that afternoon, after Smith questioned her about two letters she purportedly had written to her husband on the day after the slayings. She refused to answer on grounds it was a privileged communication between man and wife. The court upheld her.

Twice during the day, Smith abruptly dropped the subject while cross-examining Mrs. Judd. The first time came after he asked, "Mrs. Judd, you state a criminal operation was performed on Miss Samuelson. . . ." She replied, "I just know that an operation was performed. Mr. Harris told me Sammy was operated upon Saturday night." And he quickly changed his line of questioning after asking if she thought there was a good reason for Harris to go to her apartment Saturday night after the trunk had been taken there by express men. She said, "There certainly was a reason for him coming, a terrible reason for him coming. . . ." Smith cut her off.

Before introducing the surprise motion, Smith had questioned Mrs. Judd on the closeness of the death gun to her alleged victims. "How far away was the gun when the shot was fired that went into Miss Samuelson's head?"

"We were yet on the floor grappling for the gun. We were clinching. We were rolling on the floor. We were fighting for the gun."

Judge Niles asked the witness to give a responsive answer.

She continued, "We were in each other's arms—it was that close."

"How close?"

"It was just as close as the doorway—"

"Three feet away?" the attorney interrupted.

"It was not—we were both in the doorway."

"How close was it then?"

"She was trying to get the gun and I was trying to keep the gun." Checking herself suddenly, Mrs. Judd snapped, "I am not on trial here now!"

Again, Smith asked, "How close?"

"I don't know. I can't say how many inches because I was in a wild, wild fight—the most wild fight any human being has ever been in."

Not able to elicit a direct answer, Smith then asked how far away the gun was when Agnes Anne LeRoi was shot. After again asking, repeatedly, "How close?" Winnie said, "As I started to get up, she [Mrs. LeRoi] hit me again with the ironing board. I was in a half-rising position—she had the ironing board raised in her hands. I started to rise. I fired at her as she hit me with the ironing board, and we both fell at the same time. I fired in the left side of her head."

This line of questioning was believed to be an attempt by Harris' defense counsel to substantiate Mrs. Judd's claim of self-defense, thereby giving support to the contention no murder had been committed. Therefore, Harris could not be charged with being an accomplice.

At another time during Mrs. Judd's testimony, Smith accused her of having memorized certain statements. He said, "Why, when she relates the story of those killings, she pitches right in and tells a connected story. It must be memorized. She wanders off once or twice, but comes right back again. And the story she told to the grand jury is like that she told in the courtroom. She had fourteen months to figure these things out. But when she drops out of that story—the 'magic carpet' on which she rides—she is lost."

One other witness, sheriff's office fingerprint expert B. O. Smith, testified for the state on Thursday. He told of visiting the "murder cottage" about two weeks after the slayings to look for fingerprints and take pictures of the bedroom. He testified he had found a "bloody print" of what he believed "was the print of a left thumb" on a bedroom window shade. He said it was smudged and could not be identified. This testimony was an attempt to substantiate Mrs. Judd's opening-day testimony that Harris, his hands smeared with blood, had pulled down the shade.

The "bloody print" testimony became a bigger issue on Friday, the fourth day of the hearing. Over strenuous defense counsel objections, B. O. Smith and Sheriff McFadden both were put on the stand by County Attorney Jennings to further discuss the matter. Jennings produced the window shade and both witnesses identified what they believed were blood smudges.

During cross-examination, Smith asked the fingerprint expert, "It is possible, isn't it, that those smudges were placed on there by Winnie Ruth Judd?"

"Yes, it is possible."

"It is reasonable, isn't it, that she did it?"

"It is reasonable someone did it."

"Can you tell whether a woman or a man did it?"

"No, I can't."

"Might not these spots be from a spurting wound?"

"Oh, no, I believe they were caused by fingers."

"Then it is a matter of speculation as to what made two of these spots?"

"Somewhat."

"One theory is just as reasonable as the other?"

"Yes."

Smith then moved to have B. O. Smith's testimony stricken from the record, contending it did not connect the defendant. However, Judge Niles ruled the testimony corroborated that of Mrs. Judd when she said Harris had pulled down the curtain with his bloody hand after he had carried Miss Samuelson to the bed.

The fingerprint expert and Sheriff McFadden were two of fifteen witnesses called to the stand during the day by Jennings in an effort to corroborate portions of Mrs. Judd's testimony.

McFadden was asked if he had checked a license number at the request of a neighbor of Mrs. Judd's. He said he had and that it was for a car registered to the Harris Lumber Company. The car, a tan Packard, had reportedly been seen near Winnie's apartment the night after the slayings.

Most of the testimony of the other witnesses was similar to that given during Mrs. Judd's murder trial. An exception was the testimony of Marvin Hicks, employed at Union Station. He said he had seen Carl Harris at the station "right after the departure of a westbound train." Hicks, however, said he wasn't sure whether he had seen Harris on Saturday or Sunday night.

Defense counsel objected strenuously to Hicks' testimony, interrupting Deputy County Attorney Latham as he questioned the witness. When Latham rebuked Smith for interrupting, the audience applauded for the second time during the hearing. Judge Niles threatened to clear the court, and quiet was restored.

The state rested its case shortly before 5 P.M. Then Smith introduced his motion to dismiss the charge against Harris. "Her own testimony," Smith said, "is a moving account of self-defense, one that affected all of us, including the court. It is a clear case of self-defense. There could have been no crime."

Judge Niles gave Jennings and Latham overnight to prepare what were expected to be the final arguments of the hearing Saturday morning.

Carl Harris was seated in the courtroom with his wife when proceedings continued at 10 A.M., Saturday. The state opened by asking for additional time to prepare arguments against defense counsel's motion. And attorney Smith promptly introduced another surprise motion.

In submitting the new one, Smith said, "We are prepared to prove that on October 25, 26 and 27, 1931, Winnie Ruth Judd published in the *Los Angeles Times* of Los Angeles, California, her confession, and that the confession so published is a complete refutation of all charges against Carl Harris. . . . We move the case be reopened for the one purpose of questioning Winnie Ruth Judd, the accusing witness, with reference to her story upon evidence impeaching her story.

"I first learned of this situation this morning at 6 o'clock," Smith continued. "I have been convinced from the first that if we could find her first statement, before she received various theories from other persons and newspapers, we would get to the bottom of this. But it has been difficult to find it."

Smith pointed out that the *Los Angeles Times* articles appeared with this certificate: "This is to certify that the articles appearing in the *Los Angeles Times* are correct and authorized by me, [signed] Winnie Ruth Judd."

Harris' attorney then read part of the alleged "confession":

By Winnie Ruth Judd. This is my own story—the whole truth of the double tragedy which ended the lives of Agnes Anne LeRoi and Hedvig Samuelson in Phoenix, Ariz., on Friday, Oct. 16, 1931.

I have given it to my husband, William C. Judd, to dispose of as he sees fit and in order that the world may know the exact facts of the whole terrible affair.

It has been charged that I had an accomplice either before, during or after the actual tragedy. This is not true. I alone shot and killed both the women who were once my friends. I did it in self-defense—to save my own life—and for no other reason. I alone disposed of the bodies in a manner which I shall describe in more detail later. I had no help of any kind from anyone. It seemed to me the only thing to do was to hide—hide everything and myself. I was mistaken, but that is what I did in my blind terror.

Smith said he would seek to impeach Mrs. Judd's testimony in court by her purported true confession, published in the *Los Angeles Times*. Judge Niles said, "The court is disposed to know the whole truth about this matter, if it is possible. Therefore, I will permit the reopening of the cross-examination of Mrs. Judd."

The "Tiger Woman" was brought from her Maricopa County jail cell and put on the witness stand. Smith consumed nearly an hour in reading the articles. When he was finished, Winnie said, "There have been about fifty stories out, supposed to have been written by me. This is the first time I ever heard this one."

Mrs. Judd repeatedly and heatedly asserted the articles were "not in my language—I did not make that statement," and "I was delirious, and don't know what I did." After severe quizzing by Smith, she admitted many portions of the statement were "in substance" true. She said some were "in substance" what she had told her husband. But some portions of the statement, she asserted, were not true.

During redirect examination by County Attorney Jennings, Mrs. Judd noted some of the "untrue" portions.

"Where it says 'This is my own story'—that is not true. The part that says 'The whole truth'—that part is not true. October 16—that is the correct date of the fight. Where it says 'I have given it to my husband so the whole world may know'—I must say this article was published before I knew it was to be published.

"Where it says 'It is not true I had an accomplice' is not true. It is true I had an accomplice."

Jennings asked Mrs. Judd, "Why did you say at that time, if you ever did say it, that Mr. Harris had nothing to do with it?"

"I'd rather die than let my husband know [about Harris]."

The most dramatic moment of the day came shortly before the end of the afternoon session. Attorney Smith had been pressing Mrs. Judd to discuss the repacking of the bodies, an episode mentioned in the *Times* "confession."

"Did you lift Sammy from the trunk?" Smith demanded.

"No! I didn't lift Sammy—I lifted a part . . . a portion. . . ."

"And you lifted other portions and changed them?"

"Yes."

Smith abruptly ended cross-examination.

Mrs. Judd had strenuously avoided all discussion of the matter during the first four days of the hearing. She had earlier demanded and been granted constitutional privilege to refuse to divulge what took place in her apartment before the bodies were prepared for shipment. It was Winnie's first public admission of personal involvement in the actual repacking of the bodies in the large trunk, a smaller trunk and other luggage.

At the close of the session, Judge Niles granted a continuance of the hearing until Monday. Mrs. Judd was returned to the Arizona State Prison at Florence late Saturday afternoon.

Monday morning, County Attorney Jennings was granted a further continuance until Tuesday. The prosecutors of Carl Harris were now in the position of having to tear down the testimony of their star witness—Winnie Ruth Judd—to retain any hope of bringing the lumber dealer to trial.

Defense counsel and prosecution argued for four hours on Tuesday—Harris' attorneys declaring Mrs. Judd's self-defense story upheld their case, and the state arguing that Winnie was "all wrong" in her testimony, that she had committed murder.

Then Judge Niles, addressing the prosecutors, declared, "Now we have here a situation where you have proven a prima facie case by the record, but by your very next witness, Mrs. Judd, you proved self-defense. The state itself proved self-defense. . . . I do not believe there is a court in Arizona that would review this on habeas corpus and say there is anything here for the court to weigh. . . ."

"This is a very unusual situation," Deputy Latham said, interrupting the court. "I don't suppose you could find in any case in the United States a situation which brings up the questions involved in this."

"I agree," said Judge Niles, "these circumstances are unique —that there probably never has been a case presented to a court where the state is in the position first of proving a crime committed, and then in the same proceedings proving it justifiable. I want you to have all the time necessary—but I am not now satisfied with the showing." The court gave the state until 9 A.M. the next day to produce sufficient reason to hold Harris for Superior Court trial.

And at 9 A.M., Wednesday, January 25, Judge Niles said the sufficient reason had not been produced. He dismissed the complaint.

18. THREE MEN OF MERCY

LATER IN THE DAY, January 25, one of Winnie's attorneys, Arthur C. Verge, commented at his Los Angeles office, "Based on findings of the Maricopa County Grand Jury that it believed she killed Mrs. LeRoi in self-defense and upon the decision of Judge Niles in the Harris case, we are confidently hopeful that the Pardon Board will grant a full parole at her hearing." He was referring to a possible hearing before the Arizona Board of Pardons and Paroles. Verge interpreted the decision of Judge Niles in freeing Harris as proof that Mrs. Judd was innocent of committing murder.

Judge Niles, in discussing what might happen during such a hearing, said, "If they summon me the same as anyone else [as a witness], I'll go." He refused to discuss what his testimony would be.

Winnie's application for a hearing, along with an appeal for commutation of the death sentence, had been given the board before the Harris hearing. The board postponed scheduling an audience with Mrs. Judd pending outcome of the Harris case. Now, due to pressing business matters, the three members of

the Pardon Board could not agree on a hearing date. All three
—Chairman Lin B. Orme, citizen representative; Arthur T. La
Prade, state attorney general; and Herman Hendrix, state superintendent of public instruction—agreed a reprieve might be
granted Winnie unless the hearing could be held within a few
days.

Attorney Karz of Mrs. Judd's counsel hinted she would repeat her "whole truth" story before the board.

On Friday, two days after the Harris case had been closed,
the Board of Pardons and Paroles recommended to the governor an eight-week reprieve from February 17 to April 14, and
agreed on Monday, March 6, as the opening date for Mrs.
Judd's hearing at the State Prison in Florence.

Governor Moeur signed the recommendation Saturday
morning. In so doing, he unwittingly added further irony to
the case—April 14 was "Good Friday."

Later on Saturday, Dr. Judd and two members of Winnie's
legal counsel—O. V. Willson and Karz—conferred for several
hours with the "Tiger Woman" at the prison. Karz later reported, "She was very well pleased with the eight-week reprieve."

Visits from her attorneys, Dr. Judd and the Rev. and Mrs.
McKinnell broke Winnie's prison routine during the next
weeks. Then on Sunday, February 19, six state legislators visited
her and heard a dramatic plea that they aid her fight to escape
execution. After listening to her in the warden's office for more
than two and one-half hours, they expressed the opinion "she
told us the truth."

Representative E. R. Pryor of Phoenix acted as spokesman
for the legislators. "We have not made any plans whether we
will aid her. We may decide tomorrow. We even may call her to
Phoenix for a public hearing and then decide if we shall recommend that her death sentence be commuted."

Before the week was over, the Board of Pardons and Paroles,
again citing "pressing business matters," reset the hearing for
Tuesday, March 14. It was confirmed that the public would be
barred; and following Mrs. Judd's appearance, the hearing

would be continued at the state capitol building in Phoenix.

The much-delayed hearing finally began at 2:25 P.M. Tuesday, with Winnie allowed to recite her "whole truth" story before the three men with authority to show mercy on inmates of the state prison. In her application for a hearing, mercy had been sought in one of three ways: a full pardon, parole or commutation of the death sentence.

Wearing a blue and white gingham dress on which were pinned some pansies, Winnie sat in a wicker chair across a table from the board members. Members of her counsel sat around her. Also present among twenty-one persons in the small parole clerk's office in the prison administration building were Warden A. G. Walker, other prison officials and six newsmen permitted to attend as "representatives of the public."

Winnie's testimony took three hours, including two brief recesses called when she appeared on the verge of hysteria. She told essentially the same story of self-defense she had related during the Harris hearing, describing in detail events of her life, her husband, and friends after her arrival in Phoenix. When discussing her friendship with Harris, she sobbed, "I want you men to know truly that I loved my husband, and I love him still. . . ."

Amid occasional bursts of tears, Winnie gestured with a clenched fist to show how she had fought back to protect herself, how she had stabbed at Sammy with a bread knife, and how she had grabbed for the smoking automatic pistol after being shot in the hand as they wrestled in the kitchen. Winnie got on her knees to demonstrate how she had attempted to rise when, she alleged, Anne struck her with an ironing board. She then slumped back in the wicker chair, sobbing hysterically that she had only fought to save her life.

Winnie jolted her small audience with the allegation she had been told by her counsel during the murder trial that the jury was "fixed." She said she was told that among the jurors was a man who would "hang up the jury" and she would not be convicted. Then she accused Pardon Board members of trying to "influence" her to tell an untrue story on the promise her sentence would be commuted if she exonerated others allegedly to blame, and that she would be hanged if she did not. Winnie shouted, "I'm a stranger here, and I have no influence. . . ."

She then asked to be tried on the charge of having murdered Miss Samuelson, "so I can take the stand." If granted such a trial, Winnie said she would tell the same story of self-defense. She charged that her attorneys—not those who now represented her but those dismissed after her trial—had prevented her from testifying during the trial. "They wanted the insanity defense. I did not want it and I did not like some of the things they said about me." Winnie declared she had been told she would be sent to the state hospital for the insane for two or three years and then paroled in her husband's custody.

Newsmen, and even Mrs. Judd's attorneys, were excluded from a secret session Wednesday involving the condemned woman and the Pardon Board. The board was closeted with her for four hours behind locked doors.

During a brief but heated session afterwards, attorney Willson repeatedly asked that the transcript of testimony given during the secret session be read to Mrs. Judd's counsel. His requests were denied.

Mrs. Judd was not present during Willson's presentation of arguments to the board. The attorney charged that the jury which convicted Mrs. Judd of murder made a "deal to impose capital punishment only for the purpose of making her talk." Willson said the jury was influenced by four of its members to believe the Board of Pardons and Paroles would commute the death penalty, and that the threat of death would force Mrs. Judd to expose others the jurors believed might be involved in the slaying.

Willson said, "I am of the opinion that the board should hear further witnesses," and said some of the witnesses would be jurors. The attorney said, "A number of jurors have stated that if they had heard her talk as she did before Judge Niles [at the Harris hearing], they would not have returned the capital punishment verdict."

After heated debate, the board stated it would not hear testimony of the jurors. "I wouldn't believe them if they said they did it with an ulterior motive," La Prade said, "so there is no use in bringing them before me. Take those jurors to the Superior Court and let them 'confess their sins' and let the Superior Court prosecute."

Willson finally gave up on this point and turned to the question of Mrs. Judd's mental condition. "Now this woman —if she is not legally insane, she is medically insane. Her conflicting and various stories, to my mind, are expressive indication of insanity."

Orme said, "There are so many conflicting things which you try to reconcile, and you meet with disappointment each time."

The hearing would resume the following Monday, March 20, in Phoenix. Willson submitted a list of twelve witnesses. The list was promptly cut in half by the board.

The names of Judge J. C. Niles and Walter S. Wilson, court clerk, plus the four jurors alleged to have made a deal, were eliminated from the list over the strenuous objections of Mrs. Judd's counsel. Willson said, "I don't see why the board is so anxious to limit us."

Attorney General La Prade then asked why Judge Niles was wanted as a witness. "We want to show," Willson said, "that Judge Niles believed Mrs. Judd during the course of her testimony at the Harris hearing."

La Prade snapped, "His opinion isn't any more valuable than that of anyone else!"

Sunday night, on the eve of the hearing's resumption at the state capital, it was announced that Winnie Ruth Judd would not be brought to Phoenix for the remainder of the hearing. Her attorneys had requested that she be allowed to attend; and she had made a personal plea that she be permitted to face Harris. The board had subpoenaed several witnesses of its own, including Harris. As at the State Prison in Florence, the public, with the exception of six newsmen, was to be barred from the proceedings.

Thirteen witnesses—several called by defense counsel, some

by the board of Pardons and Paroles—testified on Monday; a few of them had new information to give. Among them, Kenneth Koller, the twenty-year-old son of Mrs. Judd's former landlord, discussed his part in helping Mrs. Judd move out of the 2929 North Second Street duplex into the 1130 East Brill Street apartment. He related that Mrs. Judd had asked him to take her back to the duplex because she had "forgot something." He said he sat outside in his car, and through an open window heard her say, "I went off and forgot my gun. I always keep it with me when I'm alone, so I came back for it." However, Koller said he heard no reply.

Two witnesses—a grade school student and her mother—refuted Mrs. Judd's often-made declaration that she had remained at Grunow Clinic throughout the afternoon of Saturday, October 17, the day after the slayings.

The seventh grader said she had seen Mrs. Judd "about 3 P.M." in the vicinity of the "murder cottage" and that Mrs. Judd later ordered her and playmates away from a pile of bricks on which they were playing adjacent to and on a vacant lot south of the duplex. The girl's mother corroborated these statements. She added that she, her husband and brother-in-law "smelled something burning" near their home late that night and early Sunday morning. The Pardon Board, which had called these witnesses, apparently was trying to determine if it might not have been the missing mattress, never recovered, which was being burned.

Former Judge Louis P. Russell, Mrs. Judd's first attorney in Los Angeles, testified that Mrs. Judd had given a statement to him and a shorthand reporter in the presence of Dr. Judd before she surrendered to police. He said the statement was not used because Mrs. Judd employed new counsel before her trial. He said he would reveal that statement to the board only upon the approval of Mrs. Judd. That approval was to be sought Monday night.

Sheriff McFadden was the last witness of the day. Saying he believed Mrs. Judd, he strongly substantiated portions of her self-defense story, and made some startling disclosures.

For the first time before newsmen, the sheriff gave an explanation of what had happened to the missing parts of Miss Samuelson's dismembered body. He said Mrs. Judd had told him they "fell out" while she was repacking the bodies in trunks and other luggage at her own apartment, and that she had thrown them out of a window during the train trip to Los Angeles. McFadden said she told him she "didn't know" where it was she had thrown the towels out containing the body organs.

The sheriff said Mrs. Judd first told her self-defense story to him on the second day after she was returned to Phoenix to await trial. He said she would not sign a written statement regarding her remarks. McFadden told of finding considerable evidence of blood in the breakfast room and kitchen of the LeRoi–Samuelson apartment.

Asked if he knew anything about the conversation a hotel night clerk purportedly had overheard, McFadden said the clerk had told him that Carl Harris, a lumberman from San Francisco and another man were in the hotel about 10 P.M. on the night of the slayings. He said the clerk had told him he "had a drink with them," and that they left about 10:20 P.M., returning later very excited about something.

Following testimony of witnesses, Winnie's attorneys renewed efforts to get the board to consider affidavits alleging certain jurors had participated in a "deal." The board said it would rule on the matter the next day. Again the board denied a request to have Winnie brought to Phoenix "for the purpose of advising her counsel when they shall question the said Carl Harris."

On Tuesday, even though she remained in her prison cell, Winnie Ruth Judd still made a dramatic impact on the proceedings. By means of a written statement, she refused to permit three of her former attorneys to tell the board facts about her case which she had revealed to them. Mrs. Judd's action kept Los Angeles attorney Russell, and two of her murder trial counsel—Samuel Franks and J. B. Zaversack—away from the witness stand. Attorney Willson, in explaining why Mrs. Judd did not want Russell to tell "her first story," said she and her present counsel feared he might not remember exactly what she had told him. Phoenix attorneys following the Judd case characterized her actions as "unprecedented before a Pardon Board," since she was making a final plea for life.

The board then ruled against presentation of evidence of a purported "deal" at Winnie's trial.

A feature of the morning's proceedings was Attorney General La Prade's admission he had told his own theory of the slayings to Mrs. Judd during the secret session at the prison. He said it was his theory that she had shot and killed Mrs. Le-Roi in bed, and had wounded Miss Samuelson as she came out of the bathroom, then killed her in a struggle in the kitchen. La Prade also admitted telling Mrs. Judd he believed she had dismembered Miss Samuelson's body.

Then Harris gave his first testimony in the case of Winnie Ruth Judd.

As he took the witness chair, he addressed the board: "I want to get this in the record. I have been subpoenaed here, and I am not a voluntary witness in answering that subpoena —but I am not a hostile witness. Under no conditions can it be understood that my appearance here indicates any bitterness in my mind toward anyone. I was subpoenaed at the trial. I reported there and I attended the trial every day, but I was never called. My name has been blazoned throughout the land, in an untruthful manner—whether vindictively or not, I am not judging. I am here to tell the truth—to answer truthfully all questions involving my alleged appearance at either of the houses mentioned, or of having seen or talked with Mrs. Judd after Thursday night, October 15, 1931."

The wealthy lumber dealer, under examination by La Prade and cross-examination by Willson, categorically denied he had any knowledge of the slayings, or that he aided, or arranged to have Mrs. Judd aided, in disposal of the bodies.

"The board is desirous of knowing," began La Prade, "whether or not you went to the Brill Street House Friday [October 16] at any time."

"I did not."

"Did you see Mrs. Judd there about 11 or 12 o'clock?"

"I did not."

"Did she convey to you the information she had killed Mrs. LeRoi and Miss Samuelson?"

"I never saw Mrs. Judd after Thursday night, and I was not the last to see her at that time. She was escorted to her door by another man as I sat in the car outside."

"Did you go with her to the Second Street apartment?"

"I did not."

"Did you ever see any bodies there?"

"I did not."

"Did you know Mrs. LeRoi and Miss Samuelson?"

"I did know them."

"Did you cut up a body?"

"I certainly did not."

"Did you arrange to have it done?"

"I did not."

"On Friday night—the supposed night of the slayings—were you in Phoenix?"

"I was."

"Where were you?"

"At home."

La Prade asked Harris to detail his movements after 6 P.M., Thursday, October 15. The witness said he went to the Second Street house in company with two other men, arriving at about 7 P.M. He said they remained about twenty minutes, and then went to Mrs. Judd's Brill Street apartment.

Harris said, "We sat and talked, and had something to eat and then took a ride for about twenty minutes." He said they then took another woman home who had been at Mrs. Judd's apartment, and he immediately took Mrs. Judd home. He said he then stopped by his own home for about ten minutes, then took the men to their hotel. He said he then went home and stayed there.

The lumberman attacked testimony of other witnesses that he had been seen in a hotel on or about the night of the slayings, and that he and his party seemed excited about something. "I care not who made the statements . . . they are positively untrue—I was not out of my house on Friday night."

La Prade asked, "Who was at your home?"

"My wife. My daughter was at a show, and my son was out and returned about 11 P.M. I had planned to go to a football game with my son at the stadium, but he had another engagement, so I stayed home and heard the game on the radio."

"Did you call Mrs. Judd on Saturday morning?"

"I did not."

"Did she communicate with you?"

"She did not."

"Did you see her Saturday night?"

"I did not."

"What did you do Saturday morning?"

"I was at my office." He added that he left there about noon, had lunch at home, and went to the Phoenix Country Club for a round of golf. He said it was his habit to play golf on Saturday afternoon with a certain group of men.

"Do any of these men remember whether they played golf with you that Saturday?"

"I haven't asked them."

Harris said he left the club between 5:30 and 6 P.M., had dinner at home, went to the office of a business acquaintance. He said he stayed there until 9 P.M., then went home and entertained visitors until 10 P.M.

"What did you do then?"

"I went to bed."

He said he played golf on Sunday morning, went to a show with his wife in the afternoon, and to dinner at a downtown restaurant with his son and two daughters in the evening. He said he returned home between 7 and 8 P.M. and stayed there.

Harris said he had first learned of the slayings when a physician acquaintance telephoned him Monday night, after the bodies had been discovered in Los Angeles. He said he was "shocked."

The witness was asked if he had been contacted by attorneys or other persons concerning Mrs. Judd. He said that, prior to her return from Los Angeles, he had received a phone call from a Phoenix attorney who asked if he "knew anyone connected with the case," saying he had received a call from Los Angeles, and "presumed it was a case of money."

Harris said, "I told him that if that was the situation I was not interested."

He said he received a second call from a Los Angeles lawyer who asked about the whereabouts of another man. And that quite some time later he had another call from "a man named Barber" who "had some story about knowing the McKinnells. I just figured it was another one of those mysterious calls or letters I had been receiving, and paid no attention to it."

"Did you ever have any conversation with the Rev. Mr. Mc-Kinnell?"

"No."

"Any conversation with the brother?"

"Yes."

"What did he say?"

Harris replied that Winnie's brother had phoned him, saying he was "interested in saving his sister's life," and asking to see Harris away from his office. "When he said he wanted to talk to me, I said, 'Fine, come to my office.' He said he would rather see me somewhere else. I told him I would see him in my office. He said, 'I'll phone you again tomorrow—you think it over—maybe you'll change your mind.' He called again the next day, and I told him I would be glad to see him in my office."

La Prade asked, "Did he ask you to aid or assist his sister?"

"No, he did not."

"Did he say anything about money?"

"No."

Harris said Dr. Judd had called him once during the trial, and said he wanted to see him. The lumber dealer said he told Dr. Judd he would be at his office in fifteen minutes.

"Did he come?"

"He phoned again in about thirty minutes, said he had

decided not to come, that detectives might be following him and his visit might be misunderstood. I said probably he was right."

"Have you any letters from Ruth Judd?"

"No."

"From Dr. Judd?"

"No."

"From the brother?"

"No."

"From the mother?"

"No."

Harris said he received a letter dated December 16, 1932, from a Los Angeles attorney who said he had recently been in Phoenix, but had not called on him at that time. He said the letter outlined plans for gaining clemency for Mrs. Judd, and said in part, "I feel if I should come to Phoenix again, you would be willing to aid. . . ."

"Did you answer it?"

"I did not."

"Did you receive any other letters from any lawyers?"

"None."

Turning to the self-defense story told by Mrs. Judd, La Prade asked, "Can you give us any information as to why she says those things?"

"I cannot."

"Can you give us any lead to develop any reason?"

"No, I cannot. It's a mystery to me why after a year and a half my name has been brought into this case in this way. If I had been connected with the case, Mrs. Judd certainly would have brought the charges originally."

During cross-examination, Willson tried unsuccessfully to get Harris to discuss his friendship with Mrs. Judd and the slain women. Harris would say only that what had happened before the slayings was not relevant at the hearing, and demanded that Willson "stick to the issue." He charged Willson with "delving into something that does not involve me."

Willson said, "You haven't attempted to clear your name

from the time of this tragedy until this hour, except for a statement in the *Arizona Republic*."

"I saw no necessity for rushing in for print. I made one statement. Your question is not properly put and has no bearing on the issue at hand. I have sat calmly by and suffered, knowing that the truth would come out." Harris turned toward newsmen, "I am making no refusal to answer any question directly bearing on charges against me."

Dr. Judd took the witness chair on Wednesday to tell why he believed his wife had killed in self-defense and why he was convinced she had not dismembered Miss Samuelson's body. The "Good Doctor" said that for more than three weeks after her surrender Winnie concealed from him what he now believed to be the true story—that she was not alone in the attempted disposal of the bodies. "Her second story to me, very similar to what she had told the board, I never have been able to forget or disbelieve because of the wealth of detail. . . . If one were composing a lie, why would one put so many improbable little things in it?"

Despite this, Dr. Judd said, "There is no use denying she has contradicted herself time after time. I don't know when she will do it again. Conflicting stories she would tell us graphically with a wealth of detail. Perhaps next day she would deny it and tell us she was alone. We never knew for twenty-four hours what she would say. That was the chief reason she didn't testify at her trial . . . we couldn't trust her for twenty-four hours. Once she let me write out a story for her to sign—but she wouldn't sign it. The thing that struck me first so strange," Dr. Judd continued, "was the emphasis she placed on being alone. Without being asked a question, repeatedly and emphatically she volunteered, 'I was alone.'"

He said he had told one of Winnie's attorneys about her "second story," and that she then denied to the lawyer she had said any such thing. He said she later advised him she had told it to him "privately."

Dr. Judd discussed his wife's movements before her surrender. "The newspapers remarked on 'resourcefulness' she had shown in concealing herself. It was not that. Remember now her actions in Los Angeles. She gets out of her brother's car. Now where does she go to hide? She had worked once at the Broadway Department Store. She goes to one of the few places she might be recognized—that store—and hides for the night. She met a buyer she once knew in the elevator. He didn't recognize her, but it frightened her. She knew she couldn't stay long in the store, so then where does she go? To the sanitarium where she had once been a patient—another of the few places she might have been recognized. Where does she go next day to do her telephoning? Back to the Broadway Department Store. It is interesting to show her state of mind during that period of stress, and her complete lack of planning."

Dr. Judd related various methods he said Winnie had told him she used to cut up Miss Samuelson's body in a bathtub. He said that each time he objected to her stories on the grounds of impossibility she would think a few moments and relate a new method. He said his wife had no understanding of how to dismember a body.

Winnie's husband demonstrated with a desk phone as a model how he believed it impossible for the bullet which killed Mrs. LeRoi to have taken the course it did through her head had she been shot in bed, because of the position of the bed, its head against the wall. He said it could have been possible only if Mrs. LeRoi had been sleeping with her head at the foot of the bed since the bullet ranged "backward and downward." He said, "Her story of shooting Anne in a crouching position on the floor will explain the course of the bullet, and nothing else will explain it."

Dr. Judd testified Winnie had never had any experience with surgical operations. "I tried many times when I was in Mexico to get her to help me with dressings, but she never would do it."

As Dr. Judd neared the end of his testimony, Rev. McKinnell interrupted proceedings to ask permission to ask the Doctor a question. Chairman Orme nodded that he could.

"As a physician, experienced in mental cases, do you believe that our Ruth Judd today is a woman of sound reason?"

"No," said Dr. Judd, "I do not. . . ."

"That's all!" the Reverend said.

Most of Wednesday's testimony by various witnesses was similar to that given during the trial and the Harris hearing. A grocery store manager gave the strongest support to Dr. Judd's testimony. She said Mrs. Judd had never bought a chicken that wasn't already cut up and prepared for cooking.

Dr. Judd again testified on Thursday. His only sign of nervousness was his chain smoking. He lit each cigarette from the stub of its predecessor. He held fast to his remarks of Wednesday. La Prade said, "We appreciate very much the candor and frankness with which Dr. Judd spoke. There was no holding back nor attempts to parry on his part. He is worth listening to and we want to talk to him some more." The attorney general indicated the board would have a secret session with the Doctor.

Winnie's father, the silver-haired Rev. McKinnell, gave a dramatic plea for mercy for his daughter. "I do not wish to appear as courting personal sympathy," he began. "My wife and I are not entitled to any more consideration than the parents of Anne LeRoi and Hedvig Samuelson. I may bring no new evidence, for many angles in this case are fictitious. Who mutilated a human body and who shipped certain bodies is not in legitimate consideration, for the state never charged Ruth with doing either. There are but three things to weigh: Did Ruth Judd kill Anne LeRoi, which is confessed; was it with malice aforethought or was it in a fight, and if in a fight, may it be a defensive fight; and, if punishment be deserved, what should that punishment be?

"Granted that I am supposed to be prejudiced on my child's side, while I do not want her considered as a paragon of perfection, yet in view of the judgment at which I must shortly appear, in considering her life from the dawn of responsibility to the present hour, I brand the assaults on her chastity and veracity as false. . ." His voice trembled and almost broke as he faltered.

In summing up for Mrs. Judd's counsel, H. G. Richardson

begged the board to consider itself, in fact as well as theory, the court of last resort so far as the life or death of Mrs. Judd was concerned. "There has been a lot of talk about going before the Supreme Court of the United States, but for the life of me I don't see how we can go there. We have no money. I think you gentlemen will say the last word. You might say I am asking for mercy—well, gentlemen, you are sitting here in a capacity to be merciful."

The hearing, spanning nearly two weeks of testimony including closed and completely secret sessions, was over on Thursday, March 23, 1933. By March 27, rumors were rampant of a murder trial for Mrs. Judd in the Hedvig Samuelson slaying. The rumors were dispelled on March 29, when Superior Court Judge Howard C. Speakman refused to grant another trial, saying it would be a waste of time.

Then on March 30, the Arizona Board of Pardons and Paroles gave their "last word." They denied commutation of the death sentence, and reset the hanging date to April 21, so it would not fall on Good Friday.

19. THE ELEVENTH HOUR

NEWS OF THE board's ruling did not visibly shake Winnie. She went through the next day in a peaceful mood, often smiling. Her attitude puzzled prison officials, who revealed her temper and moods had recently been uncertain—that she had tried to escape, and made threats to commit suicide rather than be hanged.

Mrs. Judd's attorneys said she still thought the law would yield and grant her life. "She is very hopeful," said attorney Richardson after a long conference with her. "She does not feel she has been given a fair chance, but she has not lost hope she will be saved. Her attorneys will stick by her to the end." Richardson said they would try to get back into Superior Court and to the Board of Pardons and Paroles, and would seek a ruling from the Arizona Supreme Court if the first two avenues were closed.

The Rev. McKinnell tried to bolster his daughter's hope with his own religious faith. He was not convinced it was God's will she should die on the gallows.

Prison authorities admitted that Winnie had attempted escape by using a saw to cut through one of the bars of her cell window in the women's ward. A guard on the main prison wall heard the rasping sounds. Upon discovery, she said her brother, Jason, had given her the eight-inch hacksaw blade, and she "wanted to be ready" if she "had an opportunity to escape." In Los Angeles, her brother, through attorney Aaron Searls, denied he had any part in a plot to help his sister escape. He revealed a warrant had been issued for his arrest as an accomplice in the escape attempt, and said he would surrender if asked. Pinal County authorities said they had no knowledge of any warrant having been issued, but that an investigation had been made at Warden Walker's request.

When Winnie began threatening to kill herself, her cell was stripped of everything she might use for that purpose. A guard was placed on duty day and night. Hers was the only cell in the women's ward that was locked at night. Had she succeeded in getting out through the barred window, Winnie still would have faced concrete, masonry and a high, barbed, steel fence. The entire women's ward area was within easy view of guards on the main prison wall.

On Monday, April 3, Warden Walker gave Governor Moeur an anonymous letter threatening to bomb the state capitol building unless Mrs. Judd was released to her mother. The writer of the letter, which was mailed from Los Angeles, threatened to place in the capitol explosives powerful enough to kill all Phoenix residents and shake the buildings "worse than the recent Pacific Coast earthquake." Calling himself "The Gangster from Germany," he demanded release of "this woman by the name of Winnie Ruth Judd for her old mother's sake." An announcement was made by the governor's office that numerous ominous letters had been received, some threatening to kill all officials unless Mrs. Judd was executed, others threatening destruction if she was hanged. The only difference in the "The Gangster" letter was the demand that Winnie be freed to her mother.

The Board of Pardons and Paroles met again on April 6 to reconsider its ruling or grant a reprieve of forty-two days to allow for possible appeal to the United States Supreme Court. The board quickly issued a twenty-eight-word statement of refusal.

Winnie nearly became hysterical when attorney Richardson carried the news to her. "She seemed to read in my face that I had bad news for her. . . . We feel that Mrs. Judd has suffered a living death already, and that if the Board of Pardons and Paroles could see fit to grant her a new lease on life, even if it erred, it would be erring on the side of mercy, and in the face of great doubt."

Richardson cited instances in which he said Mrs. Judd felt the law had not dealt squarely with her, among them the testimony before the board of two "surprise witnesses" who said they saw Mrs. Judd Saturday afternoon at the apartment where the slayings occurred the night before. Winnie maintained this was false, and that she could produce witnesses to support her charge.

Winnie's attorneys almost immediately filed in Maricopa County Superior Court a motion for a new trial, contending that the jury "had no intention that the defendant should suffer the death penalty . . . as appears by affidavits of said members to be presented to the court on the hearing of the motion." Affidavits were secured from four jurors with purported statements of two other jurors.

Juror Wallace Dooley stated, "I was the last Judd juror who changed my verdict from life imprisonment to the death penalty. I was so worried over having changed, I didn't sleep that night. Never would I have changed as I did had it not have been for Oscar Mitchell, who insisted that we would vote the extreme penalty. Then, he argued, such a verdict would make Mrs. Judd talk, including the accomplices. Oscar said he had a good political friend on the Board of Pardons and Paroles and that he would get the sentence commuted if Mrs. Judd would talk.

"Furthermore," Dooley's statement continued, "all of us jurors made an agreement, as a body, that if new evidence came to light, subsequently, and Mrs. Judd would talk, we would immediately urge the Board of Pardons and Paroles to have the sentence commuted. If it had not been for the above promise, I would not have come over to the death penalty."

Juror Ed Jorgensen's statement, in part, said, "I would have held out, but Mr. Oscar Mitchell explained to us that he had political influence and a good friend on the Board of Pardons; that he could get Ruth Judd out with life imprisonment; that we should give her a death verdict, and that would bring in the other party or parties, and he could have the sentence commuted later."

On Friday, the day after the motion was filed, Warden Walker said Winnie had begun to break, with fits of nervousness and hysteria. The assistant warden said, "It is surprising she has not let down sooner—she has an iron nerve."

In preparing to argue the motion before Judge Speakman, Winnie's counsel subpoenaed all thirteen Judd jurors, Pardon Board Chairman Lin Orme, Sr., and the attorneys Samuel Franks and Joseph Zaversack, but Judge Speakman ended the proceedings within five minutes. As he sat down at the bench the judge said, "The Supreme Court of this state has spoken on this matter repeatedly . . . so there is no question but what the lower court is absolutely powerless to reverse or interfere with any decision made by the Supreme Court. . . ."

"Do I understand," interposed attorney Willson, "that I am to be deprived on behalf of Ruth Judd—"

"I am not depriving you of one thing. I am following the law. The people of this county elected me to interpret the laws of this state. That is exactly what I am doing. I have never deprived Winnie Ruth Judd of anything, and I ask you not to insinuate anything like that. Ruth Judd had a fair trial as far as this court is concerned."

"May I offer my original affidavits?"

"This court has no jurisdiction. If you want to go to the Supreme Court and have them set aside their judgment, I will more than welcome it."

On Wednesday, attorney Karz appeared before Supreme Court Chief Justice Henry D. Ross. A request to place a petition before the high tribunal was denied, closing off the Arizona Supreme Court as a means for Winnie Ruth Judd to escape the gallows.

20. SANITY

On April 11, ten days before the scheduled execution, according to prison custom, the death watch was placed over Winnie, but the "Tiger Woman" was not taken to Death Row. Warden Walker said he was allowing her to stay in the women's ward because of her nervous condition.

Warden Walker announced he would request a sanity trial for Mrs. Judd in the Pinal County courthouse in Florence. The announcement followed two visits to the prison by Dr. E. D. Berends, physician in charge of women inmates at the Arizona State Hospital for the Insane in Phoenix. When contacted, Dr. Berends said he had been sent to examine Mrs. Judd at Warden Walker's request, "unofficially and for the warden's information."

The request mandatorily set in motion legal machinery for determination of Mrs. Judd's mental condition. Within forty-five minutes after the request had been received, Judge E. L. Green granted the petition and set 9:30 A.M., April 14, for the empaneling of a twelve-man jury.

Mrs. Judd showed no sign of interest when told of the new

trial. Fondling a prison mascot, a coal-black cat named Egypt, and four newly arrived kittens, she seemed unaware of the added scrutiny of the death watch, set to keep her from suicide until her date with the hangman.

The eleventh-hour battle to send the slender woman to the insane asylum, rather than up the thirteen iron steps to the gallows, would be waged principally in the realm of psychiatry. Among those summoned to testify for the defense were Dr. Stephens, former superintendent of the asylum who had already testified at Winnie's murder trial, Dr. Berends and Dr. Wynn Wylie, a Phoenix psychiatrist.

Dr. Stephens commented, "I made a diagnosis of dementia praecox when I went to the witness stand as the first alienist at her trial. . . . That diagnosis still stands and there has been no improvement in her mental condition during the past year, though there has been some physical improvement."

O. V. Willson, chief of Winnie's counsel, said she would not be placed on the witness stand during her sanity trial. "She is not a competent witness, hence we will not send her to the stand, though such action is discretionary with us," he said.

The state again requested the services of Dr. Joseph Catton of San Francisco and Dr. Sidney Freid of Los Angeles.

On the eve of the new trial, Winnie Ruth Judd cowered, hysterical and incoherent, in her cell. Not even Egypt and her kittens, with which she had played for hours on end, could distract her. That night, under Warden Walker's signature, fifty small white, black-bordered pasteboard invitations to Winnie's execution were issued. The invitations read, "You are invited to be present at the state prison, Florence, April 21, to witness the execution of Winnie Ruth Judd."

Mrs. Judd had seven days to live. Preliminary proceedings began on Good Friday morning, and she appeared bored throughout most of the day-long questioning of prospective jurors. She again twisted a handkerchief about her left hand, often bending forward to rest her head in her hands. She spoke infrequently, and then only to the matrons attending her. Once, when one of them rose to leave the courtroom, Winnie also started out, but was pulled back into her chair by another matron. Late in the afternoon, when someone talked to her, she responded, "I've been tormented enough and I'm tired of it." During a morning recess, she had scolded newsmen who tried to photograph her.

Psychiatrists for the state and defense observed Mrs. Judd during the day, taking down notes for testimony they would give later in the trial. Drs. Freid and Catton were allowed brief visits with Winnie during the noon hour at the nearby state prison, and Catton was spokesman for the pair.

"We are here, not as persecutors, but to express our views in accordance with justice. The Arizona law under which this hearing is being held provides substantially that if Mrs. Judd has appreciation of her circumstances and the mental capacity to comprehend the fate awaiting her, she must hang. We, no more than the great state of Arizona, desire to be charged with the responsibility of hanging anyone whose mentality is so diseased that she goes to the execution chamber unknowingly." He added that he would be glad to testify in behalf of Mrs. Judd if his observations convinced him that she was mentally incompetent under the tests provided.

Another noted California psychiatrist, Dr. Edward Huntington Williams—who had testified for the defense at Winnie's murder trial—commented in Los Angeles that he was unable to make the trip, but said he was more convinced than ever that Mrs. Judd was "absolutely crazy." He told of an incident which he said had not been officially disclosed before. "Two weeks before Mrs. Judd's trial in Phoenix, an insane woman was placed in the same jail tank with her. Mrs. Judd became infuriated until her attorney, Samuel Franks, was called to calm her. Franks discovered Mrs. Judd had obtained a butcher knife and was concealing it beneath her arm pit. When he took the knife from her, Mrs. Judd screamed that she wished to 'cut that woman's heart out, because I can't stand her.'" Dr. Williams said he had wired Arizona authorities, asking them to "bring out the knife incident."

County Attorney Will C. Truman and his assistant, Charles

Reed, questioned prospective jurors for the state. "You must," Reed admonished several of them, "arrive at a verdict exactly as though some person not under a death sentence were before you."

The first day of the trial proceedings closed with Judge Green denying a defense request to hold a night session to speed up the hearing. Preparations for the execution went steadily forward. Ten additional invitations to the hanging were to be mailed, bringing the total to sixty, but prison officials said they did not expect more than half that number. The rope for the hangman's noose was soaked before stretching under a weight of three hundred pounds. The rope processing usually took a week to ten days.

The jury, comprised mainly of ranchers and highway department employees, was named Saturday morning.

Forty witnesses were subpoenaed and six of them were put on the stand on Saturday, April 15, with Winnie and Dr. Judd both present in the crowded courtroom. Attesting to Mrs. Judd's insanity were Warden Walker, Assistant Warden Shute, and four matrons—Mrs. Ella M. Heath, head matron; Mrs. Laura Rossiter, Mrs. Mary Devore, and Mrs. Nora Stephenson, assistants.

Warden Walker said he had become convinced Mrs. Judd was insane after conferring with Dr. Berends. He had reached his final conclusion about two days before his formal trial request.

"In your opinion," asked attorney Richardson, "does she understand all the facts of the crime of which she was convicted?"

"I don't think so," Walker replied.

Assistant County Attorney Reed cross-examined the warden. He asked how long Walker thought Mrs. Judd had been insane. Walker replied that he believed she had been insane all of the time she had been in his charge (since January 1).

"Why then," demanded Reed, "did you wait until this late date to call this hearing?"

"Because I wanted to be sure."

"You dread the responsibility [for the execution], don't you?"

"Yes, I do dread it."

"Well, then, your attitude is about this, isn't it . . . you feel that instead of one man bearing so much responsibility, it should be placed on the shoulders of twelve?"

"No, I would not say that."

Assistant Warden Shute said Mrs. Judd "is absolutely indifferent. I have gone so far as to ask if she realized a noose was around her neck. She has shrugged her shoulders and laughed, and passed on to some other conversation." Shute had observed her gathering stones in the yard of the women's ward, then laying them in rows across the floor of her cell. Once, he said, she hid herself under her bed, and pulled the blankets down around the sides, so the matron in charge thought she had escaped. About six weeks before, Mrs. Judd had convinced her mother she had a razor blade in her mouth, and intended to swallow it. There was no blade.

The head matron, Mrs. Heath, testified that Mrs. Judd was convinced she was being persecuted—"but this was not being done to punish her, but in a spirit of revenge by someone." She said Winnie often "eats ravenously."

Mrs. Rossiter said Mrs. Judd "sings a lot—climbs in the window, climbs down again—slaps her hands—one minute she laughs and the next she cries—she takes her slipper off and beats herself on the back of her neck with it."

All of the matrons testified she could not possibly escape, that the reason she gave for sawing through a bar was "she wanted to let somebody else in." She did not appear to have prepared herself for death, but had made plans for the future, including flights to Alaska and Latin America.

Winnie kept the matrons occupied in court most of the day with mild attacks of apparent hysteria. When Mrs. Heath left her seat beside Mrs. Judd to testify, Winnie, apparently referring to the jurors, said, "They're gangsters and degenerates —all of them!" She started to leave her chair and was lightly restrained. Dr. Judd then took the seat beside her. On another occasion, she leaned toward her husband to demand in a loud whisper that he get out of the way so she could "throw myself out of the window." It took two matrons and Dr. Judd several moments to quiet her. At other times, Winnie chuckled and sobbed softly by turns.

After trial proceedings ended that day, Dr. Catton expressed the belief that Mrs. Judd partially feigned her courtroom hysteria. "One under sentence of death must necessarily be in such a highly strung nervous state that hysteria, at first feigned, could readily become actual." Both he and Dr. Freid could find nothing to alter their previous opinion that Mrs. Judd was legally sane. "Something may develop to cause us to change our view between now and the time we take the witness stand, but so far no such developments have appeared," they told reporters.

Both state and defense counsel despaired of completing the trial before the April 21 execution date. As sanity trials did not stay execution, Mrs. Judd legally could be hanged while the jury deliberated. Therefore, defense counsel made plans to ask the Arizona Board of Pardons and Paroles for a reprieve, to allow the jurors sufficient time.

Easter Sunday represented a one-day recess, but to Winnie Ruth Judd it was one of five days she had left to live.

The first technical testimony of the trial—offered by Dr. Berends and Dr. Judd—was given Monday. Judd, speaking as a physician with many years of psychiatric practice, declared, as in the previous trial, that his wife was suffering from dementia praecox. "God himself," he said, "could not coach that woman to act insane—all she has to do is act natural." Describing her mentality as "entirely inconsistent," he said, "At one moment she is in a state of exultation, in another moment she is quiet —from intense dejection she rises to the most supreme exhilaration."

While Dr. Judd was on the witness stand, Winnie suddenly screamed wildly at the whole courtroom. "You bullies! You cowards! You gangsters! Quit torturing me! Quit taunting me!" When two matrons put their hands over her mouth, she bit them, and continued screaming.

"Where is the warden of the penitentiary?" Judge Green demanded.

Warden Walker hurried to Mrs. Judd, lifted her from the chair and took her bodily from the courtroom, one foot dragging on the floor.

"Let me alone!—let me alone!—quit torturing me!" she yelled as spectators scrambled to get out of her path. She beat her free arm in the air and kept screaming after Walker and a matron put her down on the courthouse lawn and attempted again to quiet her. But her screams became so loud Judge Green ordered the bailiff to "tell the warden he must take the alleged insane person out of the hearing of this jury."

She was lying on the ground, beating her heels on the grass and still screaming when Warden Walker took her to his car. After a half-hour ride over the Florence countryside, Winnie was returned to the courtroom. She was at first smiling, then became somber, but quiet.

Testimony continued. Dr. Berends agreed with Dr. Judd that Winnie was suffering from dementia praecox. "She is lacking in judgment, lacking in reason and insight and apparently suffering from illusion. She is unable to take care of herself, is a menace to herself and others. She is unable to concentrate and lacks attention. Her speech is abnormal, irrelevant and delivered under great pressure." He said Mrs. Judd was not malingering.

Mrs. McKinnell proved a spirited witness, sparring with a number of the attorneys. "He knows she's insane," she said vehemently, looking at Assistant County Attorney Reed, "but he wants to hang her!" Once when Willson stopped her, she snapped, "And he's a pill, too." She told the jury, "There is insanity on both sides of my family. I have always felt that insanity was on me to some extent and on Ruth even more. I want you to know that girl is insane and has been more or less insane all her life."

As proceedings drew to a close Monday, Warden Walker took unofficial note of rumblings of unrest from within the state prison walls and of a "grapevine" message from prisoners sent out to Dr. Catton, telling him he had "best watch out for himself" if he found Mrs. Judd sane and ever entered the prison walls.

Defense counsel said a petition for reprieve had been given the Board of Pardons and Paroles, and that telegrams were sent to United States Senators Carl Hayden and Henry Ashurst of Arizona, urging them "in the interest of justice to Winnie Ruth Judd and the fair name of Arizona" to lend their "full support and influence for an immediate reprieve."

A telegram from Ernest Whitehouse Cortis, secretary of the Men's League of Mercy of the United States, organized to prevent the execution of women in the United States, said, "Please notify Mrs. Judd I am leaving Tuesday at daybreak for Washington to personally plead with President Roosevelt in her behalf. Ask her to pray for my success. Tell her to trust in God."

Lengthy testimony was given on Tuesday by three defense psychiatrists. Dr. George W. Stephens, who had testified during Mrs. Judd's murder trial, told the jury, "I feel she has deteriorated since." Referring to a hysterical outburst by Winnie that morning, Dr. Stephens told the jury, "That was just an outburst, such as may occur in dementia praecox. She is unstable. I'm making my diagnosis in this case now purely on the fact that this woman is delusional. She has a persecution complex —she dislikes people without rhyme or reason—she dislikes officials. I have a letter in my pocket which she wrote to her husband. That letter shows a paranoid trend regarding the prison warden, her mother, her father, her attorneys. She speaks of 'John Robert' and says she is going to see him when she dies." "John Robert," as explained the previous day by Dr. Judd, was her name for a child who never existed.

Drs. Huffman and Pinkerton agreed Mrs. Judd was not faking insanity. Dr. Pinkerton said a picture of a truly insane person "is just like a jigsaw puzzle—you can't see the picture unless all the pieces fit. The ordinary person knows of and feigns only two kinds of insanity. One is your gibbering drooling idiot, the other is your raving maniac. They attempt to feign one or the other, and they jump right into the last stages." He ascribed Mrs. Judd's outbursts to "the same emotional pressure that prevents her telling a connected story—that pressure piles up until the emotions break under the stress."

During cross-examination, attorney Reed attacked a statement by Dr. Pinkerton that he had received no compensation, nor expected any, for his services during the trial. "Don't you know as a matter of fact, Dr. Pinkerton, that the expenses on behalf of Mrs. Judd are being financed by the Hearst newspapers?"

"Now here . . . wait!" attorney Willson interrupted. "Now, I object to that . . . and charge this counsel with misconduct and ask that the jury be instructed to disregard the remarks of counsel," he shouted. "I want to announce right now in open court that that is absolutely false."

"We intend to prove the fact," Reed insisted.

"You can't prove it!" Willson countered.

"If you take the stand, I can prove it."

"I will take the stand any minute you want me to."

Judge Green asked Reed, "Do you want to show the witness is interested in this case?"

"I want to show who is financing this case."

"Are you going to show he is getting compensation?"

"I expect to."

Willson again interrupted. "Now that this is before the jury, let us have it out right now. I want to take the witness stand, as will any lawyer or physician engaged here, and we will show that not a dollar has been received in this case in the way of a fee for medical or legal men here since the commencement of it, of our taking hold of it, a year ago."

The discussion was finally ended when Dr. Pinkerton said, "This is the first I have heard of it." Rumors had circulated since the beginning of the trial that William Randolph Hearst was financially involved.

State and defense counsel engaged in another heated debate just after Judge Green announced recess until Wednesday, and informed the jurors, "You are to be placed in the custody of a bailiff and kept together for the remainder of this trial."

"May it please the court," said County Attorney Truman, "we wish the record to show that it was the defense counsel who requested this action, and that we did not desire it."

E. W. MacFarland, one of Mrs. Judd's counsel, leaped to his feet. "That is the most gross error I ever saw committed in a court of law."

"It is an error," Judge Green concurred, "but it is done now. . . . I think the jury understands it is not to allow any such things to affect its judgment. The order was agreed upon between counsel. The state did not oppose." The request had been made earlier in the day, and granting of it by Judge Green was mandatory. Reports were brought to his attention that jurors had been reading newspaper articles about the trial.

That day the Board of Pardons and Paroles, in the absence of Attorney General La Prade, granted Mrs. Judd a one-week reprieve, until April 28. Winnie's counsel had asked for three weeks, expressing their intention of taking the case to the United States Supreme Court if the jury found Mrs. Judd sane.

Judge Benjamin B. Lindsey, founder of the Juvenile Court system and famed as a champion of "companionate marriage," sent a telegram to the Pardon Board in support of defense counsel. "In interests of justice and humanity I urge you to grant Winnie Ruth Judd a reprieve until May 13 so her case may be fully and adequately presented to court and allow time for action at Washington. America expects Arizona to give her a square deal. Please do your part without fail."

The reprieve—the fourth for Winnie—came just three days before her scheduled execution. She did not react to the decision.

Earlier in the day, the possibility of a mistrial was avoided when medical treatment of a juror during recess enabled him to return to the jury box. Suffering from an abscessed ear, he said he would be able to last out the trial.

After testimony by the defense psychiatrists, Dr. Freid engaged in a lively discussion with newsmen. "She is suffering from a state of great fear and is thoroughly frightened," he said, adding she was not insane. "But wouldn't you be frightened," he asked reporters, "if death were as near for you as it is for her? Her actions in the courtroom yesterday afternoon were an emotional outburst, not uncommon for a woman. Many women whose minds are not mentally unbalanced have such outbursts over trivial matters, but it only goes to show that she is under a highly nervous strain."

A reporter asked, "But, Dr. Freid, what about Mrs. Judd's blank stare during the proceedings here?"

"Look here," he replied, emulating the stare for several minutes.

"Then, should Mrs. Judd be shamming insanity, what do you think of her ability as an actress?"

"She has great histrionic ability."

Both Drs. Freid and Catton interviewed Mrs. Judd on Tuesday night. They reported that she had adopted a mute attitude, refusing to answer questions, and talked of inconsequential matters or played with her kittens.

That night the twelve jurors bedded down on cots in the same barn-like room that served for the trial during the day. A cold rainstorm descended on Florence before they retired, and wood fires were lit in stoves along two walls to chase the damp from the big, drafty room.

When proceedings resumed, Dr. Stephens and Dr. Wynn Wylie, a Phoenix psychiatrist, testified briefly and Mrs. Judd's counsel abruptly rested its case, catching the state off guard. County Attorney Truman and his assistant, Reed, asked for and were granted over defense protests a four-hour delay in which to round up and confer with witnesses. The state then paraded several witnesses to the stand. Gordon Wallace, clerk of Judge Niles' Superior Court in Phoenix, said he believed Mrs. Judd knew she was under sentence of death when she appeared at the Harris preliminary hearing. Thad Frazier, prison parole clerk, described Winnie's story at the Pardon Board hearing as connected and intelligent, and a member of the Maricopa County Grand Jury as well as Pardon Board Chairman

Lin Orme, Sr., and fellow board member, Herman Hendrix, all said they believed Mrs. Judd was fully aware she was to be hanged. Pressed for an opinion of her present mental condition, Hendrix declined to commit himself, saying he had not observed her in that regard.

Mrs. Judd exploded during Orme's testimony when he said Mrs. Judd revealed to the board during a secret session at the prison that she would attempt to impregnate herself if the board ignored her plea for a life sentence. "She said that she wanted to save her life and she wanted us to commute her—"

Winnie, sitting, half-hunched, suddenly became a volcano, hurling screams and accusations. "You told me," she screamed, raising her right arm toward the board chairman, "that if I would not exonerate Carl Harris, you would kill me! I said, 'Please don't kill me because I am going to have a baby.' You said if I exonerate Carl Harris you would not kill me. That is all I said. Carl Harris . . . where is he . . . where is Carl Harris? Make him come up here. Listen . . . come up here! Carl Harris, come here! He said Carl Harris, and unless I exonerate Carl Harris he would kill me and I said you won't! Where is Carl Harris? Get him! Mash his brains over the ceiling like a dish of oatmeal! I said, 'Get Carl Harris.' Because he said Carl Harris, if I exonerate Carl Harris, 'we won't kill you.' 'If you don't exonerate Carl Harris, I will kill you!' I said, 'Don't kill my baby!'"

Again Warden Walker and matrons forcibly took Mrs. Judd from the courtroom. She was returned after a brief walk about the courthouse grounds. Back in her chair, she once again subsided into apparent abstraction.

On cross-examination, Willson demanded of Hendrix if he had not seen Mrs. Judd "in hysteria, wailing and crying."

"Yes."

"Did you consider that the manifestation of merely a nervous woman?"

"I have seen high school girls act worse."

"Would you say she is sane today?"

"Me? I have made no observation."

"You don't know now, then, whether Ruth Judd comprehends her surroundings?"

"Well, I think she did Saturday."

"What makes you think so?"

"Orme and I were sitting in the rear of the room while the jury was out. I said to Orme, 'I would like to see Mrs. Judd face to face again.' She looked around, then turned her eyes away—and called us four names."

"Oh, so that is why you think she is sane!"

The state asked for and was granted an early halt to proceedings Wednesday afternoon.

That day a letter circulated through the Arizona State Prison. Composed in the institution's "underworld," it said:

A grapevine message from 700 of the boys in the Arizona State Prison who have watched Ruth Judd from that night 14 months ago when the sheriff's car drove up with her:

We all know Ruth Judd is insane, just as we all know she is broke. So does anyone else who is sane. We are all wise as to who is behind the whole deal and whose money is paying those fancy doctors and other witnesses against her, and we have all made up our minds that if Ruth hangs, those responsible will follow her to hell in short order.

There are 700 of us here, and we will all be free some day. There won't be any rioting here—we all respect Warden Walker and Cap Shute too much to make things tough for them—but don't forget some day, some way, the guilty ones will have to pay.

After she has gone through the trap and is pronounced dead, the state will hire a preacher to preach her into heaven. If she is good enough to be preached into heaven, she is good enough to live on this earth of ours.

In Phoenix, announcement went out that a 3 P.M. mass meeting of Winnie Ruth Judd sympathizers would be held Thursday in the Free Methodist Church, Fifth and Adams streets. An address, "Should Ruth Judd Hang?" was to be delivered by the pastor of the Phoenix Fundamental Tabernacle. An evangelist and several state legislators were scheduled as special guests.

The state called its "big guns" to the stand on Thursday. Although several Arizona psychiatrists and doctors attested to their belief in Mrs. Judd's sanity, the testimony of Drs. Freid and Catton brought an overflow crowd of spectators.

Dr. Freid said he found "no evidence of any insanity, or any delusions—no hallucinations, no illusions—no evidence of any behavior belonging to the category of insanity. I saw none of the behavior that goes with dementia praecox—I saw behavior that goes with deliberation; behavior that goes with a self-serving attitude of mind. I reached the conclusion she didn't because she chose deliberately not to talk.

"She is disagreeable to her parents. She treats them miserably. I was not particularly impressed by that. When a person has a particular purpose in mind, they carry out that purpose —and what greater purpose than save one's life?

"I considered her family history and I felt it possibly is a bit tainted—but knowing many sane individuals have insane relatives, and knowing I had examined such patients of tainted heredity, it did not count for much.

"I feel this lady is in a nervous condition. I feel she is under a great strain. She is depressed—seeking refuge from a terrible situation. She stands the strain better than I could, if I were in the same situation. I think the woman is in a neurotic state. I think she is nervous—and she is scared to death almost—but I think the reaction to save herself is perfectly normal."

Dr. Catton then took the stand. "Family history helps explain insanity in an individual, but it does not help you to say an individual is insane.

"I know Mrs. Judd does not talk in certain instances, but whether or not she is able to talk on those occasions, frankly, I do not know. I am not so smart I cannot be fooled. I believe about 60 per cent that this woman has a definite prison psychosis, or insanity. I believe with the other 40 per cent the picture she presents may be fraudulent."

Dr. Catton said Mrs. Judd "is sane" according to the legal

definition. "I am driven, in spite of the fact this woman is mentally ill and sick, to stand on the fact in this record—that she does know what is going on. I believe it is a fact that, as long as society—at this moment unfortunately—is arrayed against Mrs. Judd, her ideas of persecution are in a way sound—not under the circumstances a true delusion at all. It is my opinion that her present mental condition had its birth in feigning and simulation. Beyond a doubt, she is suffering from a condition I would term 'neurosis of the condemned.'

"It is my belief that neurosis is made up in part of simulated symptoms, and in part consists of mechanics beyond Mrs. Judd's control. It is my opinion beyond any doubt this subject is not suffering from dementia praecox in any of its forms. Mrs. Judd never has been the type of personality from which an insanity of that type might spring. Certain of Mrs. Judd's symptoms, if believed truly present, must be 'psychotic' or insane. Such psychosis as is present, it is my opinion, will disappear, if commutation be granted, within a period of weeks, or months at most."

Dr. Catton tempered his testimony given during Winnie's murder trial, saying she was legally sane, but medically insane. He expressed regret that the legal definition of insanity as propounded by the court bound him to "the factual statements which have found their way into the record" rather than allowing him to relate "what might be my personal wish in regards to a statement of Mrs. Judd's condition."

The state failed to produce the rest of its witnesses, and state and defense counsel agreed to close the case without further presentation of testimony by either side. Assistant County Attorney Reed needed time to prepare his closing arguments. Deputy Court Clerk Wylie Parsons said a delay would be granted because of "physical inability of Reed to prepare and present his argument tonight." Reed had lost much sleep in preparing his case, and reached a state of exhaustion.

Recesses, summing up of arguments and Judge Green's instructions to the jury consumed most of Saturday. The jury was instructed it could return only one of two verdicts—that

Mrs. Judd was sane or insane, under the court's definition. Arizona law required a vote of at least nine of twelve jurors to find commitment to the state asylum. A verdict of sanity, however, would seal Winnie's April 28 fate with the hangman.

Jury deliberations lasted an hour and fifty-seven minutes, with five ballots taken. At 7:14 P.M., the jury foreman, a railroad section boss, called the bailiff and said, "We are ready to come in."

By agreement of counsel, the verdict was to be read before Mrs. Judd was brought into the courtroom. Court Clerk Tom Marks read introductory remarks, slowly and deliberately. Then he hesitated, while the whole courtroom took a deep breath. Finally came the words: "Do find her insane."

The silence broke under a storm of applause. Attorney Willson leaned on the jury box, visibly affected. Colleagues rushed to his side, offering congratulations.

As the verdict had been read, Mrs. Judd was getting out of a prison car. She was close to the courthouse when the clapping of hands thundered out a message that the matrons with her clearly recognized. Winnie Ruth Judd showed no sign that she knew she was victor in this battle. As she was led to her chair in the courtroom, County Attorney Will C. Truman faced the jury. "The state has no objection to your verdict."

As Winnie sat down, Dr. Judd, his face flushed with emotion, sat beside her, took her hand and put his arm about her shoulders. "You will not be hanged. Everything is all right. Do you hear? You are going to the hospital."

Winnie showed no sign of hearing. She stared blankly across the counsel table. Several women spectators rushed to Winnie, caressing her, even kissing her. She just stared.

Warden Walker said, "I think the jury vote established that my judgment was correct in deciding to ask for the trial. I am very glad that I did it."

Mrs. McKinnell expressed her gratitude to the jury. As she was doing so, Dr. Stephens went to congratulate Mrs. Judd. She recognized him, and took his hand. "I'd like one of your kittens," he said.

"I'll give you one of them, too, even though I only have three left. I'll give you Tom, but you can't have Angel."

Moments earlier, Winnie had broken her silence with the declaration, "Lin Orme can't have any of my kittens."

After her brief exchange with Dr. Stephens, Mrs. Judd was hurried back to her prison cell.

21. DO UNTO OTHERS

WINNIE WENT TO bed early, quickly falling into deep slumber. She did not awaken until nearly 9 A.M. Sunday. After breakfast, a matron marcelled her hair. Then wearing a plain blue gingham dress and black pumps, Winnie spent most of the day playing on a patch of grass with Egypt and the kittens.

Her husband and parents visited her during the day. Many others also went to the prison, hopeful of a Sunday visit with the woman who had so dramatically been snatched from the gallows, but they were denied admittance. Other inmates in the women's ward ignored her.

Winnie was in a carefree mood. Throughout the day she talked intelligently and displayed keen interest in activities about her. She stopped winding her handkerchief about her left hand. Once, while sitting on her cot, Warden Walker called attention to her old mannerism. Winnie looked down, smiled sheepishly, and wrapped the handkerchief several times.

On Monday morning, Judge Green signed the papers committing Mrs. Judd to the Arizona State Hospital for the Insane, and directed she be taken that day to Phoenix. Mrs. McKinnell visited Winnie shortly before her departure, leaving when her daughter became enraged and threatened to kill herself during a discussion of family affairs.

Mrs. Judd had resumed the nervous wrapping and unwrapping of the handkerchief when she was escorted to the warden's car. Winnie's chief concern during the trip were Egypt and two kittens. Hospital officials said they would allow her to keep the cats "for awhile," hoping it would quiet her.

Winnie abruptly shed her unconcern as the car rolled into the grounds of the asylum at Twenty-fourth Street and Tempe Road. "Look at them—the bunch of morbids," she shouted, noticing several newspaper photographers. "They've made a shell out of me, and they're not going to take any pictures of a corpse. They can't taunt me any more. They can't take any more pictures of me!"

Dr. Berends placed Winnie in a small room in Ward D, to remain under observation for at least thirty days.

Asylum officials said Mrs. Judd would be regarded as "just another prisoner." The "Tiger Woman" was finally free of the gallows, but there was one catch (as in such cases): if she were ever certified sane, she would be returned to prison and executed.

Winnie adjusted quickly to asylum life. Within a few months, she gained the reputation of a docile patient who would do anything asked of her by doctors, attendants and other inmates.

But during those early months of her transition from the more restricted and confined life of the state prison, her only authorized visitors were her parents. They had moved to Phoenix soon after the sanity trial, determined to be near their daughter and to carry on the fight for her complete freedom.

The Rev. McKinnell was already a seasoned campaigner in seeking to aid Winnie. After her murder trial, he had walked the streets of Phoenix soliciting signatures for a petition requesting a new trial. Before the Board of Pardons and Paroles turned down a plea for clemency in early April, 1933, he wrote Governor Benjamin Bakin Moeur, "We are not afraid of a legal trial and have exhausted every legal means to get a retrial. There is not an attorney in the country who, when shown our evidence, but will decide that to the present she has not had a lawful trial. . . . Now if by persuasion of advice given the Board of Pardons and Paroles you can save the state expensive costs of litigation and the judiciary of the state the disgrace that will follow the publicity of such legal actions, it will do great good."

On July 15, 1933, Rev. McKinnell submitted a petition for a full pardon for his daughter, basing his plea on grounds and evidence previously presented: self-defense, "bruises on Mrs. Judd's body," affidavits of the jurors concerning a deal made to convict her so that she would tell the whole truth, and her fifteen months' imprisonment under the sentence of death. This and other pleas of a growing legion of friends were unsuccessful.

During 1934 and 1935 Winnie's parents established a close friendship with Mrs. Ethel Mayberry. She helped Winnie's parents promote the Townsend Plan, the famous plan of Dr. F. E. Townsend for national economic stability and old-age pensions.

The McKinnells often talked to Mrs. Mayberry about Winnie. When Rev. McKinnell suffered a stroke which left him partially paralyzed, and he could no longer visit his daughter, the McKinnells asked Mrs. Mayberry to visit her for them. To do so, she had to go to the state capitol building and get a signed permit from the governor, then ride out to the asylum on a streetcar.

Mrs. Mayberry's daughter, Gail, in a letter to the *Arizona Republic* many years later, told about her mother's efforts to help Mrs. Judd, and Mrs. Judd's efforts to help others:

> From time to time, the media manage to drag up and rehash the Winnie Ruth Judd case. But to my recollection, there have never been any articles about the woman she is and the service she gave to the hospital.
>
> Every time a new doctor came, her privileges were

stripped from her and she had to start all over, just to get the privilege of helping and serving her fellow patients.

No one knows how many thousands of dollars she saved the state by the work she did in relieving the nurses and helping wherever needed. We came to love and admire her very much as we watched the self-sacrificing service and love she gave to the patients at the hospital. No matter where they moved her or under what treatment, she spent her time helping the patients and nurses.

When she was in the building with the elderly, she planted flowers and put bouquets in their wards, preparing foods they could eat, reading with them and feeding them. She took complete care of six babies and children when the children's wing overflowed. She did all the washing and ironing, cooking, feeding and care.

She was placed in the young women's wing. There, Mother got her a sewing machine and gathered formals and party dresses. These Ruth carefully washed and ironed and altered so that the girls could dress up for the dances and programs arranged by the therapy department of the hospital. Mother gathered costume jewelry and party shoes; and in the winter, warm jackets and skirts. All of these were cared for by Ruth for the girls.

Ruth was a talented beauty parlor operator and used this as therapy for the patients, giving many of them the first feeling of pride and a step up the ladder of recovery. Many of them were helped to gain a feeling of personal pride and to be well again through her aid.

Some beauticians complained, and her equipment was removed and she was denied this service. The fact that the ones she helped could not get out to the shops and had no money to pay for it, did not seem to enter into the decision.

She helped in the craft work and made beautiful things to brighten the rooms and develop the skill of the patients who had lost their ability and will to go on.

As anyone who ever knew her would tell you, she was a

help and comfort and inspiration to all who came in contact with her. Surely the years of service have earned her the right to peace and an end to the persecution by the newspapers.

There are some who remember the years of love and service she gave to her surroundings at the state hospital.

Mrs. Judd had operated a "beauty culturist business" for several years when it suddenly became a political hot potato in April, 1939. Dr. Louis J. Saxe, superintendent of the hospital, ordered that her practice for employees and a "few outsiders drawn by curiosity" be stopped. It was reportedly fashionable in some social circles to be able to announce "I had my hair done by Winnie." Dr. Saxe's directive followed newspaper publicity giving letters written to the governor and other state officials by the Arizona State Board of Beauty Culturist Examiners, charging "unfair competition" because of Mrs. Judd's low prices.

In June, 1939, Governor Robert T. Jones held a conference with three members of the Board of Beauty Culturist Examiners, accompanied by eleven beauty shop operators outside. It ended in a row when Governor Jones refused to hear the shop operators.

"I am not interested. These people are all being paid with public funds and we cannot take any more time than is necessary," he said, pointing to several state employees in the room.

Mrs. Ware, chairman of the examiners, interrupted, referring to the shop operators, "They are the public that supplies the funds."

"I didn't call those women."

"It'll make it tough on you not to see them."

"I'm not running for office, and you can go out and tell them that. I'm trying to protect those poor helpless people in the hospital and I'm going to do it, so good day."

Governor Jones had already said he believed Mrs. Judd was being persecuted in the matter.

A few days later, Winnie Ruth Judd took an overdose of sleeping tablets, and was in a coma for two days.

Although very much agitated over the loss of her "paying customers," Winnie did not give up the free enterprise system. She started a "laundry business," washing uniforms for hospital attendants, who paid her ten cents each.

By early October, 1939, Mrs. Judd had earned over $30. She continued laundering despite warnings of friends that Phoenix laundries might stir up trouble because of her competition and low price. In mid-October, Winnie, according to a friend, sent $20 of her savings to Dr. Judd, now residing in a government hospital in Sawtelle, California, so that he might come visit her. She had not seen her husband in all the years since her commitment to the asylum. Her only communication with him had been through frequent, sometimes lengthy, letters which he answered.

Winnie asked a friend to buy her some clothes, with the last of her savings, saying she was expecting a visit from her husband the following Sunday. The friend bought a purple rayon dress, a pair of black shoes, a pair of tan stockings and six bottles of a soft drink, so Winnie could entertain her husband. Dr. Judd did not keep the appointment his wife had talked about.

Apparently very much disheartened, Mrs. Judd continued talking about leaving the hospital, as she had since the beauty culture episode. At various times, she talked of visiting her husband in California, of going to South Africa to become a missionary, of returning to Mexico. She spent hours crying because she was not allowed to visit her ailing father.

22. A RAGE FOR FREEDOM

ON THE NIGHT of October 24, one day after the eighth anniversary of her surrender in a Los Angeles funeral parlor, the "Tiger Woman" escaped. She did not attend a Tuesday night dance arranged by the therapy department. Instead, she artfully transformed an assortment of boxes, bath towels, cosmetic containers and bottles into a dummy resembling herself asleep under the bedclothes.

At about midnight, Winnie showed up at the home of her parents at 1328 East Moreland Street. Mrs. McKinnell urged her to stay there during the night and return to the hospital in the morning. Winnie refused. After writing a letter to Governor Jones, which she asked her mother to deliver the next day, Mrs. Judd walked out into the night.

The escape was not discovered at the hospital until 10:45 A.M., Wednesday. Attendants did not bother to check, as she habitually slept late. Only after someone expressed the belief Mrs. Judd may have taken more sleeping tablets, did a nurse go into the wire-mesh room to awaken her. Forty-five minutes later, the escape was reported by hospital authorities to the

Maricopa County sheriff's office and the board of directors of the state institutions.

Within hours, Winnie Ruth Judd was once again the West's most widely hunted woman. In San Francisco, Dr. Joseph Catton said he believed Mrs. Judd would try to resume normal life if not recaptured. "I think she will attempt to pick up the threads of normal life in some distant city, either as a secretary or a nurse. She will think she is clever enough to evade the police in that manner."

Dr. Catton recalled Winnie's love for Mexico and said she might try to escape across the border. Also believing that a possibility, Sheriff Lon Jordan broadcast to every border point of entry from California and Texas a request that records be checked to determine if she had entered that country. Officers were alerted in San Luis Potosi, Mexico; Los Angeles; New Concord, Ohio; Darry, New Hampshire; Rock Rapids, Iowa; Albuquerque and Los Lunas, New Mexico; Detroit and other cities from which Mrs. Judd had received recent correspondence from friends, to find a clue that would lead to her capture.

In Sawtelle, California, Dr. Judd issued a plea for his wife to surrender. "If my words can reach her, this is what I say to my wife: 'Surrender to the nearest officers of the law, wherever you are, for only disaster awaits you if you attempt to remain in hiding or to continue your flight.'" Dr. Judd expressed a "fervent hope that Winnie Ruth will give herself up—she can gain nothing by her escape."

It was early evening, Wednesday, before Mrs. McKinnell got to see Governor Jones. She agreed with him that Winnie's action "was a very foolish thing." This is Winnie's letter which she gave the governor:

I am only going to see my father and husband. I have a right to.

My husband coaxed me to surrender to the police. I did and look what happens. Dr. Saxe tortures me. Even Hitler would not torture his prisoners when they surrender. I was not overcome, so I had to surrender. Only a coward would torture one helpless.

I am helpless because I trusted fairness. I do not get it. Dr. Saxe says I have no privileges. I did have until he came here. He took them away. For 18 months I had yard parole, could sit on the yard alone or with my family. I never abused a privilege or broke a trust. Dr. Saxe took my privileges away because he hates me.

I am persecuted by the Catholics.

At this point, a portion of the letter was apparently missing. It continued:

. . . him $20 to come on. But he can only stay one day. $20 just to see him two or three hours. Two hundred hours' work to see him two or three hours, and now they have ordered him I have to visit him in Mrs. Lassiter's presence, my bitter enemy. [Bertha Lassiter was a matron.] I will not.

Tonight I am running away. I hate everyone who has forced me to do it. May God punish them. I want to be a good patient. I like you. I hope you may be governor again. You have been kind to me and I do not want to do anything ever to hurt you.

I am desperate to see my father. I am going to see him tonight, then somehow see my husband and I will surrender to you on condition you promise me Dr. Saxe will be forced to leave me alone.

I will not run away. I do not want my freedom illegal.

The letter was unsigned.

Dr. Judd said he believed his wife's escape was not a plot hatched over a long period of time, but that "she acted on the spur of the moment, as insane persons often do."

Investigators believed otherwise. They said her escape was the culmination of a carefully laid plan—that all of her arrangements were made, not to receive and entertain her husband, but to enable her to equip herself with clothes for her flight without attracting attention. They said several letters, particularly the one to Governor Jones, were part of the plan. One investigator said, "It looks as though it worked perfectly." He said that Winnie's declaration to the governor that she would not run away was a ruse to throw officers off her tracks.

Attendants and patients alike were puzzled at her escape, relating how she liked them and was always doing little acts of kindness for them. Winnie spoke Spanish fluently and often served as an interpreter in the handling of Spanish-speaking patients.

When Winnie had previously threatened to run away, her mother always tried to dissuade her. Mrs. McKinnell on one occasion reportedly said, "Your father needs me, Ruth, but when he is gone you can have my life, if you want it."

On Thursday, Y. C. White, executive secretary to the governor, said it was "perfectly obvious" Mrs. Judd hadn't simply walked through a locked door. Hinting that he believed she had received either inside or outside help, White said he would press his inquiry until the "person or persons responsible" had been found. A door through which Winnie had apparently fled was supposedly locked at all times.

A physician was called that day to the McKinnell residence. Mrs. McKinnell said her daughter's escapade had further impaired Rev. McKinnell's health. Earlier in the day, Sheriff Jordan and his chief deputy, Ernest Roach, searched the McKinnell home "as a precautionary measure." They found no clues.

On Friday, Dr. Saxe, just returned from a curtailed vacation in Southern California, conducted an all-day probe at the hospital which brought to light nothing he didn't already know.

The Peoria, Illinois, *Journal* reported that a former pastor of Phoenix had walked into its office declaring he was present when Mrs. Judd recently talked about escaping. The Arizona attorney general telegraphed Peoria police, "Interrogate him fully," and the police said they would in "four or five days."

From Los Angeles came a report that two men, residents of an outlying tourist court, "positively identified" a police photo of Mrs. Judd as that of a woman who had stayed there Wednesday night.

A $100 reward for information leading to Winnie's capture was posted Saturday by the acting Arizona governor, Dan Garvey.

An informant told Austin, Texas, Sheriff Lee O. Allen that he might be able to reveal information about the escape, but authorities discounted his story.

At Eagle Pass, Texas, Dr. E. F. Gates reported a woman resembling Mrs. Judd had come to his door the night before to get some medicine analyzed. He said the woman fled when he tried to question her. Dr. Gates said he had treated Mrs. Judd a number of years earlier when she and Dr. Judd lived in Tosita, Coahuila, Mexico, about ninety miles southwest of Eagle Pass.

Dr. Saxe concluded his probe Saturday, saying he was "satisfied in my own mind there was no open door" through which Mrs. Judd could have fled. He said, "One thing is evident—the ward was left free for a time that evening," and one of the attendants had apparently neglected her duty.

Asked if he would punish Mrs. Judd upon her return, Dr. Saxe said, "Of course not. This is not an institution for punishment. She would be treated as she always has been."

Dr. Judd was brought to Phoenix, where he secluded himself in a hotel, hoping to attract Winnie there. Mrs. McKinnell visited him on Saturday, but by late Sunday, Dr. Judd's whereabouts had become a mystery.

On Monday, long before daylight, the Rev. Michael Payton ran into the sheriff's office, shouting: "I just let Ruth Judd out near the hospital!" The Tempe minister said his wife had seen a woman standing in their yard Sunday night as they were getting ready for bed. He went outside to approach her and recognized her as Winnie Ruth Judd. Taking her inside, they talked for three hours. He and his wife pleaded with her to return to the hospital and prayed with her.

Rev. Payton said Winnie told him she had left a house in Phoenix about dusk, walked south on Seventh Street to Van Buren and then to Tempe. Several times during the nine-mile walk, passing motorists stopped and offered her rides, but she declined. Mrs. Judd told the minister she had spent the first night of her freedom in an orange orchard near the hospital, then moved to a vacant house on Seventh Street. She said she had scratched her initials with a piece of glass on a window sill.

The minister said he had finally persuaded her to get into his car, acting on her own suggestion that he take her to the home of a friend. He drove to the hospital, slowed down and again pleaded with Mrs. Judd to let him take her inside so she could surrender. But when Winnie threatened to cut her throat with a razor, he said he was too frightened to use force. Winnie directed him to turn north off Van Buren onto Twenty-fourth Street. When they reached Roosevelt Street, just north of the hospital grounds, Winnie said, "Stop. This is good enough." Rev. Payton let her out—it was about 2 A.M.—then drove downtown to the sheriff's office.

Sheriff Jordan and several deputies went to the place where the minister had let Mrs. Judd out, and began a thorough search. Their only "find" came before noon, when they located an unoccupied duplex at 701 East Brill Street, at the corner of Seventh Street. On a window sill of the duplex apartment were scratched the initials "WRJ" and beneath them "10-29-39." The sheriff found prints of bare feet in the dust, and bits of a half-green orange peel. The men continued searching until dusk on Monday.

Hospital guards and attendants at the asylum grounds had found a small case that Mrs. Judd had with her during her visit with Rev. Payton. The case contained a half-green orange, a can of soup, a can of spaghetti, a small jar of salad dressing and a small jar of jelly, plus three shoes, a red sweater and photographs of Mrs. Judd's parents.

About 7:50 P.M., she was seen sidling away from the home of the hospital engineer. She had apparently gone into the house for food. As a dozen guards and attendants closed in, Mrs. Judd quickly headed for the back door to the ward from which she had escaped six days earlier. She made it to the door, and rapped. Other attendants took her to Dr. Saxe's office.

"Well, here I am!" she told Dr. Saxe.

Winnie had spent part of her freedom hiding in the asylum's cemetery. When Dr. Saxe pressed for details of how she had eluded searchers, she "just became more and more hysterical." She was given sedatives, then talked briefly to Governor Jones, who had returned from San Francisco, postponing his vacation pending further developments in the Judd hunt. "I told you I would come back and give myself up, and I did," she said. "I kept my word to you. I wanted to see my father, I saw him and talked to him, then I came back and gave myself up like I said I would."

Three hours after Mrs. Judd's return to custody, Dr. Saxe allowed her to be photographed, but would not permit any reporters to talk to her. Newsmen received a description of Winnie from the hospital engineer at the moment of her return. He said she was shoeless, her stockings all but torn off, her feet and legs bruised as though she had fallen down frequently in the darkness. She was dirty. He said one ankle was sprained and she had fashioned a brace for it from a girdle she apparently had been wearing when she escaped. She was wearing an old brown overcoat and a drab blue hat pulled over her ears.

Dr. Saxe promised to "get the whole story with all the trimmings just as soon as I feel she is physically able to give it." The following day, on Tuesday, Dr. Saxe said the case was closed as far as the hospital was concerned. A key to her ward door had been found on her person after her return to custody, a key that had been recorded as "lost" months before. Dr. Saxe said Mrs. Judd would not be allowed to visit her parents nor permitted to wander about hospital grounds. He said her beauty work had never been taken away entirely, but admitted she was not and would not be allowed to do work for attendants or outside clients. Mrs. Judd would be kept for a while in her box-like wire-screened cubicle.

In a brief interview, Winnie repeated that she had left because she wanted better treatment and wanted to see her parents. "I heard my husband was in Phoenix, but I did not get to see him."

Mrs. Judd was kept in solitary confinement for the next four weeks. She was then given back her ward privileges, allowing her the company of other inmates.

On Sunday night, December 3, 1939, thirty-four days after her return, Winnie Ruth Judd fled again. She apparently walked through the same "locked" door she had used on her first escape. Governor Jones announced the escape from his sickbed at home, after hearing the news from Dr. Saxe, who was also ill at home.

Investigators for the governor were told by attendants that at 6:30 P.M., Winnie was sitting on the edge of her bed, nervous and distraught. At 7 P.M., she was gone. She made no attempt this time to conceal her disappearance. Nineteen hospital personnel immediately scoured the hospital grounds, remembering Winnie's statement that she had hid part of the time during her first escape in a cornfield and graveyard on hospital property. They did not find her.

Twelve highway patrolmen and several sheriff's deputies were sent to strategic points to cut off her escape. Other officers were stationed at the McKinnell home. Winnie did not show.

Her parents again asked that the arresting officers "be gentlemen" with their daughter. The ailing Reverend expressed annoyance that neither he nor his wife had been allowed to see their daughter since her first escape.

Investigators, failing in every attempt, again advanced the theory that she may have had outside help of some kind. Her vanishing had been too complete for only a half-hour's start on the searchers. Hospital nurses said only a wine-colored dress and low brown shoes were missing from her wardrobe. She had gone out into the chilly night air without a coat or hat.

By the early-morning hours of Monday, bloodhounds from the Arizona State Prison at Florence were on Winnie's trail. The hounds lit out in a huge semi-circle from her ward building to the southeastern corner of the hospital grounds, losing the scent where the trail led across the pavement of Van Buren Street.

A few hours later, it was revealed that Mrs. Judd had entered the home of the Rev. Robert V. Spencer between 8:30 and 9:30 Sunday night. She gained entry by cutting a screen. She took a coat, sweater, two oranges, part of a box of crackers and a partly-filled carton of milk. Winnie left two notes—one to Rev. Spencer, the other to Governor Jones. The note to Rev. Spencer, who was the pastor of the Free Methodist Church at Fifth and Adams streets, expressed regret at her theft, and promised that the articles would be returned by mail and that her mother would pay for any damages. Winnie also expressed dissatisfaction with conditions and treatment at the hospital: "It's either this or suicide."

Rev. Spencer gave the note for Governor Jones to Mrs. Mc-Kinnell. Asked by the governor's agents for the note, Mrs. Mc-Kinnell said it would be delivered only by Dr. Judd.

Hounds were taken to Rev. Spencer's parsonage. They lost Winnie's trail a block away, in a vacant lot at the southwest corner of Fourth and Adams streets.

Police later received reports that a slim woman, about thirty-five years old, had pried her way through a window of another Phoenix home, between 11 and 11:30 A.M. on Monday. The woman took a fork from a cabinet drawer, ate the filling from a pie on the kitchen table and left, disturbing nothing else. Neighbors who had seen her enter the house believed her to be a relative of the resident.

By late Tuesday, the note for Governor Jones still had not been delivered and investigators could find no additional clues as to Winnie's whereabouts.

On Wednesday, Dr. Judd arrived in Phoenix. He said he would deliver the note to the governor, and serve as "bait" for his wife's capture. Contents of the note were not revealed.

No trace of Winnie could be found anywhere. After her disappearance, turmoil raged in Arizona State Hospital for the Insane. Dr. Andrew F. Tombs, hospital physician, handed in his resignation on Thursday. He was the fourth physician to do so in as many months. There was now only one staff physician to provide care for nine hundred patients. Rumors that Dr. Saxe would soon be replaced were quashed on Saturday by Governor Jones, who reaffirmed his confidence in Dr. Saxe's administration. The governor said immediate action would be taken to acquire a competent staff of physicians. He added that Dr. Saxe might be running the hospital with an entirely new staff of personnel if the "bickering and fighting" didn't stop. A Phoenix doctor who was asked to join the hospital staff said, "I never would be able to live down the political stigma and my private patients would go running."

Dr. Judd's vigil as "bait" failed to lure the escapee. But on Friday, December 15, 1939, shortly after the noon hour, Sergeant James Stahl of the Yuma Police Department noticed a woman he thought might be Mrs. Judd. He trailed her for thirty minutes. Seeing the superintendent of the Arizona Department of Liquor License and Control, Sergeant Stahl asked him to also observe the woman and see "if that isn't Mrs. Judd." They followed her down a street and into a drugstore where she made a phone call. As she came out of the drugstore, Sergeant Stahl asked her to enter a waiting police car. She declined at first, saying she was a hitchhiker named "Marian Burke." But she finally got into the car and was taken to the office of Yuma County Sheriff T. H. Newman.

The sheriff noticed an object at the back of the woman's head, just above her neck. A local physician, who had known Mrs. Judd when she lived in Yuma more than ten years earlier, examined the woman, confirming her identity as Mrs. Judd. He removed the object, a safety razor blade knotted into her hair with chewing gum. She told Sheriff Newman she kept it for suicidal use, "If I felt I had to do it."

Mrs. Judd was disheveled, her stockings torn and her shoes— new ones her mother had given her the afternoon she escaped —badly worn. She said she had walked all but about 24 of the 198 miles to Yuma. The physician said she was "badly bruised practically to her waist."

At about 3 P.M., Mrs. Judd was taken by car to Phoenix,

accompanied by Sheriff Newman, Sergeant Stahl and two matrons. During the trip, Mrs. Judd pointed out to Sheriff Newman various places she had been, and others she had circled to avoid being seen. She revealed her drugstore phone call was to friends in Los Angeles, asking them to arrange for Dr. Judd to come to Yuma that night to meet her at the home of a long-time friend. Mrs. Judd said she did not know her husband was in Phoenix.

Sheriff Newman stopped in Gila Bend to have a tire repaired. While there, a truck driver said that the week before he had given Mrs. Judd a ride for eight miles to Theba, his destination.

It was at Gila Bend that Winnie first saw reporters who had set out from Phoenix to meet her car. She recognized one of the reporters and told Sheriff Newman, "I have been wanting to see a reporter for a long time, but at the hospital they never would let me."

Mrs. Judd talked candidly with the reporters, and gave them a twelve-page statement carefully written in longhand. The statement, which Winnie said she had written before her escape, was addressed to the Arizona State Legislature. In it were named the person Mrs. Judd said had dismembered Hedvig Samuelson's body, and another person she said had arranged for the "operation." Mrs. Judd elaborated on points discussed in her letter and on other topics pertinent to her case for reporters at Gila Bend, later at Buckeye when the party stopped for dinner, and during the remainder of the trip.

Winnie repeated the self-defense story essentially as she had given it nearly seven years earlier during the Harris preliminary hearing, and during a clemency hearing before the Arizona Board of Pardons and Paroles. In her letter, she pleaded for the right to stand trial on the charge of murdering Miss Samuelson.

A reporter asked Mrs. Judd if she believed she was sane. She replied, "I should either be given the chance to testify in court, or should be given the proper treatments for insanity."

She said she had received no medical care at the hospital and got "only mistreatment."

She expressed an earnest desire to be allowed to talk alone with Governor Jones. "When I got back last time, they shot me full of hypodermics. The attendant told me, 'I lost thirty-six hours' sleep over you,' and he put his knee in my back and shot me with the hypo and said, 'I guess you know why you're getting this. You talk too much.' When Governor Jones came out to see me, I wasn't able to talk to him. That stuff constricts your throat so you aren't able to talk. I was hazy. I just vaguely remember his being there."

Mrs. Judd said that, although she had been promised the opportunity to see her parents, she had not been allowed to do so. "They put me in a straitjacket."

The subject of Mrs. Judd's hairdressing activities was also thrashed over again, and she wrote a letter to the newspapers but was kept from sending it. "I took care of patients that no one there would put a hand on. I did more than hairdressing. I got up in the middle of the night and changed bedding for some of them. At times, I literally slaved there."

Mrs. Judd added, "I could have gotten away many times. That door was open for days before I left the first time. There were other times I could have left."

When Sheriff Newman's car reached the outskirts of Phoenix, Winnie began to cry. She gradually became more hysterical the closer she came to the hospital. Her twelve-day "vacation" officially ended at 8:15 P.M., when the car rolled through a gate and onto asylum grounds. She was taken immediately to a new ward, one more "escape-proof."

23. UNLOCKING THE "SEPULCHER"

W<small>INNIE</small> R<small>UTH</small> J<small>UDD</small> faded from the public eye almost to the point of obscurity during the next several years. In July, 1941, she gained some prominence when a self-appointed "committee of nine" asked the Arizona Board of Pardons and Paroles to reconsider her case. The committee asked the board to hold a public hearing to determine if the death penalty hanging over Mrs. Judd was an obstacle to her treatment for dementia praecox and to take "appropriate" action.

The Pardon Board took no action, and the committee's efforts quickly died out. However, her father never let up in his letter-writing campaign. During the last months of his life—almost to July 1, 1942, the day he died—he wrote one or two letters weekly to Governor Sydney P. Osborn, despite a paralysis of his right hand (through great effort, Rev. McKinnell had learned to write with his left hand), but unknown to him, his letters were never mailed. Herbert Wagner, who cared for the Reverend, revealed in later years that he had been directed not to mail the letters. Wagner would not say who had given him the direction, but indicated it came from friends of the family who believed the letters would do more harm than good in helping Mrs. Judd's cause. He never read the letters, he said, always turning them over to someone else, except on one occasion when Rev. McKinnell wrote a poem about the United States flag and showed it to him. Wagner disobeyed the order and mailed that letter, and Governor Osborn sent an appreciative response. The poem was read at Rev. McKinnell's funeral.

During the last few months of his life, Mrs. Judd was occasionally allowed to visit her father. Wagner said it would have been easy for her to have walked away from the house. But Winnie had promised she would never try to escape when allowed to visit her father. "And she never did," Wagner said.

Within three years, Dr. Judd also died, Mrs. McKinnell was committed to the Arizona State Hospital for the Insane as a fellow patient with her daughter, and Mrs. Lottie Connors —who had been chairman of the "committee of nine"—became Mrs. Judd's court-appointed guardian.

In mid-1945, Dr. Jeremiah Metzger, then superintendent of the asylum, recommended to the Arizona Board of Pardons and Paroles that Mrs. Judd's death sentence at least be commuted to life in prison. He said such action would clear the way for effective treatment leading to the possible recovery of Mrs. Judd's sanity. The board took no action, saying it had no responsibility to alter the sentences of convicts committed to the asylum until they were mentally capable of appearing before the board at the State Prison.

Winnie Ruth Judd took matters into her own hands on May 11, 1947, escaping for the third time. She left her second-floor room at about 9 o'clock Sunday night, unlocking a door opening to a stairway and another outside door, and walked through a gate, supposedly locked at all times.

At 2:45 A.M. on Monday, Sheriff's Deputies Bill LaFever and Jerry Heffelfinger woke up Winnie's guardian to question her. Mrs. Connors said, "I've always told her I couldn't hide her if she came around here."

At about 8:15 A.M., Mrs. Judd was found lying asleep in a furrow in a large grapefruit tract about a half-mile north of

Indian School Road. The manager of the property was walking through the grove with his dog, Blondie, when he saw the woman. Blondie barked, waking Mrs. Judd. She asked if the dog would bite, and he said it wouldn't. Mrs. Judd got up and left hurriedly.

"I didn't think about the Judd woman until after she started to walk away through the trees," the manager later recalled. "Then I remembered the tail end of a news broadcast—something about Winnie Ruth Judd escaping—and I went back to the house and called the sheriff."

She was captured at 10:15 A.M. that day in a pasture southeast of the fashionable Arizona Biltmore Hotel by Deputies Ez Harris and Dave Davenport. She had covered nearly three miles from her furrow bed, and was kneeling behind the gate of a dilapidated old corral when Davenport walked up and took hold of her arm. Her freedom had lasted only thirteen hours. She was carrying a pillowcase full of clothing, sugar and grapefruit, and had changed from her hospital uniform to a blue street dress. Her hair—despite her night out in the open—was in nearly perfect condition.

Winnie told a reporter she was perturbed because hospital Superintendent Dr. John A. Larson "wouldn't let her" visit her mother in the hospital infirmary. "Yesterday was Mother's Day. I asked to see her, but he told me I could see her for only five minutes and then under three guards. I didn't see her all day. . . . I was simply going to some place to draw some kind of a plan to help my mother."

This time, the "Tiger Woman" discussed her sewing and "fancy work," which included making dresses for dolls. "I've got to do something to keep my mind occupied, but Dr. Larson has taken my sewing privileges away from me. I just can't sit in a room and brood. He told me if I would tell the truth about my tragedy, he would restore my liberties, but my . . . there are some things about my tragedy that I don't even know myself."

About ten days before her escape, Mrs. Judd had been moved to Ward B from the hospital infirmary where she had been allowed to care for her eighty-year-old mother. Dr. Larson said she had "too many liberties" in the infirmary and that the ward was the proper place for her.

"My mother is all I have," Mrs. Judd told the reporter. "She needs me. She is just like a baby. You have a mother, don't you . . . ? The attendants, who are all very nice, give my mother routine care. I want to give her special care."

Sheriff Boies took Winnie to his office for processing and Dr. Larson, the hospital superintendent, came to escort her back to the asylum. He had earlier used the term "connivances" in explaining the escape. Mrs. Judd spoke crisply to him now: "I hope you won't be there long."

He replied, "I know you do."

Almost a year later, on May 2, 1948, Dr. Larson revealed he had written to Evo De Concini, Arizona attorney general and member of the Board of Pardons and Paroles, recommending Mrs. Judd's death sentence be commuted to a lesser penalty. "It is preposterous—a paradoxical situation—when people are dumped out here under death sentence, to expect us to be able to treat them." Relatives had refused permission to subject her to shock treatment, knowing if she regained her sanity she would face execution.

The attorney general said that certain board members were afraid that if the death sentence were commuted, efforts would then be made to get her a total release.

Winnie's mother was eventually moved to Ward B in a room adjoining that of her daughter. Mrs. Judd was allowed to care for Mrs. McKinnell, and she again became a "model inmate." She seemed contented in this role of nurse. Many of her other privileges, including that of hairdresser, were also restored.

Then on November 1, 1951, Dr. M. W. Conway took over as the new superintendent. Winnie heard rumors that she might be moved to a ward away from her mother, and told attendants she would commit suicide if they were separated.

Mrs. Judd was returned from a show on the ground floor at 9 o'clock on Thursday night, November 29. At 10 P.M., an attendant found her giving fruit juice to her mother, now eighty-five years old and unable to talk. Then the attendant and others were called to another part of the ward to calm a violently disturbed patient. When this task was accomplished, another check was made at 10:30 and Winnie Ruth Judd was gone. When they saw a rope and an open window in her mother's room they thought she had carried out her suicide threat. However, instead of finding Winnie's body dangling somewhere between the second-floor window and the ground, they found a makeshift ladder anchored to Mrs. McKinnell's bed and hanging most of the way to the ground. The ladder had been cleverly woven from yarn, cloth and pieces of electric cord. Winnie had used a screwdriver and pliers to remove a heavy steel screen from the window and apparently scampered down the ladder, dropping the last several feet. A bag containing her personal belongings was later found inside an eight-foot-high locked gate.

The "Tiger Woman," now forty-six years old, had planned her escape better the fourth time around. Remembering the bloodhounds that trailed her in 1947, she had spent the previous several days laundering over and over the bedding and clothing she was to leave behind. The only scent the hounds could pick up was laundry soap, and they wouldn't leave the hospital grounds.

This time officials were in for a surprise. Throughout the West, police were notified to be on the lookout for the famous Mrs. Judd, but by midday Friday, only two calls came in from persons who thought they had seen Winnie. The sheriff's radio dispatcher said the lack of public reaction was "amazing. Ordinarily, when someone as notorious as Mrs. Judd is at large, we get hundreds of reports from people who think they have valuable information."

Sheriff Boies said it was "anybody's guess" where she would show up next. No organized search would be made because of the uncertainty as to which way she was headed.

Winnie's mother was wide-eyed when investigators entered her room to examine the window and ladder. Attendants said

"Granny" (as they called Mrs. McKinnell) did not realize what had happened.

Late Friday afternoon, Mrs. Marie Mason of 221 North Eighth Street, a former attendant at the asylum, reported the theft of a fur coat and several other items of clothing. At 9:05 P.M., two policemen saw a woman wearing such a fur coat in front of a house at 712 North Eleventh Street. Approaching her, one asked, "Are you Winnie Ruth Judd?" As the woman started walking in a driveway, he asked, "Do you live here?" The woman said, "Yes," but residents of the house said they did not know her. Winnie Ruth Judd then admitted her identity. Her freedom this time had lasted twenty-three hours.

She told the officers, "Why did you have to pick me up? I've served twenty years out there and I think I should be turned loose. I had a tragedy twenty years ago that I wasn't wholly responsible for. I wish you boys would turn me loose . . . I'm awfully tired. I have walked all day. I'd like to sit down."

The capture had been made because police patrols were concentrated in the vicinity after it was learned Mrs. Mason was on writing and speaking terms with Mrs. Judd. Mrs. Mason, who knew Mrs. Judd well, said that when she discussed the burglary with an investigating officer she did not realize Mrs. Judd had been in her apartment. "If I had known Ruth had taken my clothes, I never would have reported her. She took care of me when I was ill, when no one else paid any attention to me."

When told Mrs. Mason had notified police about the burglary, Winnie said, "She was a good friend, and now she's double-crossed me."

At police headquarters, Mrs. Judd explained her need to escape: "I became seized with panic and fear at the coming of the new superintendent and I heard he was going to call a criminal board. I was afraid they'd transfer me to a criminal ward away from my mother. . . . I'm not really a criminal. I'm not like those gangsters. I've never hurt anyone."

Seeing newsmen and photographers, she cried, "I don't want anything to do with newspapers. I'm a very sick woman and

I don't want my picture taken. If you were sick, you wouldn't want your picture taken, would you?" Finally, consenting to be photographed, she said, "Well, okay, but I won't smile. I don't feel like smiling, would you?"

Asked how long it took to weave the escape ladder, Winnie replied, "Quite some time . . . I've got a wonderful story—I've got it all written, but I couldn't lift the bag I put it in over the fence."

It was little wonder she couldn't carry the bag over the fence. The large laundry bag contained a variety of clothes, sewing materials, books, writing paper, tools, cosmetics and dozens of snapshots. But hospital attendants did not report finding a manuscript.

Rambling, Mrs. Judd talked about friends in South America who ran a leper colony. "I wish they'd send me down there so I could work with those leper children. They're like me. They're just outcasts. But I could do them some good. I could teach embroidery, crocheting and a lot of other things that I've learned while I was out at that place."

Mrs. Judd said several times, "I need friends. I haven't got anyone left. . . . When I lost my husband I lost everything." Winnie coughed and said, "See, I'm a very sick woman. I have cried constantly ever since doctors told me that I have cancer in the breast. They told me if the lump didn't go down they'd have to operate and I didn't want them to do that."

Two state hospital employees took Winnie back to the asylum. Her room was bare except for necessities. All of her beauty equipment—rinsers, shampooer and hair dryer—had been removed. Other restrictions were not yet decided.

An editorial in Saturday afternoon's *Phoenix Gazette* discussed the Arizona State Hospital's inability to keep inmates confined. The editorial concluded, "Whether or not Winnie Ruth Judd should have cheated the hangman in 1931 is pretty much beside the point today. The important thing is that people like Winnie Ruth Judd should not be permitted to roam at large. Now that she has been recaptured, Dr. Conway should see to it that she has no opportunity to repeat her frequent walk-outs. When an insane murderess can pry her way out of a state mental hospital with a pair of pliers and a screwdriver, it's obvious that some changes should be made."

Dr. Conway suspended the attendant responsible for Mrs. Judd's care at the time of her escape, saying the action "is the first step to cleaning house." The loose handling of Mrs. Judd was "not the fault of any one attendant. You have to go higher up than a ward attendant when you blame someone for bad administration. In this case that blame can be put on the unskilled administration which this hospital has been under for many years." The superintendent said Mrs. Judd "has had entirely too many privileges in the past, and has been treated as a private patient. In the future she'll have the same status as other patients." He said she would not have any more opportunities to "make an escape ladder from articles in her room."

Meanwhile, Dr. Conway ordered a hospital shakedown. A half-dozen knives were discovered in the men's ward and a man convicted of murder was working in the butcher shop handling cleavers. Dr. Conway began a study of assignments of other inmates considered dangerous.

In the Sunday *Arizona Republic,* an editorial questioned Mrs. Judd's insanity. It said, "She certainly is smart enough to fool everybody around the Arizona State Hospital for the Insane—and allegedly insane."

On Monday, Dr. Conway took the one step Mrs. Judd had feared most—he ordered Mrs. McKinnell transferred to a separate ward building. Winnie would no longer be close to her mother.

There were ninety-four patients in the darkened television-viewing room. One of them slipped away from her chair, quietly sprung the catch lock on a door to a stairway, and hurried nervously upstairs to the third-floor storeroom. There she put the finishing touches on a forty-eight-foot-long rope improvised from restraining harnesses. She anchored one end of the rope to some bedsprings, removed screws from the wired window, and dropped the rope out into the darkness. Then she eased herself through the window and slid down the rope, falling the last fifteen feet to the ground. The woman got up and ran in the shadows to the fence, now nine feet high since the addition of a one-foot tier of barbed wire. She scaled the fence and disappeared.

Winnie Ruth Judd had escaped again. Number five was an 8:30 P.M. caper. It was Saturday, February 2, 1952.

Four persons reported seeing a black 1948 Hudson sedan with California license plates backed up to the west gate as though it were waiting to make a quick getaway. They said two women were in the car. A search was launched to find the car.

Meanwhile, hospital attendants revealed it would not have been difficult for Mrs. Judd to gain entry to the storeroom. They said she had had periodic access to it to mend clothes for other patients. And she had become very adept at picking locks —someone reported she could open a door "with only a toothbrush."

One attendant said Winnie's winsome ways and sweet disposition had gained her many friends at the asylum. "Mrs. Judd has a tendency to tilt her head to the left when she laughs. She has a very melodious voice, and when she addresses a person, she looks straight at him and smiles. . . . Although Mrs. Judd dyed her hair recently, streaks of gray still show through the coloring. She is actually forty-seven years old but looks much younger—about forty." She said Mrs. Judd kept no jewelry or rings, but habitually wore freshly laundered clothes.

The attendant added, about the recent escapade, that Winnie "has a driving force that will make her do anything that she decides to do."

Few phone calls came in from persons believing they had seen Mrs. Judd. When search efforts failed to turn up the mysterious black sedan, efforts were concentrated on questioning persons who had recently visited her.

Staff psychiatrist Dr. Dean Archer said Winnie recently had boasted, "Someone will help me escape," and Dr. Conway revealed he had received a tip a week earlier that Mrs. Judd was getting outside help to escape. Sheriff "Cal" Boies expressed doubt that Winnie had actually escaped down the rope. The knots were not pulled tight enough to support her weight. "She must have had help getting out some other way."

Dr. Conway concurred: "I think she probably put the rope out of the window to mislead any searcher." The rope was hanging from a south window while the door she would have used faced north.

A Tuesday editorial in the *Arizona Republic* commented, "At the very least her frequent escapes give the state a bad name, for the sensational crime figure is front-page news across the country." The same day, an editorial in the *Phoenix Gazette* said, "Some way should be found to curb these recurrent attacks of wanderlust in inmates like Mrs. Judd."

Helga Swenson, young owner of the Paradise Grill at 4037 North Nineteenth Avenue in Phoenix, revealed that Mrs. Judd had written her the day before her escape. One of Winnie's closest friends, Miss Swenson said, "Mrs. Judd was a wonderful person. She gave me courage to start my personal business on a shoestring and got her friends to help me finance the venture. She was like a mother to me. And I know how Ruth felt. Living for twenty years in that hospital. She lived on hope alone. She waited and waited for freedom for years. She believed persons who promised to help, but always grieved when nothing happened."

This passage was in the letter to Miss Swenson: "Helga, I want you to live a clean life. Have a business, a home, and comfortable happiness. I've introduced you to my friends, good people, and I know you won't fail me. I know you realize how I feel toward you. I feel love. I feel fear for you, but I don't feel jealousy over the good luck you seem to have had lately."

Mrs. Lottie Connors, Winnie's guardian, scotched rumors of a fortune Mrs. Judd had allegedly acquired during her many years at the asylum. "She has less than $500 in her bank account and hasn't touched a cent in more than a year. She can't touch the account unless I co-sign the checks."

At 4 P.M., Tuesday, a woman called the sheriff's office to say that Mrs. Judd would return to the hospital within twenty-four hours if she received assurances by the Maricopa County Grand Jury through the newspapers that she would be given a hearing. An anonymous woman caller also phoned Mrs. M. W. Conway, the hospital superintendent's wife, at 8 o'clock that night. The twenty-four-hour promise was made again.

Mrs. Conway reported the call to the sheriff's office. The next morning, Captain Stanley Kimball appeared before the grand jury. Within hours, a formal statement signed by the acting grand jury foreman was issued to the press: ". . . we will issue a subpoena for her appearance immediately upon her return to the Arizona State Hospital."

The old question was raised whether or not an insane person could testify at any hearing and County Attorney Warren McCarthey explained: "Insane persons were barred from testifying in court up until recently, when courts agreed that some insane persons were competent to testify."

The grand jury's assurance of a hearing appeared that afternoon in the *Phoenix Gazette,* but not until the next morning in the *Arizona Republic.*

At 11 A.M., Thursday, a secret conference was held at the asylum, including Dr. Conway, Sheriff's Deputy Herb Barnes and two unidentified men.

At 10 o'clock Thursday night Mrs. Judd walked up to Dr. Conway's residence and rang the doorbell. When he opened the door, she said, "Here I am." They talked for forty-five minutes before Winnie was returned to the hospital. The conversation was interrupted by a woman telephone caller, asking if Mrs. Judd had arrived safely. Dr. Conway said it was the same person who had talked to his wife on Tuesday night. He denied that the secret conference earlier in the day had anything to do with Winnie's surrender.

Dr. Conway verified the outside help that Mrs. Judd had received and reconstructed the events after his discussion with her. She had gone down the rope, hurried to climb the fence, walked through the asylum graveyard and headed north. In a shack she found a dark cloth coat, and continued to a prearranged meeting with persons who were helping her. Mrs. Judd said she had flashed the storeroom lights twice to signal the car's occupants she was ready to leave. The previous night she had flashed the lights four times to indicate she was not ready.

Mrs. Judd, Dr. Conway said, was moved from place to place —at least four or five times—to avoid capture. He said she returned to the institution "half-heartedly. She came back because the situation was unpleasant where she was staying. She was anxious and frightened."

Dr. Conway quoted her as saying, "I've lost faith in anyone doing anything for me." Her original plans, the superintendent said, had been to flee from Phoenix by airplane, ultimately going to Guatemala. She didn't want to go to Mexico, where she could be quickly extradited and returned to Phoenix.

When Mrs. Judd surrendered, she looked like a different person. "It was a moment before I recognized her—she looked so attractive," Dr. Conway said. "She had her eyebrows plucked, her hairline raised off her forehead, and seemingly wore some type of makeup which erased wrinkles and other signs of age from her features."

Friday morning, newsmen were allowed to submit written questions for Winnie to answer in writing, but not to see her. Some of the questions and answers were:

Question: How long have you been planning this escape?
Answer: I do not plan escapes. It's just that I've been in a sepulcher of living dead for twenty years. As long as I knew I could escape, I pacified myself, but when I read articles of tightening up and putting more nails in the coffin, I got panicky and escaped.

Q.: Did you have help in making your escape?
A.: No.

Q.: Did you offer to surrender if the grand jury would permit you to testify before it?

A.: I wrote the grand jury two months ago asking them to investigate why my case was in politics. Twenty years ago, the Board of Pardons and Paroles came to see me and told me, "If you will keep everything quiet, as soon as public sentiment dies down, we will do likewise for you."

I waited six years—twelve years—three times six years—and then was told by a Rev. Hofmann of the Pardon Board, "Mrs. Judd, the Pardon Board is between two political factions in doing anything for you."

The whole thing was crooked. My husband said he could raise the money, but he would not trust my life to those dirty double-crossing dogs.

Q.: Are you satisfied with the treatment you have had at the state hospital under the present administration?

A.: They treat every patient kindly at this hospital.

Q.: If you did receive help, was it by local people?

A.: No one helped me escape. I cut through a field behind the hospital, through the country up to the Grand Canal. Local people helped me return, not escape, because they knew I was a patient and had hurt myself badly. They cried and cried and said they wanted to see me free legally.

Dr. Conway said he would not let Mrs. Judd testify before the grand jury unless compelled to do so. However, he admitted she would make an excellent witness because of her good memory. He said she remembered every detail of what happened in 1931, and would relish the chance to tell it.

Commenting on the Judd case, Governor Pyle said, "I think I can understand Dr. Conway's attitude. . . . He has a patient in his care, a mental patient, and he dislikes the idea of her being further disturbed when in all probability little, if anything, is to be gained by it. On the other hand, if Mrs. Judd is subpoenaed for a hearing, she will be made available."

A *Phoenix Gazette* editorial Friday afternoon said, "As this editorial is written, Winnie Ruth Judd is back in the Arizona State Hospital. Whether she will still be there by the time the *Phoenix Gazette* reaches the streets is anyone's guess. For the famed murderess apparently can walk in and out of the hospital at will, with cars waiting to take her away and bring her back. She has friends who can take care of her when she is loose, and who can make deals with the hospital authorities before returning her to their care. All of which is strange, considering the brutality of her crime. But many old timers who were here at the time of the trial say that all the facts didn't come out."

The mystery surrounding Thursday's secret conference in Dr. Conway's office was solved Friday when reporters discovered the identities of the two mystery men. They were the Rev. A. R. Hudson and Ralph J. Tucker, a private detective.

Rev. Hudson said he was merely "an old friend of Mrs. Judd's family" and had been working to gain her freedom since she was judged insane in 1933. He said he had affidavits from jurors which, when presented in court, would prove "Mrs. Judd was railroaded to protect other persons." Photostatic copies, he said, might be submitted to the grand jury. "I must have dynamite in my possession—and several persons would like to get their hands on the evidence I now have. Some unknown persons have broken into my home and stolen pictures and other papers which have a direct bearing on the case I'm trying to prove."

Tucker said he had been working on the Judd case more than two months. "I have been retained by private interests who do not want to be named at this time. But I have found some evidence which might make it possible to identify my clients soon." He said some of the court records in the Judd case had disappeared. "And some of the evidence used has been taken, too. I've found a receipt which indicates the death gun is now in the hands of an official who played a large part in the case." He said bullets taken from the death weapon had also been signed for by the same man who took the gun. "But now we know where we can find these bullets, and will make good use of them when the time comes."

Deputy Barnes said he was convinced an underground existed among hospital employees and patients. "And Winnie is their queen. She seems to have a hypnotic influence over some of the patients." Dr. Conway admitted there was a well-organized letter-smuggling system in the hospital, in which both attendants and patients participated.

Governor Pyle and O. D. Miller, chairman of the hospital board of control, both conducted investigations of Mrs. Judd's latest escape. They agreed there was no "arch-conspiracy," but that it was accomplished with the aid of personal sympathizers among patients and friends on the outside. Miller issued a statement saying, "It appears that none of these persons had any ultimate plan in mind other than simply to help her get away from the hospital if that was what she wanted to do."

Late Sunday night, February 10, an unidentified assailant slugged fifty-eight-year-old hospital dietician Don Wood. He had given authorities their first tip after Mrs. Judd's February 2 escape. He was the first person to report having seen a dark sedan parked near hospital grounds shortly before Mrs. Judd was reported missing. Wood said a man entered his apartment on the hospital grounds and struck him "with something besides his fist."

24. THE GIFT OF LIFE

On Monday, Winnie got her chance to tell her story to the Maricopa County Grand Jury in a plea for commutation of her death sentence. A subpoena had actually been issued several days earlier, but kept secret. Dorothy Loofsboro, supervisor of nurses, and Clyde Jackson, chief male attendant, took Mrs. Judd to the county courthouse. Sheriff Boies met them at the rear of the building and escorted them on a circuitous route through the building to a third-floor office to avoid the crowd gathered in the courthouse to see the celebrated "Tiger Woman." Obviously interest in Winnie was reaching a peak again. The bailiff was alerted that Mrs. Judd had arrived, and she was taken into the courtroom at approximately 1 P.M.

Mrs. Judd wore a gold-and-flower print dress. Her hair was tinted red, and she wore makeup and a strong perfume. She emerged fresh and smiling from the grand jury chamber at 5 P.M. The discussions during the four-hour session were kept a closely guarded secret. Reporters heard that other persons might be called before the grand jury later in the week.

The man who prosecuted Mrs. Judd during her murder trial

—Lloyd J. Andrews, then well known throughout Arizona as "Dogie" Andrews, a friendly, easy-going Phoenix attorney—broke a long silence on the case of Winnie Ruth Judd because he was irked at accusations that she had been railroaded to protect other persons.

"I've been listening to this sort of eyewash ever since the conviction, but I find the present outburst pretty hard to stomach. While I admit the right of people to express their opinions, I also feel it is high time a few solid facts were held up for scrutiny. Mrs. Judd killed a woman in cold blood, confessed the crime in her own handwriting, and was found guilty. . . . The rest is a baffling hodge-podge based on rumor, falsehood, and innuendo. . . . The jurors were all deeply religious men who got down on their knees and prayed for guidance before deciding on the verdict."

Andrews shot back a comment on whether or not Mrs. Judd could dismember a body: "People say now that she must have had the help of a skilled surgeon. More baloney. In trying to sever a leg, the person doing it attempted to cut through a thigh bone. Does that sound like the work of a surgeon or of an amateur butcher?

"This thing has been boiling within me for twenty years. It just had to come out. I have no views at all on Mrs. Judd's present mental condition. . . . My current interest in the case is to try to set the record straight. I feel that my own position in the case has long needed to be vindicated. It has seemed to me that if the people knew the facts they would not be so ready to jump to this woman's defense. Mrs. Judd's case was thoroughly reviewed. What else is there to say?"

On February 13, the grand jury voted unanimously to recomment commutation of Mrs. Judd's death penalty to life imprisonment, and resolutions were sent to the Board of Pardons and Paroles and Governor Pyle. At a special session on May 5, the Pardon Board recommended commutation of the death penalty. The final decision now rested with Governor Pyle.

The governor signed commutation papers for Winnie and another patient five days later. "In the case of Mrs. Judd, three superintendents of the state hospital have, since April, 1945, urged that her sentence be commuted on the premise that no patient of such an institution should be denied the opportunity to recover from insanity because of a sentence of death. Mrs. Judd's confinement has placed her in the position of having already served more than twenty years of a life sentence." He went on to say that to execute her at any time in the future would, in effect, be exacting a double penalty for the crime for which she was convicted.

The decision set a precedent. It was the first time in Arizona history that mental hospital inmates had death sentences commuted to life imprisonment while still in the charge of a mental hospital.

Dr. Conway said Mrs. Judd "registered quite a little joy when I informed her of the governor's action. She has promised not to attempt any more escapes."

25. NOT STRONG ENOUGH

AND WINNIE RUTH JUDD didn't attempt any more escapes —for six months, when she took one more little holiday on Thanksgiving night. (It was not until the 1960s that she became notable for her six-and-a-half-year disappearance.)

About 7 P.M. on November 27, 1952, she complained of a headache and backache, suggesting a hot bath might relieve the aches. Wearing a green skirt, green sweater, brown and black saddle oxfords, and carrying a bathrobe over her arm, Mrs. Judd went to her bath. Attendants saw her start running water in a first-floor bathroom tub and close the door. Fifteen minutes later, when nurse Erma Dow opened the door to check on Winnie, she was gone. The wire-mesh screen of the bathroom window was cut.

Dr. Conway maintained that the hospital "was not strong enough" to hold Mrs. Judd. "You can't hold that type of woman in a paper sack."

Within twenty-four hours, three employees in Mrs. Judd's ward had been fired, and a search begun for two former employees believed to have been involved in the escape.

A well-made, but obviously homemade, sign mysteriously appeared at the Twenty-fourth Street and Van Buren asylum. It warned, "Drive Slowly—Inmates Escaping."

And that Saturday afternoon, the *Phoenix Gazette* commented in a strong editorial: "The Winnie Ruth Judd cult probably will applaud Mrs. Judd's escape from the Arizona State Hospital. But the average citizen will begin to wonder whether Mrs. Judd is bigger than the State of Arizona. . . . One conclusion is inescapable. If and when Mrs. Judd is captured . . . the authorities should be told to keep her in the hospital 'or else.' If a dungeon has to be constructed, that should be done. And every effort should be made to find out who is helping the murderess. Ruth Judd and her friends have thumbed their noses at the sovereign State of Arizona long enough."

Late Saturday afternoon, a policeman and detective went to the home of Mrs. Lottie Connors, Mrs. Judd's legal guardian. Under a large pile of clothing in a closet, they found Mrs. Judd.

Discovered, Winnie said, "Why don't you leave me alone. I'm so tired of being locked up—it has been long enough."

She remained calm until Dr. Conway said she was "dangerous and a troublemaker." Tears clouding her eyes, she told reporters, "I don't quarrel with the other patients or the attendants. They've helped me escape. Nurses have hidden me on the grounds until I could get away. Attendants have hidden me in their homes—five of them helped hide me in their homes last time I escaped. Would they do this if I were dangerous? Would they have kept me in their homes? Would some of the best people of Phoenix have entertained me?

"Oh, I've been out a number of times." She explained that before Dr. Conway came to the hospital she had been allowed to leave the hospital for a day at a time on passes: "I've eaten with friends at nice restaurants—places like the Golden Drumstick."

She said all of her privileges had been taken away, following her previous escape, and added a new note: "I want a sanity hearing. . . . All I want to do is get out and get a job and live a normal life." In other words, she now thought that if she were declared sane, she might gain her freedom.

In February, attorney Harold E. Whitney filed a petition for a writ of habeas corpus in the Maricopa County Superior Court seeking Winnie Ruth Judd's release from Arizona State Hospital on grounds that she was being "unlawfully held and detained" by Dr. Conway. It further charged her detention was illegal and in violation of the United States Constitution and statutes and rules of the Superior Court because, "the said Winnie Ruth Judd is not insane within the meaning of Arizona law governing the commitment or detention of persons to and in the State Hospital for the Insane." Filing of the petition was the first step in an effort to gain a sanity hearing. This began three and one-half months of legal shuffling that ended without benefit to Mrs. Judd. The petition was dismissed, and the sanity hearing was not held.

At the State Hospital, the round-the-clock watch continued in an effort to keep Winnie put. A special security room with the most effective escape deterrents available was being equipped for the "Tiger Woman." Before a maximum security room could be made ready, she was kept in a cell room with specially constructed bars. Matrons accompanied her at all times. She was allowed out of her room twice a day to care for a fishpond and a bed of flowers. Most of the time in her room she spent on needlework and reading.

In early November, 1953, Mrs. Judd was allowed to attend funeral services for her mother, Mrs. Carrie McKinnell, eighty-seven. In mid-November, she was treated to a day at the State Fair in Phoenix, going unrecognized and ignored by the fair crowd.

During a brief interview a month later Winnie said, "I'm so low right now I'm not even interested in helping myself. . . ." But she gradually regained her privileges during the next few years under the administration of hospital Superintendent Dr. Samuel Wick. By late 1956, she was serving as a hospital attendant, had cooking privileges and walked unattended between buildings. Dr. Wick said she was always under observation.

In December, 1956, legal action by Phoenix attorney Arthur Mackenzie Johnson attempted to gain a judgment of sanity, then parole to the free world. Johnson said he had been hired by "the many friends of Mrs. Judd," who had obtained for her a job as a helper in a South American leper colony. When Johnson asked the chairman of the Board of Pardons and Paroles to bring Mrs. Judd's case before the board, he was told, "It would be a waste of time."

Winnie Ruth Judd again marked time until December, 1958, when her brother, Jason, made a personal request to the Pardon Board. He asked that his sister be released and her sentence commuted to time served. The chairman, this time in a letter sent to Jason, said the board had rejected the request on the ground that its jurisdiction had ceased when the "Tiger Woman" was declared insane in 1933. Jason's appeal to the Arizona attorney general brought no results.

In May, 1959, doctors at the asylum said they believed Winnie had given up her fight for freedom, and because of this resigned attitude, her mental condition was beginning to improve. They declared that she had become "especially talented" in painting and ceramics, caused no trouble and agreeably complied with hospital regulations.

26. MASQUERADE

WINNIE RUTH JUDD left the quiet life, when on Monday night, October 8, 1962, she proved for the seventh and final time that the Arizona State Hospital could not hold her. This time the outcome was far different than before. Nobody saw Winnie again for years. Dr. Wick said, "A door apparently was accidentally left open," and that nobody had plotted her escape beforehand. James McNulty, chairman of the hospital board, said, "We feel she has contributed far beyond the average patient," and that she "might be staying with friends in the Phoenix area."

The escape was reported casually, police Patrolman Everett Ford dispatched to the asylum to take a "missing person report." Attendants told him Mrs. Judd had recently said she wanted to "leave the hospital so she could clear up some matters." They did not know what the "matters" were. Mrs. Judd, now fifty-seven years old, was described as not dangerous.

Her escape brought a "so-what" response from authorities. Sheriff Boies and Assistant Police Chief Charles Hodges said their agencies would not assign special details to search for the "Tiger Woman."

Such comments as these were common:

A Superior Court judge: "I hope she makes good her escape this time."

A police sergeant: "If she had been sent to jail at Arizona State Prison for life, she'd be out now. So what difference does it make if she's free now?"

A police radio dispatcher: "People just don't seem to care about whether she gets out or not. And you can say I'm just about in the same boat."

A police jail matron: "Why don't you leave that poor woman alone? I and a lot of other people think she's already paid her debt to society but none of us has guts enough to do anything about it."

Dr. Wick refused to make a public statement about Winnie's sanity. Asked if it were true he had privately told members of the hospital board she was sane, he said, "I don't recall saying that. My memory blanks out on that." He begged off on any discussion of the Judd case, saying that too much attention was being paid to what should have long been forgotten.

Few reports came in from persons claiming to have seen Mrs. Judd. But Minnesota Senator Homer Carr told police he had seen her at the Minneapolis–St. Paul International Airport. "If that isn't her, she must have a double." It wasn't her.

In Los Angeles, Attorney Richard Cantillon, who had helped arrange Mrs. Judd's surrender in 1931, sent an open letter to Winnie through the press. "Friends have retained me to represent your legal interests [and] . . . intend to reopen your case in the courts. They ask that you follow instructions. Please do."

A week after her escape, Mrs. Judd's clothing was found on the roof of a shed four blocks north of the State Hospital, but no other clues could be found. No one stepped forward with information.

During the next three months, she was reported seen in New Mexico, Reno and Santa Barbara.

In February, 1963, the nation was reminded of her latest escape when an entertainer gave her a toast on the Jack Benny television show.

Wherever Winnie Ruth Judd had gone, she had left a cold trail.

Susan Leigh Clark lived the life of student and companion to a blind woman in a town in central California. She often rode the bus downtown to shop, and to attend a school where she studied practical nursing. Occasionally, she went to the nearby military cemetery to visit her husband's grave.

In the fall of 1963, she took a job as housekeeper for Mrs. Virgil A. Nesbit, an elderly lady of the town. Susan ran the house. She cooked, cleaned, shopped and cared for Mrs. Nesbit. For her services, she received room, board and $400 a month. She earned a few dollars extra as a babysitter for well-to-do families in the neighborhood.

Susan loved children. Over many months she built up a cache of things she hoped to take with her someday to Paraguay. She dreamed of working with children whose parents lived apart from them in a leper colony. Susan had a considerable assortment of bright greeting cards ready to be cut and pasted. She carefully collected ceramic molds, packing them neatly for later use in teaching craft classes. And she kept her talent for hair-styling at a professional level, hoping to pass this talent on to girls and young women in Paraguay.

Everybody seemed to like Susan Clark. Mrs. Nesbit's son, Harold, and her daughter, Mrs. Barry Wyckoff, appreciated the loving care with which Susan attended their mother. She was employed by Mrs. Nesbit for over four years until the elderly matron succumbed to a heart attack. The family retained Susan after Mrs. Nesbit died. When the estate was finally settled eighteen months later, in mid-June, 1969, Susan Clark had been remembered by a bequest of $10,000. Dr. and Mrs. Barry Wyckoff provided her a cottage at their home. She became their housekeeper.

A very important event happened earlier that year. In late April, Mrs. Florence Copeland, the forty-seven-year-old wife of a psychiatrist in a nearby suburb, was bludgeoned to death on the patio of her home. It was reported that a car seen near the murder site was found to be registered to Susan Clark and that subsequent investigation showed another person drove the car. When the Contra Costa County Sheriff's Detective-Sergeant David Gardella questioned Susan Clark, he was reported to find "something fishy" in her story. Some of the things she said bothered him. He started the laborious task of fitting together pieces of an odd puzzle. A solution was reportedly passed to him from Sergeant Joe Walsh, who, in mid-June received a tip from a person whose identity officials allowed to remain anonymous. Fingerprints were checked on the car. On June 26, Sergeant Walsh telephoned Dan Roth, chief criminal deputy to Maricopa County Attorney Moise Berger in Phoenix. He wanted information about Winnie Ruth Judd.

Later in the day, Sergeant Walsh was contacted by reporters. He refused to talk to them. Arizona State Hospital Superintendent Dr. Willis Bower said he had been contacted by Walsh. He said he had received crank calls about Mrs. Judd, "but this one isn't a hoax, that we know. This is a bona fide investigation by a police agency."

The state attorney general's office and the county attorney's office argued as to which had authority in the case. There was no outstanding warrant for her arrest.

Lieutenant Robert Sang of the Contra Costa County sheriff's office in Martinez, California, criticized Maricopa County officials for releasing information about this query to the press. "Someone there [Phoenix] blew the whole thing out of proportion. She has not been located here. . . . There had been several rumors in the past that Mrs. Judd had been seen in the area. We just made a routine inquiry to Phoenix to see if there was a warrant for her arrest in case she should be located."

The next day, Friday, June 27, 1969, Susan Clark was approached by deputies as she walked two poodles near the Wyckoff residence. She was wearing a blue dress. After lengthy conversation, she agreed to accompany the deputies to the sheriff's office, when advised she could go voluntarily or be arrested. As Lieutenant Sang later recalled, "She looked like a sweet little old lady with a slight limp. Very much like somebody's mother, chubby and pleasant looking."

At the Contra Costa County sheriff's office, Susan Clark's fingerprints were taken. They matched prints taken from her car, which had previously been compared with the fingerprints of Winnie Ruth Judd. She was placed under arrest and booked into the county jail as a fugitive. Winnie clung to her identity of Susan Clark, domestic, and she asked that a San Francisco attorney, Melvin Belli, be contacted for her defense.

In Phoenix, Maricopa County Attorney Berger announced he would ask Governor Jack Williams and State Attorney General Gary Nelson to start extradition proceedings. On Saturday, Contra Costa County Sheriff Walter Young said his prisoner would be returned to Arizona.

Also on Saturday, the prisoner conferred in her cell with Belli. He said he would represent Winnie Ruth Judd "or whoever she is" at the extradition hearing.

Meanwhile, attorney Eric Redmond, who had lived across the street from Mrs. Nesbit, said Mrs. Judd was "a harmless, sweet, likable, motherly woman" who was "clearly rehabilitated." As Susan Clark, she had baby-sat for Redmond's two-year-old daughter. Although not a criminal lawyer, Redmond said he would do what he could to help Mrs. Judd. "Looking back, maybe you could see something a little peculiar, but she really was almost too good to be true. She is clearly rehabilitated by any standards. We have no doubt about her ability to take care of our child."

Another neighbor of Mrs. Nesbit's, Dr. Herbert Allison, said, "We all liked her very much. When Mrs. Nesbit had a stroke about two years ago, Mrs. Clark took the very best care of her."

Dr. Allison's cook, Amy Bates, said, "I used to ride around with her in the car. You mean she's a murderer?"

And Harold Nesbit said, "She was a wonderful friend and a very good housekeeper. I just can't believe this."

Winnie Ruth Judd was arraigned Monday morning before Mount Diablo Municipal Court Judge Sam W. Hall. He denied a plea by Belli that Mrs. Judd be released on her own recognizance since she had been a "responsible citizen" in the community for six years. Belli did not contest his client's arraignment for escape from Arizona State Hospital; however, he said, "We do not acknowledge that she is either of the persons charged [Mrs. Judd or Susan Clark]." Judge Hall placed the fugitive under $125,000 bond, and set July 14 as date for a preliminary hearing.

Chaplain Paul Strickland of the Arizona State Hospital confirmed a report that a friend of Mrs. Judd had received Christmas cards from her since her seventh escape in 1962. He said the cards had been postmarked North Pole, U.S.A., and gave no clue as to her whereabouts. Postal officials said it was common practice to send bundles of cards to certain towns where they were then individually postmarked.

California authorities admitted Monday that Mrs. Judd's possible involvement in the Copeland murder case was still being investigated. Asked if she was a suspect, Lieutenant Sang said, "We are not overlooking the possibility."

Back in Phoenix, County Attorney Berger prepared extradition papers for Mrs. Judd's return to Arizona, and sent them to Governor Williams for his signature.

Belli countered from California with the reply he would "demand a hearing" before Governor Ronald Reagan to fight extradition. While agreeing that fingerprints don't lie, Belli would not concede that his client was really Mrs. Judd. He blasted the taking of fingerprints as a system stripping the individual of protection. He protested that eventually the police could "change heads and take a leg off" to prove a person's identity.

He described his client as a wonderful person: "Everybody likes her." He said he didn't know what had happened in Phoenix in 1931, whether the convicted murderess had been insane, or whether the motive might have been sexual jealousy or self-defense. But Belli said she "has got a hell of a story to tell now. I'm trying to peddle it for her." He reportedly had contacted a national magazine, but the publication was undergoing a format change and decided against doing the story. The California attorney said if Arizona decided not to press for extradition, "Then we would just leave her out here and she could come over and be my housekeeper."

On Thursday, July 3, Superior Court Judge Roger Strand issued from Phoenix a bench warrant for Mrs. Judd's arrest. The warrant charged she had escaped from custody of the superintendent of the Arizona State Prison while confined in the Arizona State Hospital. It was forwarded to California authorities.

During a July 5 long-distance telephone interview with Tucson radio station KTKT, Belli said he hoped Arizona's chief executive wouldn't want his client back if she was proven to be Mrs. Judd. But he stated, "I think we all know that she is Mrs. Judd." He quoted her as having told him, "If you talk to anyone in Arizona, tell them, 'I didn't leave because I didn't like them. I just didn't like the place they locked me in.'"

On July 9, Governor Williams made formal request to Governor Reagan for extradition of Mrs. Judd. He asked Reagan to notify Maricopa County Sheriff John Mummert if and when the request was granted. But two days later, Reagan, on advice of California Attorney General Thomas Lynch, rejected the request for "legal and technical" reasons. The extradition papers were returned to Arizona for modification. A spokesman for Reagan would say only that the papers were found to be "not in order." County Attorney Berger drew the assignment of getting the papers in order for resubmission.

The papers had not been resubmitted by Monday, July 14, when "Susan Clark" faced Judge Hall during the preliminary hearing to determine her true identity. This was done quickly. She told the Judge, "Yes, I'm Ruth Judd, known to my friends as Susan Clark. My legal signature was Ruth M. [Marian] Judd. They called me Winnie, but it was not my legal name."

Mrs. Judd asked to be allowed to return voluntarily to Arizona to seek a judgment of sanity and a pardon. She said she wanted to be legally free to secure a passport for travel to

Paraguay. Judge Hall denied the plea, ordering her held without bail pending extradition. Deputy District Attorney John Hatzenbulher explained that Maricopa County authorities had requested this action. The judge continued the hearing until August 4 to allow time for extradition papers to be amended and returned to California. Attorney Belli said he would still press for a hearing before Governor Reagan when extradition papers were received.

The "Tiger Woman" spoke confidently during a press conference after the hearing. "I feel I have paid my debt to society. If I could go to the leper colony, I could take care of the children; I could do their hair, and I could be a medical assistant." She said "many people" knew her identity during her six and a half years as Susan Clark. Some of them, she said, had telephoned to ask about making a movie of her life.

Mrs. Judd, as she had often done during nearly four decades as Arizona's most celebrated "murderess," told a story of self-defense. "I haven't talked about it for years, and it is hard to live in the past when you have been concentrating on living in the future." She hinted that a doctor, now dead, had helped her dismember Hedvig Samuelson's body.

Attorney Belli, nodding toward Winnie, said, "She sits here as a human being exemplar." He asserted that if there was such a thing as complete rehabilitation, "Mrs. Judd represents that."

Nobody at the press conference made reports concerning the Copeland murder or speculated on why "Susan Clark's" car had been seen near the Copeland residence. The license number was later attributed to a person who was among the doctor's list of patients. However, the doctor subsequently denied that he kept a record of such numbers. The murder was never solved, and police later reported Mrs. Judd had no connection with it.

During the next two weeks in Phoenix, both legal and State Hospital officials remained tight-lipped about the case of Winnie Ruth Judd. County Attorney Berger declined to go into detail but said one of the reasons why the first extradition papers were returned was failure to include the original murder trial verdict and sentence. State Hospital Administrative Assistant Tom Warnken said Superintendent Dr. Willis Bower did not want to comment on the case for fear his remarks would be "interpreted or misinterpreted." Dr. Bower, who took over direction of the asylum after Mrs. Judd's seventh escape, later said, "I don't know Winnie Ruth Judd, and if I did I wouldn't talk about her." But he said the hospital would re-examine a person who had been absent from the institution without authorization, and if the person was found sane, he would be released. "Obviously, if there is a hold on a patient, then that detainer is honored and we hold the person until the proper authority arrives." In Mrs. Judd's case, if she were to be ruled sane, she would be transferred to the State Prison at Florence.

A "man-on-the-street" type series of news interviews in the *Phoenix Gazette* indicated women were more sympathetic than men toward Mrs. Judd. Typical of the comments made by women were these:

A Phoenix motel manager: "She might as well be let go now. She's got all her stuff prepared to go to Paraguay. She has paid for her crime. Let her do some good in the world."

A housewife: "Mrs. Judd has proven herself to be a respon-sible citizen. I feel she should be able to live the rest of her life as a good citizen."

Most of the men interviewed said they believed Mrs. Judd should be returned to Arizona to serve out her sentence. The harshest comments were made by a nineteen-year-old college student: "I think she should be subjected to capital punish-ment. I'm not a sadist, but if she is put up again she is liable to get loose again, and no telling what she will do." However, a few of the men interviewed were impressed by Mrs. Judd's reported good behavior during her lengthy freedom in Cal-ifornia. A service station operator said: "I think she's all right. If she can travel and do the things she's done in Cali-fornia since her escape, I guess she's providing for herself. Peo-ple just don't provide for themselves unless they are sane."

On July 30, 1969, Acting Governor Wesley Bolin signed Ari-zona's revised extradition request for Mrs. Judd's return from

California. The request included a complete file on her case in compliance with a new California extradition law. Bolin, secretary of state, signed the papers for Governor Jack Williams, who was attending the Western Governors Conference in Seattle.

Three days later, Governor Reagan stepped into the case, scheduling an extradition hearing for his office on Friday, August 8. This action resulted in the removal from Judge Hall's agenda a hearing previously scheduled for his court on August 4.

Before Reagan could hear the extradition proceedings, a *Phoenix Gazette* editorial revealed a meeting between then Maricopa County Attorney Dick Harless and J. R. McFadden, former county sheriff, that had taken place in 1939. According to the editorial, McFadden told Harless that Mrs. Judd had become frantic after the slayings. She walked a mile to her apartment, called a man friend at a speakeasy and took him to the 2929 North Second Street duplex. The man friend told Winnie he would take care of the bodies with help from a doctor. McFadden also told Harless that he had learned a considerable amount of money had been raised by friends of the three women involved to provide a murder trial defense for Winnie. There was a condition attached to the money—that Mrs. Judd would reveal no names. Harless and an investigator checked McFadden's story with Winnie at the State Hospital, in 1939. She verified what the former sheriff had said. McFadden, although claiming large sums of money had been involved in the case, had received none himself and died two years later a pauper. A collection was taken to pay for his funeral.

On the eve of the hearing in Reagan's office, *Dragnet* was bumped from Phoenix TV station KTAR for airing of an exclusive interview with Mrs. Judd. The interview had been filmed earlier in the Contra Costa County courthouse in Martinez, with attorney Belli sitting in on a three-way chat, including newsman Joe Patrick. Mrs. Judd again said she had killed in self-defense, and gave the name of a doctor who had dismembered Miss Samuelson's body as a Dr. Brown of Phoenix. Belli said that if his efforts to halt the extradition failed, he would move to have her declared sane and her sentence "commuted to time served . . . for I don't know anyone in the West who has served more time for murder than Mrs. Judd."

Herbert Ellingwood, Governor Reagan's legal affairs secretary, presided over the hearing in the governor's Sacramento office. Reagan was not present during the hour-long proceedings.

Belli told Ellingwood, "This woman who stands before you now has been rehabilitated as much as any woman can be." He said if she were not, "rehabilitation is a mockery. . . . This woman hasn't had an official adjudication of her sanity. The only instance of aberrancy in her whole life was that horrible crime. She's done three times more time than she should have done." He said the usual time served on a life sentence in Arizona and California "is seven to ten years."

Harold Nesbit and Mrs. Barry Wyckoff said Susan Clark had given their mother "kind loving care." They said they didn't think she was a menace to society.

Mrs. Judd told about her work as a housekeeper and student of practical nursing. "I want to stay, I love it here. . . . When you've spent all that time in a mental hospital, you're just glad to have a home and peace and quiet. . . . I escaped trying to get something done in my case. Every time the doctors tried to get a sanity hearing, they were fired. I had to prove myself sane.

"I never tried to hurt anybody who threatened me." She said a man who knew of her past "blackmailed me . . . that's where most of the money [her $400 salary] went. He wanted to sell me for a movie; he wanted to sell me to Truman Capote for a book."

At the close of the hearing, Ellingwood said, "I'll make my recommendation to the governor within a couple of days." He indicated Reagan would make his decision on extradition "within ten days."

Announcement of Reagan's decision was made by his press office August 14, six days later. In a prepared statement, he said, "After a thorough evaluation of all legal and factual matters in this case, it is my conclusion that there is no basis on which to refuse to honor a requisition of the governor of Arizona." He said there were "certain legal defenses to extradition, none of which have been raised in this case."

Citing Belli's remarks that Mrs. Judd had been rehabilitated, Reagan said, "However, the proper forum in which to consider matters such as Mrs. Judd's rehabilitation, her mental condition and questions of parole is Arizona, the state in which the crime was committed and where Mrs. Judd was convicted and sentenced."

On Monday, August 18, 1969, Winnie Ruth Judd was flown back to Phoenix. Accompanied by Sheriff's Deputy Ralph McMillen and his wife, Mrs. Judd reached Sky Harbor Airport in the late afternoon.

"Susan Clark" had come home.

27. THE GOVERNOR'S DECISION

EARLIER ON MONDAY, Larry Debus announced he would take over Winnie's fight for freedom upon her return to Arizona. The thirty-two-year-old lawyer, who had quit his post as a deputy Maricopa County attorney in June, said he would work on the Judd case in association with Melvin Belli. The San Francisco attorney had previously outlined defense strategy. He said the goal was to have Mrs. Judd declared sane, sent to the State Prison, and then work from Governor Jack Williams down to the Board of Pardons and Paroles in an effort to gain her freedom.

Even before Mrs. Judd's plane landed in Phoenix, Maricopa County Superior Court Judge Howard V. Peterson signed a writ of habeas corpus presented by Debus, and set 9 A.M., Wednesday, as the time of a hearing. The purpose of the hearing would be to discuss and determine who had the legal right to hold Winnie. Debus and his law partner, Jerry Busby, served Sheriff's Deputy McMillen with the writ as he deplaned with the "Tiger Woman."

Mrs. Judd, wearing a violet dress with a short-sleeve bolero of the same color, was hurried into a waiting car and taken to the county jail. Although her cheeks were well rouged and her auburn hair fluffed around her face, she looked tired and worried.

On Tuesday, a spokesman for Winnie's defense said a writ of habeas corpus would be sought against State Hospital Superintendent Dr. Willis Bower if Mrs. Judd were readmitted to the asylum. Obtaining a sanity hearing would be the purpose of this writ. In discussing efforts to gain freedom for Winnie, the spokesman said, ". . . we are not going to be able to do it without favorable publicity."

During an interview Tuesday in the county jail with an *Arizona Republic* reporter, Winnie Ruth Judd talked about "Susan Clark":

"I was somebody else and I tried to forget the past. In this atmosphere, with all the love I had, I was happy for the first time in my life. These people loved me. I was not insane Winnie from the insane hospital. I was Susan Clark and I was loved. I want to go back and work for Dr. and Mrs. Wyckoff. I've had six years of love and happiness. I have been in heaven. From my window, in the beautiful bedroom of the Wyckoffs' home, I could see the bridges and all the lights of the town."

She said she had been in California only one day after her last escape when she had to ride a bus downtown. "And do you know what, I got off that bus facing an attendant from the Arizona State Hospital. 'Ruth,' he said, and I just looked mean at him and he looked away, thinking he had made a mistake.

"I wasn't afraid of the police. In fact, I was walking down the street when a small boy—about two years old—was almost hit by a bus. I ran out and picked him up and I spent all that morning riding about with a policeman looking for the boy's mother.

"When I went to work for Mrs. Nesbit, I couldn't even go to the grocery store. I had to learn. I ran the house and I had to take care of the money. Oh, I hadn't cooked in twenty-nine years, but Mrs. Nesbit wanted me to cook. So I went to bed with my cookbooks every night. I was determined to make good."

Her biggest scare came when a ruby ring belonging to Mrs. Nesbit disappeared. "Oh, I was so scared. The ring was insured and the insurance investigators would be all over me because I was responsible for everything in the house." The ring was found in a repair shop.

Winnie showed signs of bitterness when she spoke of a niece's husband. He had driven her from Phoenix to California following her seventh escape, she said, and had received money from her since. "He just used me." She would not name the man for fear of hurting her niece.

That day Winnie was examined by Dr. Eugene Almer, a Phoenix psychiatrist, and then transferred from the county jail to Arizona State Hospital. The next morning Judge Peterson dismissed the writ and Mrs. Judd was placed in custody of the hospital. Debus said he and his client were "tickled pink" over her early transfer to the hospital: "Mrs. Judd has no business being confined behind bars," and the transfer had put her "among friends." Another writ would not be filed against Dr. Bower unless Mrs. Judd were to be held in the asylum as insane.

The hospital population had dropped from about "2,000 inmates" to "1,079 patients" since Mrs. Judd left there in 1962. "She left an insane asylum. She returns to a hospital," according to an administrative assistant. She was being kept in a private "seclusion room," not in the maximum security ward building. Mrs. Judd was to undergo psychiatric "assessment and evaluation" to determine if she "does or does not need hospitalization."

In the Friday morning, August 22, *Arizona Republic*, an editorial about the case of Winnie Ruth Judd concluded, "The flamboyant San Francisco lawyer, Melvin Belli, can be expected to put on a great show if he appears before the Arizona Board of Pardons and Paroles in behalf of Mrs. Judd. Not because of his histrionics, but because enough is enough. We believe Arizona will be serving the joint causes of justice and mercy if it turns Winnie Ruth Judd loose to live the rest of her life as a functioning member of society."

By noon a hospital guard and a nurse had escorted Mrs. Judd to the Arizona State Prison after Dr. Bower announced that examination revealed no cause for her to be kept in the mental institution.

Mrs. Judd carried with her a dozen red and white carnations, sent to her by a friend who had been a patient of Dr. Judd's more than forty years earlier. Winnie clutched the card that accompanied the flowers: "Keep your courage up!"

"I will. I will," she said.

The "Tiger Woman" was assigned No. 8811, the same identification she had worn at the prison in 1932 and 1933, which was the oldest worn by any inmate there. At this time, the latest number in the prison's chronological numbering system was 29466. Winnie's number had already been stenciled in black on the right pocket and on the back of a simple blue-and-white checked knee-length dress that she wore during an interview at the prison. She was still somewhat apprehensive. "Oh, I know that my attorneys want to strike while the iron's hot. But I'm afraid that there'll be more pitfalls.

"But everything seems to be going all right now. I expected to stay at the hospital for one to three months under examination before they sent me here. I was really surprised. Nobody could have treated me better than those people at the hospital."

Mrs. Judd indicated she didn't want to dwell on the past. "You know it's an unhealthy mind that lives in the past. I have to look to the future."

Arizona Attorney General Gary Nelson immediately ruled that Mrs. Judd must get credit for the twenty-nine and one-half years spent in the State Hospital as time served in prison. The average time in prison for life-termers was eight to ten years. Not counting escape time, Mrs. Judd had actually spent twenty-nine years, 154 days in the asylum. Asked if the board might ignore his opinion, Nelson said, "They can read the law as well as I can. It obviously applies exactly to Mrs. Judd."

The law Nelson referred to was ARS 31-224: "When it appears that the prisoner has sufficiently recovered that he may be returned to the prison without further risk, he shall be returned to serve the unexpired term, and the period he was confined in the State Hospital shall be counted as though served in prison."

The next day Arizona legal authorities ruled out criminal prosecution of Winnie Ruth Judd for her seven asylum escapes. Escaping from prison had long been defined as a crime in Arizona, but another long-standing law stated that the insane were incapable of crimes. So, Winnie's escapes were not considered crimes.

Attorney Debus formally filed a petition to the Pardon Board on September 3, 1969, asking that Mrs. Judd's sentence be commuted to time served, indicating that she would return to California to live and work for Dr. and Mrs. Barry Wyckoff. The hearing was scheduled for October 27.

Attorneys Belli and Debus represented Mrs. Judd at the hearing before the three board members—Chairman Keith Edwards of Sun City, Walter Michael of Phoenix and Abe Cruz of Tucson.

"I really think God feels I have suffered long enough," Winnie told the board. She was continually comforted by Belli during questioning, which dwelt at length on the possibility Winnie might benefit financially from publishing her story. Edwards and Michael repeatedly questioned her about rumors that the story of her life was to be published or exploited in some way. At one point Michael declared, "I want to be sure crime doesn't pay."

"I personally have no intention to do any writing," Mrs. Judd said.

"Would you waive all remuneration?"

"Yes. I don't want money. I just want peace," she replied, obviously upset by this line of questioning.

Noticing her discomfort, Cruz politely said, "Please calm down. It is not my intention to upset you."

Winnie affirmed that a nephew had driven her to California after her last escape in 1962. She said he "pressured me into buying a car and giving him money. He used me as a pawn, telling me he could turn me in." She denied reports that a check by California police of a car registered to "Susan Clark" led to her capture. Mrs. Judd said her identity was revealed by the nephew, since she had run out of money and could no longer provide him with loans he demanded.

In a shaking voice, Mrs. Judd said, "I have no hatred against anyone. I have tried to help everyone in the hospital and on the outside. I tried to do everything that was right."

Talking about the Wyckoffs' home in California, Winnie said, "They have a little ranch. It is nine miles from the bus station. There are lots of dogs and cats and birds. And if I go, I'd be very happy if you could come to see me someday."

The Wyckoffs were among seven witnesses testifying that Mrs. Judd was "fully rehabilitated." A Phoenix physician testified that she "is not in the best of health," citing old tuberculosis scars, a thyroid growth, hypertension and a family history of cardiovascular disease as supporting reasons.

Belli briefly addressed the board following questioning of witnesses by Debus. "She has served more time than any woman in the western United States for any crime." He asked that Mrs. Judd be returned to California, and concluded, "There is no opposition to that request. She now is sane, has a job and an exemplary history there."

Four days later—on Halloween—Board Chairman Keith Edwards released a six-page statement with reasons why Mrs. Judd's application for commutation of her life sentence had been denied. It was a two-to-one decision, Edwards and Michael voting against freedom for Mrs. Judd, Cruz favoring freedom.

The lengthy statement indicated Edwards and Michael had strong doubts about Mrs. Judd's rehabilitation. "If, as the record shows, she was insane during her time as a fugitive and alleged rehabilitation, then she would not be capable of rehabilitation. On the other hand, if she was actually sane, then she was a fugitive from justice and in violation of the criminal laws of this state and was therefore not subject to rehabilitation."

The report said Mrs. Judd's explanation of how her car came to be near the house in the Copeland murder case in California —the investigation of which supposedly led to "Susan Clark's" capture—was "vague and unsatisfactory." An issue was made of this point despite the fact that Winnie had been absolved by California authorities of any possible guilt in connection with that murder, which had remained unsolved.

Continuing, the report said Mrs. Judd "completely escaped the verdict of the jury and the penalty prescribed by it, whether by subterfuge or providence. . . .

"From the standpoint of punishment and incarceration, Mrs. Judd has been very fortunate indeed. To observe the application of punishment in this case from beginning to end, one wonders if it could not be singled out as the case more disposed to induce and encourage crime, rather than act as a preventative."

The statement lashed out at asserted lack of emotion by Winnie over the death of Mrs. LeRoi. "The record does not disclose, nor at any time during the hearing did Mrs. Judd show any evidence of remorse for the brutal murder of her girlfriend, Agnes Anne LeRoi. . . . If, as is claimed by Mrs. Judd, she has suffered enough punishment for this brutal crime, still, she has at least been privileged to live to suffer it, while her innocent victim, whom we must assume had as great a desire to live as her murderer, and certainly as much right, lies cold in death."

Concluding, the report said, "The board is unable, after thorough search of the record, to find any recommendation of mercy from any judge, juror or prosecutor involved in the trial of this case."

Attorney Debus appeared stunned by the decision. "We hadn't anticipated this. There is a lot more here than meets the eye." He suggested that Mrs. Judd "is entitled perhaps to some sort of public disclosure of circumstances that brought the board to this conclusion."

Belli was less kind. Contacted at his office in San Francisco, he said the decision "was a shock to me, just as it must have been to all of Arizona. I think the board was born too late. They should have been born at the time of the Spanish Inquisition and the Star Chamber period."

He said the action was "the most Victorian thing I've ever seen in my lifetime—utterly unbelievable. There was uncontradictory testimony that Mrs. Judd has a cardiac condition, there was no opposition, nor no adverse claim by the state, and she was involved in no problem [referring to the Copeland murder] in California."

Belli said legal action might be taken against the board, possibly in the federal District Court or in the Arizona Supreme Court. "For one thing, her parole hearing was opened with prayer. That's unconstitutional, and I think I'm as religious as the next man. I'm going right into court on it." This assertion understandably puzzled parole officials, for when Belli spoke at the hearing, he had complimented the board, saying, "I am impressed that you open your meetings with a prayer."

Several days later, on November 5, Belli was still flaming. Alluding to Parole Board members Edwards and Michael, he said, "Two of those board members must be sick. There is something very sinister in this . . . either someone or something is being protected." He said he would petition the court to have them undergo psychiatric examination. Expressing wonder that Governor Jack Williams would let them continue to serve on the board, Belli added, "I am utterly and completely furious about this. It is one of the blackest marks on your state." Belli later wrote in a letter, "I'd like to borrow your whole Parole Board for my next Halloween party."

Meanwhile, Abe Cruz issued a minority statement saying he did not subscribe to the Parole Board statement. Edwards, in defending the Parole Board statement, which one newspaper columnist termed "medieval, frontier-style phraseology," said phone calls and letters coming to his office favored the decision, seven-to-one. Scoffing at defense charges, Edwards said, "I can't see anything on the writing [in the statement] that could be questioned."

Governor Williams said he planned no intervention in the case of Winnie Ruth Judd. Commenting on mail pouring in daily, Williams said out-of-state mail overwhelmingly favored Mrs. Judd's release, while mail from Arizonans was "about 50-50."

On December 4, 1969, Attorneys Belli and Debus filed a suit in Maricopa County Superior Court asking that the board be forced to recommend that Mrs. Judd's life sentence be commuted. The suit charged that the board's action "was an arbitrary and capricious abuse of discretion for the reason that no scintilla of evidence was before the board upon which it could base the finding of facts and conclusion. . . ."

For seven months, the issue bounced around in the Arizona courts. State Attorney General Gary Nelson fought the suit, contending that probation and parole are matters of grace, not of right. Therefore, courts are without authority to force favorable Parole Board action as a right. Nelson argued that the board's decision was final. "It's their decision, whether people agree with it or not." Ultimately, the Arizona Supreme Court upheld a lower court ruling that no court could substitute its opinion for that given by the board.

Winnie Ruth Judd stayed in prison. Her legal counsel did not seek a second commutation hearing before the board during the remainder of 1970, though such requests could be made six months after the first hearing. Debus later explained that a hearing was not requested then because he wanted the board to realize Mrs. Judd could live inside—as well as outside—the prison walls as a responsible person.

Some observers speculated that the delay was due to the gubernatorial race between Governor Jack Williams and challenger Raul Castro. Williams won and began his new term in office in January, 1971.

On January 8, Walter Michael, now chairman of the Pardon Board, confirmed that there had been a request for another commutation hearing, and Tuesday, February 16, was set as the date.

Mrs. Judd, now sixty-six, her hair having gone from auburn to gray since her 1969 confinement in the State Prison, made an impassioned plea for freedom before familiar faces—Michael, Edwards and Cruz. She was teary-eyed throughout most of the ninety-minute hearing, but lost her composure only once, near the end of proceedings. She said she felt ill and left with a matron for a few minutes after commenting, "I don't want to throw up in here."

Debus called upon Dr. Herbert L. Collier, clinical psychologist at St. Joseph's Hospital in Phoenix; and Dr. Otto L. Bendheim, the psychiatrist in charge of Winnie's case from 1938 to 1942 at the State Hospital.

Dr. Collier reported findings of a December 29, 1970, examination of Mrs. Judd. "She is entirely within the normal range, except for the area dealing with depression." He attributed this to her imprisonment. "She showed a tremendous need to do good. . . . It seems she is very tuned in to the needs of other people."

Dr. Bendheim supported Dr. Collier's views, adding that Mrs. Judd showed no trace during a January 19 examination of the psychosis that had been diagnosed forty years earlier.

Mrs. Judd told the board, "I want you to know I would never do anything in my life you would be sorry for," and again testified she had no desire to write her story or have anyone else write it.

Board members were admittedly worried about any hold Melvin Belli might have over Mrs. Judd in the way of a contract which would give the attorney the right to publish her story. She said there was no contract, and Debus affirmed that he was now Mrs. Judd's only attorney. He said friends and relatives had paid his client's legal fees, and if such a contract existed, Mrs. Judd had been legally insane until her 1969 transfer from the State Hospital to the State Prison. Any contract negotiated before that would be void.

In closing, the board indicated strings would be attached if Mrs. Judd were to be paroled. Attorney General Nelson was asked to draft a document assuring that she would not be able to benefit financially from telling or having someone else tell her story.

One week later, on February 23, the board voted two-to-one

in favor of asking Governor Williams to commute Mrs. Judd's life sentence to time served; Board Chairman Michael cast the dissenting vote.

Governor Williams, on his return from the National Governors Conference in Washington, D.C., three days later, said it would be "quite some time" before he decided whether or not to free Mrs. Judd. Williams still had not made a decision when interviewed April 14 by *Phoenix Gazette* reporter Lois Boyles. He discussed his unusual relationship with the case of Winnie Ruth Judd. He had worked with Phoenix Radio Station KOY at the time of Mrs. Judd's murder trial in 1932, together with Jack Stewart. He said Stewart reported the trial for KOY and "I rewrote it." Actors took the roles of the real trial participants and read Williams' script during nightly broadcasts.

Adding to the irony of Williams' situation was the fact that, at the time of the trunk murders, he also worked parttime as a railroad baggage man at Union Station. "I could well have handled one of those trunks. Whoever would have thought this would ever come back to haunt me like this?"

The governor said he wanted to make a completely thorough study of the case. "There is no deadline. If I had to rush, I'd keep her in there." He said he felt Mrs. Judd was in no hurry. "When I make a decision, I want to make the right one. I want to know in my own mind that I have done my best."

In early August, rumors began circulating that the Parole Board might reconsider its recommendation. Board member Edwards had suffered a heart attack on July 30 and the ailing Cruz had been replaced by Walter Gomez Jacobs. Board Chairman Michael denied the rumors.

In San Francisco, Melvin Belli said the entire nation would be horrified if Williams did not free Winnie, who was now reported to be in failing health. "Arizona will be disgraced if this woman were to die in the State Prison before Governor Williams made a decision." Belli revealed on August 9 that he had met secretly with Williams a month earlier to make a personal plea for Winnie's freedom. Questioned about the meeting, Williams snapped, "If Belli says we had a secret meeting, then we

had a meeting. He told me he wanted it kept confidential."
Williams later said Belli's action could not help Mrs. Judd's
case. Mrs. Judd was reported under sedation after learning of
Belli's involvement with the governor.

Several times during the next two months, Williams stated
he did not want to be pressured. Once he hinted that if people
didn't stop pressing him, he would let Mrs. Judd stay in prison.

Finally, after 245 days of consideration, Williams made his
decision—on October 27, as he departed for a vacation in
Spain: "I have given this matter long and deliberate thought
and I concur with the unanimous feeling of the Board of Pardons and Paroles." He commuted Mrs. Judd's sentence to "time
served and her maximum sentence shall remain life imprisonment."

Timing and wording of the announcement were masterful.
The press had no time to question the governor before his departure, and he had satisfied himself that the board's feeling
was unanimous. Michael, who had voted against commutation,
said he had later changed his mind after several talks with the
governor. Williams had effectively placed final responsibility
with the board. Winnie's sentence was commuted, but the
board now had to decide whether to grant parole.

"I'm sure the conscience of the governor will be better now
that this has been done," Belli said in San Francisco.

In Phoenix, Larry Debus said Mrs. Judd "had been going
downhill for a long time" because of the anxiety caused by the
long wait, and now was very happy.

The board hearing was now scheduled for November 29 and
lasted an hour, with witnesses testifying concerning Mrs. Judd's
rehabilitation. But the questioning centered on the possible
sale of the Judd story. Both Edwards, now chairman, and Michael indicated a desire that she not get involved in such a
sale. Edwards said, "I don't believe anyone should benefit financially from this—you or anyone with whom you come in
contact." Winnie, after revealing that a man "high up politi-
cally" had approached her in prison about selling her story, said
she would comply with any rules the board might lay down.

At one point in the proceedings, Michael asked Mrs. Judd, "How do you feel about capital punishment?"

She replied, "I'm against it."

Michael then observed, "Over the last forty years we've made great strides in dealing with crime. Had your crime happened today, you might have gotten only five years' probation."

The vote was unanimous in favor of parole, with certain stipulations to be formally spelled out at a later date. The date of actual release now depended upon the speed with which Arizona's legal machinery could act, and upon an interstate compact agreement by California, where Mrs. Judd must live. Parole would not be granted if California authorities refused to allow her to live in that state.

In early December, Arizona officials sent parole papers to Sacramento, but quickly withdrew them. Final papers were not prepared and signed until December 21, 1971. The official parole proclamation included this stipulation:

Along with all other parole conditions imposed upon her as a parolee by the State of California, a further condition of parole is that Winnie Ruth Judd, Arizona State Prison 8811, shall not engage in any act or acts, directly or indirectly, or allow any other person to so engage to sell, commercialize or otherwise to promote the sale or utterance in any form of a story depicting her life or any part thereof.

The wheels of justice suddenly began to move. With secrecy, Winnie Ruth Judd was taken from the Arizona State Prison at 1:30 A.M., Wednesday, December 22, 1971. A cousin and other friends drove the one-time "Tiger Woman" away in a car bearing California license plates.

On Christmas Eve, Winnie reached the affluent California suburb where she had lived so happily. She arrived during a driving rainstorm, and she had a cold. But she was home with the Wyckoffs. Winnie Ruth Judd was free.